TIME TO REIGN

TIME TO REIGN

16 Success Stories of Female
Entrepreneurs Creating Their
Queendoms

Queens In Business

TIME TO REIGN
16 Success Stories of Female Entrepreneurs Creating Their Queendoms
© 2021 Queens In Business

ISBN: 9798544627852 Paperback

Edited By: Marjah Simon-Meinefeld, Esquire - Author Writer's Academy

Cover Designed By: Tanya Grant - The TNG Designs Group Limited

The strategies in this book are presented primarily for enjoyment and educational purposes. Every effort has been made to trace copyright holders and obtain their permission for the use of copyright material.

The information and resources provided in this book are based upon the authors' personal experiences. Any outcome, income statements or other results, are based on the authors' experiences and there is no guarantee that your experience will be the same. There is an inherent risk in any business enterprise or activity and there is no guarantee that you will have similar results as the author as a result of reading this book.

The author reserves the right to make changes and assumes no responsibility or liability whatsoever on behalf of any purchaser or reader of these materials.

This book also comes with a complimentary bonus pack including a downloadable electronic copy of the book, printable posters and an exclusive never-been-seen bonus chapter. These bonuses will support you in starting or scaling your business by giving you more strategies, stories and even more motivation to get there! Get your free bonus pack here: https://bit.ly/time-to-reign

Acknowlegements

By Chloë Bisson

Founder of Queens In Business

Since starting my journey of entrepreneurship, I'd dreamt of creating a movement for female entrepreneurs and it was all made possible by these incredible women.

Firstly, my five co-founders; Carrie, Marjah, Shim, Sunna and Tanya. This movement would never have been possible without your belief in me and my mission. Thank you for jumping on the rollercoaster with me!

I want to give a special thank you to Alex, our Operations Team Leader, for being my right hand in getting Queens In Business to where it is today.

I want to give a special thank you to Shim as our Club Manager for keeping us all in check, organised and on target with making our mission a reality.

I want to give a special thank you to Tanya for your incredible eye for design and creating the beautiful artwork that symbolises everything we stand for in the QIB Club.

Finally, I want to give a special thank you to Marjah whose dedication to the success of this book has been unmatched. You and your team have done a brilliant job in bringing this book to life and on behalf of all of the co-authors, thank you for all of your hard work.

Dedication

This book is dedicated to all of the women in the world. You matter. We see you. We hear you. We understand.

With love,
Queens In Business Club

Table of Contents

Introduction

One thing is certain – life happens. Things that we want and things that we don't want impact us every moment. When we get what we want, life is wonderful! We celebrate, cheer and float. But just as sure as the shifting of the sun rising and setting, so shifts the events we face. When the adversities of life challenge us, when hardships befall us, the only question is – what do we decide is the meaning of that moment?

For far too many, those difficult moments stop us, limit us, and even break us. But there is another choice. This work is the compilation of 16 women. When faced with defining moments, they chose to rise up over the odds. The choice to decide the course of their destinies, despite the odds, continues to impact the world. These women created businesses that impact communities, and now will hopefully inspire you on your voyages through your life moments.

No matter what field you are in, or want to be in, we believe you will find parallels between your life and the lives of these 16 women around the world. With different cultures, backgrounds, trainings, and professions, we find that we are similar in many ways. As we find our voice, use our intuition and take action shifting our lives, we become free. We want this for you as well.

Just for you, 16 women openly share their truths and pull back the curtain on their journey to creating their queendoms. As you read the stories, see that you are not alone in your experiences. Your journey does not have to be a solo one. Please apply these lessons to your own life and business to shortcut the time it takes to create and up-level your queendom.

This book also comes with a complimentary bonus pack including a downloadable electronic copy of the book, printable posters and an exclusive never-be-seen bonus chapter. These bonuses will support you in starting or scaling your business by giving you more strategies, stories and even more motivation to get there! Get your free bonus pack here: https://bit.ly/time-to-reign

Time to reign!

Your Life, Your Empire, Your Rules

Chloë Bisson

Multiple Award-Winning Business Owner and
International Speaker

Queens In Business

"Sometimes you have to get knocked down lower than you've ever been, to stand up taller than you ever were." --- Unknown

Getting Knocked Down

It was 2016. I sat in the office, looking out the window to the dark grey January skies. There was not even a glimpse of sun between the dark clouds and the rain smashing against the window.

I could hear people rushing up and down the corridors. The printers and faxes churning page after page. But the office I was sat in was deadly silent. I waited.

The door opened and Mr. R walked in. Now, Mr. R had been my boss and mentor in the company for the last four years. He taught me everything I knew. We had a great relationship and always got on, but today something was different.

"Chloë, you've done a brilliant job managing your team and training up the new staff. The work you've done during your time with us has been incredible."

I could feel in the air there was a "but" coming.

"But unfortunately, things have changed since you've been gone and I'm afraid I'm going to have to let you go."

Surprisingly, I said nothing. There were no words for how I was feeling. I was numb.

I'd been at the company on and off for over four years. I help them grow the company from 25 employees and one office to 250 employees and three different offices. I moved my whole life to different cities to help them set up and grow their offices and for what? To be cut loose without a second thought.

Now for many people that lose their jobs suddenly, it hurts. But for me, the pain was a little deeper. I had just got back after being unwell for six months diagnosed with severe clinical depression.

I had given my all to this company and prioritised it over everything, including my mental health. I had burnt out and ended up being so unwell that I was unable to work for six months. I was told by doctors that it was unlikely that I'd ever be able to go back to work again. They even advised me to consider an "easier career", but that wasn't part of my plan.

Being off work, I felt so guilty that I couldn't be there to "pull my weight". That guilt motivated me to get better so I could get back to work and step up again.

So, to go through all of that and find out that I wasn't needed anymore, that they were dropping me just like that, was like falling to the floor and being kicked whilst I was down.

I felt betrayed.
I felt used.
I felt like I was nothing without my job.

It took me a few weeks to come to terms with what had happened and accept that the "dream life" that I had been fighting for was gone. I realised the hurt and betrayal that I was feeling was a result of my own mistake.

I had placed so much reliance on my job to make me happy that when it was gone, I didn't know who I was anymore. I had defined my ability to succeed based on what my boss told me, based on my work appraisal and based on feedback from others. I had given up my freedom to work 12-hour days to build someone else's dream. I had given up my happiness to do what kept my employer happy.

I realised there and then that I had to take ownership and responsibility of my own happiness, my own success, and my own freedom.

First Taste Of Freedom
After losing my job, I finally felt free. It was a weird sensation of frustration and anger towards my ex-employer. But at the same time, an amazing feeling of freedom. The freedom to choose, freedom to think, freedom to live, freedom to enjoy and freedom to be whoever I wanted.

But there was a lingering thought in my mind - how could I sustain this freedom?

I couldn't just not work for the rest of my life, despite what all the doctors told me.

I had to find a vehicle that would support me, mentally and financially. I wanted something that would help me maintain this feeling of freedom.

In my career in the corporate world, I worked on everything from accounting to compliance to recruitment to learning and development. I suppose you could say that came with the job of transforming a small business into such a large organisation; if something needed doing, we just had to step up, learn how to do it and get it done.

Just before I lost my job, I was responsible for coaching and mentoring some of the trainees in the business and I absolutely loved it.

I remember thinking to myself how amazing it would be if I could spend all my time just talking to people - coaching, mentoring and training them to be the best versions of themselves.

So, when I suddenly lost my job and was thrown back to square one, I had the opportunity to change my path. There was a tiny voice inside my head that said "maybe I could do coaching, training and mentoring full time". It was like a faint whisper that was very quickly shut down with a much louder voice saying:

"I'm not good enough to do that."
"I don't have enough experience to do that."
"People won't pay me for that."
"Dream jobs don't exist."
"I need a real job."

And before I had a chance to even consider the idea, my logical brain had muted it and moved on to start looking for a "real job".

But then I got an email from one of the trainees that I used to coach as part of my corporate job. She asked if I would be interested in coaching her privately.

"Me? You want to pay me to coach you?"

I was speechless. She explained how much I'd helped her before and how she wanted my help to apply for her next promotion.

Before I even knew what I was doing, I said yes, and we booked in our first coaching session.

Word quickly got out and within a couple of weeks I had three clients, all from my previous employer who were paying me privately to continue to coach and mentor them.

I know they were doing it because they saw value in what I had to offer and how much I could help them but what I don't think they ever really knew was how much they helped me.

They helped me see the value in my knowledge, my passion and my ability, not just to help myself but to help others. Seeing the value they placed on me helped me to believe in my value too.

Belief Is Everything
People often say "seeing is believing". When someone asks "Do you believe in ghosts?", most people answer "No, I've never seen one". The assumption is that because they haven't seen one, they don't exist.

But in reality, if we've never seen something, does it mean it doesn't happen? Does it mean that it's not possible?

As women, we are very rarely the first to achieve in society. Traditionally we've followed in the footsteps of our male counterparts that have done it first. Being able to vote, being able to get a mortgage, even being able to go to work. Women were only able to do those things because men had done them first. Putting it simply, we saw men achieve it and so we believed we could achieve it too.

And this is where many women struggle in business. Whilst seeing is believing is a concept that is programmed into us, the truth in business is actually the opposite.

The winner in business is the one who can believe it before they see it. The one who can create something based on a belief, a gut instinct, before they see the result.

Take businesses like Apple, Microsoft, Coca Cola, Amazon, Uber, Airbnb – they were all innovative in their products. They are all responsible for bringing a brand-new concept to reality. They all believed in something that had never been done before and they made it happen.

There are many different psychological principles and beliefs that come into this thought process but to keep it simple, if you believe you can do it, believe in yourself, believe in the process, believe in the possibilities, this is when you will begin to see the results.

But this belief doesn't always need to start with us.

I remember the first time my business mentor, Jessen James, told me he wanted me to speak on his stage at an event he was running in Amsterdam. I just laughed. I thought he was joking. Turns out he was being deadly serious and the event was just a few weeks away.

"How am I supposed to speak on stage?"
"What am I supposed to talk about?"
"What if I run out of things to say?"
"What if I speak too quickly?"
"Why me?"

And here we go again. That loud voice telling me why I wasn't good enough.

Because here's the thing, we are often our worst enemies. For every success, we find holes. For every win, we find failures. For every compliment, we find flaws. For every belief, we find doubts, just like that loud voice telling me why I shouldn't speak on stage.

Now normally, I would have listened to the loud voice and ignored the tiny whisper in my mind. But this time, it wasn't a tiny whisper in my mind. It was a very successful international speaker telling me why he wanted me to speak on his stage.

Whilst I had no idea how I was going to do it, I saw his belief in me and said I would do it.

The event came and despite being absolutely terrified, battling the voices and the panic attacks, I got on stage and spoke for nearly two hours. It was amazing! It was the beginning of my speaking career and a game changer for my business. But it all started because he believed in me. His belief in me helped me see what was possible.

So, whilst "believing is seeing", it doesn't always have to be your own belief that helps you see the result. Listening to those around you, your mentors, your community and your cheerleaders, listening to their belief in you can be the boost you need to achieve what you want.

Being Uncomfortable
"The Only Constant in Life Is Change." - Heraclitus

One of the biggest lessons I learnt when running my business is that the only thing that is certain is that things always change. From customers preferences to competitors' products, even social media algorithms, nothing ever stays the same for very long.

And the key to being successful in business is to surrender to the fact that things are forever changing.

The irony of the whole situation is that many people start their business because they want stability, they want to build solid foundations and have certainty in their lives. But how is that possible when so much is constantly changing, right? I still remember when I asked one of my first business mentors about this and she told me I needed to "get comfortable being uncomfortable".

I was furious because quite frankly, I didn't want to "get comfortable with being uncomfortable". I didn't want to be uncomfortable at all. The whole point of me starting my business was to feel more stable and secure than when I lost my job. The idea of being uncomfortable really wasn't appealing to me.

But over my years in business, I realised what this concept really meant.

It's not about "getting comfortable with being uncomfortable". The way I prefer to see it is controlling what you can and preparing for what you can't.

Let's use the example of getting paying clients.

We'll never be able to control if we do or don't have paying clients but we can control the action that we take to get paying clients. If our previous strategies to get clients stop working, we can control our attitude towards finding new ways of getting paying clients.

We can also prepare by having a buffer in our bank account as a worst-case scenario.

Therefore, we control what we can and prepare for what we can't.

I've always been a bit of a control freak so acknowledging that there were things in my business that I'll never be able to control was a very difficult thing to accept.

In fact, in life there are more things that are outside of our control than those that are within our control. So, it's more productive to focus on what we can control rather than what we can't.

Putting it simply, there are two things that we can control; how we think and how we act. These are the most important drivers for success that arguably have the power to make or break your business and thankfully, they are connected.

The way we think drives the way we act which drives the results we achieve. This is also known as the BE DO HAVE principle. What we HAVE is driven by what we DO which is driven by how we are BEing.

Everything we achieve always comes back to the thoughts we had that started the process.

Many people will argue that you don't have 100% control over your thoughts. As someone who has battled several clinical depression, anxiety and suicidal thoughts, we may not always be able to control our thoughts, but I believe we all have control over how we fuel our minds and monitor our thoughts.

I remember when I started my business that everyone was telling me it's all about "mindset" and if I'm honest, I thought it was all

B.S.. I was a very logical thinker, believing that anything was possible with the right strategy, with or without the right mindset.

But what if the strategy stops working? No matter how amazing your business is or your systems, your campaigns, your branding, your marketing, your products; if you're not working well, they won't either.

How you think will define how you act which will define the results you achieve. Your thoughts are the fuel of your business.

Asking For What You Want

The first step to challenging our minds in business is to tune into what we really want. Why are we even in business in the first place? Where do we want to go?

It's like driving to a new destination that you've never been to before. You get in the car, pick up the Sat Nav and program it to start your journey. What's the first thing the Sat Nav programs? Usually where you are right now.

What's the next thing? Where you want to go. You have to type in your desired destination in order to start your journey.

But in business, how many of us actually start with our desired destination in mind?

I know I didn't. When I started my business, I had no idea what I wanted nor what my long-term plan was, I just knew what I didn't want and that was a job.

Most female entrepreneurs are exactly the same. Many start their businesses because they have an idea but don't necessarily know what they want from it all or WHY they even want it.

And this absence of considering what we want isn't just in our businesses. We rarely think about what we want in any aspects of our lives; what we actually want for ourselves.

As women, we've been trained and programmed over generations to always care for others. We've always been nurturers. We are mums, we are daughters, we are wives, we are sisters and with every single role, there is an expectation to care for others. But why is there no expectation to care for ourselves?

Biologically, women are on this planet for one reason; to be a host and a vehicle to create life. We have been given life so that we can give life to others – no wonder so many of us struggle to prioritise ourselves.

So, for many of us it's completely alien to actually ask ourselves, "What do I want?" and when we do ask that question, our minds go completely blank. Not because there aren't lots of things that we would love but because we haven't been allowed to want before. Many of us didn't even know we could.

But here's the thing.

Not only are we allowed to "want", we are allowed to dream. We are allowed to achieve. We are allowed to be whoever we want to be. Who says we can't?

Here are the questions that I ask myself to keep grounded and stay in tune with my purpose in life:

1. What do I want?
2. Who do I want to be?
3. What do I want to achieve?
4. What do I want to create?

You can use these questions whenever you want to connect with yourself, on a regular basis or if ever you feel lost or stuck.

Notice that all of those questions are "what" and "who" questions, not "how" questions. When you ask yourself "what" or "who", it allows your mind to open and to dream. When you ask yourself "how", it actually limits your ability to dream to only what you believe is practical or possible.

As soon as we begin to ask for what we want, we start to expand our minds to the real possibilities of our businesses.

Another exercise I love to do with my clients is an imagination exercise.

Ask yourself:
"If I had a blank piece of paper and I could create anything I want, what business would I build?

- What would it look like?
- Who would my clients be?
- What would I offer them?
- What would my role be?"

When you truly allow yourself to dream, the game changes. You start to believe in what could be, you start to see the potential and you start to attract opportunities to make it happen.

Less is More
Once we've accepted and connected to what we're able to control, the next step is to prepare for what we can't.

But how do we prepare for something we can't control?

Well, imagine you're about to organise your child's 4th birthday party. You know there are going to be about 30 accident-prone kids running around, almost looking for ways to hurt themselves. You can't control them but you can prepare. You might decide to invite more adults to share the responsibilities, less kids for you to watch over yourself. Or you might decide to have a smaller party, less children means less risk in theory.

The concept here is to reduce the amount of moving parts in as many ways as possible. The same goes for business. The secret is to keep it simple. The less moving parts, the less work required and the less that can go wrong.

One of the gifts that all entrepreneurs have is the ability to create. We love to come up with new ideas and new strategies. We are naturally innovators. We see someone doing something and think "Oh I'd love to do that too", and a new idea is born.

But this can be a curse in business. The more ideas we have, the more products we create, the more work required to make them successful.

For example, if we have four products that all require our attention they each get 25% of our time. That means that it will take us times as long for them to be successful than if we just f one. And let's be honest. Time is money. If we tak the results, it is costing us money too.

So, the key is to keep it simple. Less

- Focus on one business
- Focus on one product.

- Focus on one niche.
- Focus on one sales strategy.
- Focus on one social media platform.

Keep it simple until it works. Only when it's operational, profitable and scalable, do you move onto the next project.

For example, Airbnb didn't start with offering accommodation, experiences and trips all over the world. They started with not just one city but actually just ONE property. As soon as their concept was getting traction, they branched out to look for more properties in the same city and found more people that would want to rent out their homes. As soon as the concept became extremely popular in their city, they then extended to new cities and so on.

But it all started with just one thing.

After about two years in my business, I had online courses, I had an academy, I had face to face events, I had 1:1 coaching sessions, I had group mentoring programs and I had a VA agency.

It's safe to say I definitely had more than just one thing.

I was stressed, I was overwhelmed, I was constantly putting out fires, hiring and firing staff, working 80 hours a week and getting paid less than I did if I was working 9-5 in my old job.

So, when I came across this principle of "the one thing", it was a game changer. I saw how wrong I had been doing it and more importantly, how I could do it a lot better.

stopped selling almost all products from my services and d on just one. I stopped trying to grow all of my social media platforms and picked one. I closed my VA agency and focused on my mentorship programs as that was where my heart was.

I streamlined everything and I ended up multiplying my revenue by five times. The shift was incredible. Not only did my sales and profits go up but also my mindset completely levelled up.

Clearing your schedule, clearing your to do list, clearing your mind and only focusing on one core thing is game changing.

I was so much more productive, so much clearer and so my business grew.

Once I'd mastered the foundations of that one thing, I then began to build more on top. I launched the Queens In Business Club, I wrote my best-selling book and then the whole thing continued to grow.

From there, I was featured on the cover of Global Woman magazine following in the footsteps of incredible women like Jennifer Aniston and Scarlett Johannsson. I spoke on stage alongside Kim Kiyosaki and I've since been featured on BBC, Fox, ABC, NBC, CW, London Business Magazine, Business Woman Today, Foundr and some incredible media outlets. Today I'm an international speaker, a multi award-winning entrepreneur and manage multiple six and seven figure businesses.

Now I know this may feel very far away from where you are now and you may be thinking, "But Chloë, how can I get there? I'm just starting out."

The point is simple.

The simpler you keep it, the stronger the foundations and the bigger the empire you can build on that.

The simpler you keep your products, your marketing, your sales, and your message, the stronger the foundations of your business will be and therefore, the bigger the success can be in the future.

As a result of all that, I get to spend my time now training women all over the world in building their own businesses and that's the reason I created Queens In Business.

Because it is my belief that as women, we don't just have to settle for the norm. We don't just have to settle for what our "biology is created for". We now have a path that other women have created for us. We are making waves in the industry. There has never been as many female entrepreneurs on the planet than there are today and I'm so proud to be one of them. I'm even more proud to be helping other women come out their shells and build the business of their dreams.

The time is now, Queens.

It's your time to get what you want.

It's your time to build the foundations of your dream life.

It's your time to be proud to be you.

It's your time to reign.

About Me

If there is only one thing you need to know about me, it is this - I believe that all women have what it takes to be successful female entrepreneurs. Women have the right to create their own businesses, their own income streams and their own happiness.

Also known as The Automation Queen, I am a number one bestselling author, international speaker, multi-award-winning entrepreneur. Managing multiple six and seven figure businesses – and I've only just turned 30!

As a chartered accountant at the age of 21 and director by the age of 24, my success came to a sharp halt when I was diagnosed with severe clinical depression at the age of 25. After months of growth and recovery, I knew I was meant for more than the "normal" path. This is when I began my journey of entrepreneurship.

Since then, I've been featured on the cover of Global Woman magazine, spoken on stage alongside Kim Kiyosaki and been featured on BBC, Fox, ABC, NBC, CW, London Business Magazine, Business Woman Today, Foundr and some incredible media outlets.

Today I run Queens In Business, a training organisation that teaches female entrepreneurs how to build successful businesses to work less and earn more. To date, I have helped thousands of women build their online businesses and make their dreams a reality!

Toxic Success

Shim Ravalia

Founder

The Gut Intuition

"Choose to put yourself first and make you a priority. It's not selfish, its necessary." --- Keysha Jade

If you can read this whole chapter without any distractions and I have your undivided attention, then the key messages I have for you will sink in. However, if you find yourself getting distracted, multitasking and flicking through page after page, then you definitely have some work to do. So, grab yourself a cuppa, switch off any distractions around and get comfortable as you go through this journey with me.

What Is Success?
"What does success mean to you?"

This was a question one of my mentors asked me on a coaching call back in 2017. I thought about it momentarily and wrote in my journal exactly what success meant to me at the time. What it felt like! Even, what it smelt like!

I wanted the Porsche! The beach house! Six figure business, making a shed load of profit every year and I wanted the dream team to enable my success.

Before my entrepreneurial journey began, I worked a full-time job at a private health club. The kind of job that had attractive perks, but it robbed me of any social life and allowed me the occasional weekend off.

There was a major lack of spontaneity, fun or play for me, only boring shifts and with no room to grow or learn. I had enough and something needed to change fast! I became uncomfortable with being comfortable. I did a 360 turnaround in 30 days, going from employed to self-employed for the first time ever. This is how my first business was born.

I would like to say the rest is history but where's the fun in that!?

The biggest lesson embarking into entrepreneurship is that it's not a destination that is reached, it's a process. However, the quality of this process and approaches are dependent on the quality of your health and one's capacity towards resilience.

It was an incredibly exciting time to be starting my own business. Finally, something new! Something exciting! Creating something of my own and on my terms! I had this idea that there will be a long queue of clients outside of my door, money will be rolling in and life will be good.

I realise now how naïve and immature my mindset was around money and how a business actually ran behind the scenes. I guess you could say I was impatient and wanted everything quickly, a bit like a child impatiently waiting for the ice cream from the ice cream van.

The worst piece of advice I have received is 'Fake it till you make it'. When I heard this, I instantly felt rather yuck and out of sorts. The way I understood this advice was I had to be someone else to be "successful" and for people to respect me. The sad thing is, this advice is what many people tend to take on board and implement.

Having an idea, creating it from scratch and actually running with it was no easy feat when I first started out. The hardest thing to look after within business was...ME!

My biggest belief today is how I look after my physical, my emotions and my mental health. This shows up in how I run my business. Of course, I learnt this the hard way but then again, I'm so glad I did! As you are reading this, you might sit back, take a deep breath and smile; knowing you don't have to make the same mistakes as I did. I believe you'll get a lot from what I have to share with you.

The world of entrepreneurship is never without ups and downs but that's to be expected right? Not to me! For the first three years of running my business, I ran it from the mindset of the employed rather than that of a business owner. I used to think how hard can it be? I'll get the clients which equals money in the bank which equates to spending and happy days! Actually, when I zoomed out it wasn't unrealistic. To get to this stage required patience, planning and perseverance without a shadow of a doubt.

Seventy-Six Pence
One cold January evening, I opened my laptop, procrastinating and dreading to just look at my bank account, deep down my intuition was telling me something didn't feel right. I logged in and I had 76 pence left in my account. 76 pence?! My heart sank, my mind was racing and my inner critical voice got increasingly louder. I worked so hard and I was so damn busy with clients but it didn't quite reflect this on what was in my bank account at the time. In all honesty, I felt like a failure.

At times, I would cringe at the thought of when someone would ask me how my business was going. I'd always reply back, "It's going really well thanks," with a smile on my face, knowing full well that wasn't the case many times.

Looking back on this now, I realised just how much I attached money to my success. Being successful meant a certain amount should have been in my bank account.

This is toxic and I wouldn't advise this approach at all.

I obsessed over money and I hoarded it at times and then freely spent it too. A clear sign of my toxic relationship with money was not opening and looking at my bank statements. I'd just avoid it altogether. I was hitting and hoping with no real plan in sight. I carried a lot of guilt and shame around creating my own money as well as asking for help too.

Before I really understood the energy of money and how to improve my relationship with it, I was very much a martyr around money, doing everything by myself. There is nothing wrong with asking for help around money. My parents were an absolute godsend when it came to helping me out. Without them, I wouldn't be where I am today.

The moment I realised that my finances were not healthy was the time I got up, shrugged my shoulders and got to work to find a way to turn my business around. There was no way I was letting it go. I felt deeply that there was another way.

At the time, there were a lot of free events going on where one could turn up and learn from a coach/mentor, and they then sell you a program to join. I've lost count of how many of these events I attended. The one thing I do admire about myself is that giving up was never an option. But when the bank account is close to empty and I still wasn't getting anywhere with hitting the six figures I dreamt of, this does equal desperation and making decisions from fear rather than using my intuition.

I cannot tell you how many times I had been in front of experts where they pitched with fear and unfortunately it really did feed my insecurities around money. It led me to take action from a place of lack rather than abundance.

The point is there will be times when you will face challenges in business and in health that seem impossible to turn around. Many experts and gurus will tell you that they can help you make six figures in 30 days, which is not true. It's important to really do your due diligence. Suss it out, ask questions and use your intuition to make a good decision for you. Don't fall prey to your ego that's screaming at you and freaking out!

We can apply this strategy to anything in life. Remember to take a few deep breaths, keep calm and then move forward. (How very British, ha-ha).

New Level, New Devil

A few months down the road, I found a coaching program that fitted well with the kind of help I was looking for. I went to their free workshop, signed up to their 3-day event on my credit card and off I went. I started to feel that I really was able to turn this around and actually get somewhere financially with my business at the time. I then signed up for a one-year coaching program, again on the credit card! I grew up with the belief from my parents that credit cards were really bad for debt, so you can only imagine that inner dialogue that was going on in my mind at the time. But I did it, and I was so glad I did. Credit cards are a godsend when you use it wisely, for the things that yield a return on investment.

One thing I did notice about some of the 3-day events was how much it became a drink/party fest! I had never seen so many health and fitness professionals get smashed on a 3-day event. There were times with the excitement of learning, meeting new people and just being in a totally different environment, I got carried away partying, staying up till 2am in the morning.

Now you can only imagine the hangover on day three trying to concentrate on learning about Facebook® ads and websites (yawn)! It made me question, "How much did I really take in if I haven't given my body the rest, the food, the recovery it needs to function at its best?"

I believe there's a time and place for socialising/partying, but not so much when you are making some serious changes to your business. It can cloud your judgement due to the lack of sleep and skew your decision making. And of course, the result is piss poor action.

Not to sound like a party pooper, but I feel celebrating your wins can come in all sorts of ways. It doesn't have to be the typical toxic approach that I grew up with in the East End, where walking in a straight line on a Friday night was impossible because there was always something to celebrate. If I had celebrated all my wins in life with alcohol, I would have needed a new liver or I would be dead.

The business really took off. Within eight months, I started to make £5K plus which was an amazing result. The pressure that came off my shoulders never felt so good, and I felt that I was able to finally stop worrying and actually enjoy running the business.

However, the more money that came in, the more obsessive I became at making more. I did not stop to celebrate my wins at all and just wanted to reach the next level every month. I've never forgotten this saying that someone once told me "New Level, New Devil". I took this to mean to just keep going but once you get there, then what?

As a result of this, making more money gave me a good leg-up in the right direction. It motivated me to do better, pay more attention to the numbers in my business and offered opportunities to scale it to another level. However, that wasn't the full picture, it was a small piece of the jigsaw puzzle.

The shadow side of making more for me at the time was I didn't see my friends much or family. I stopped exercising because I was juggling so much in one go. I had mastered the "art of multitasking" like a pro. I also didn't eat a balanced diet because I always felt I didn't have time - so something quick and easy to eat within 20 minutes was my go-to almost every day. I didn't sleep so well due to the mountain of work I had with my clients' caseloads. I realised actually running a business and working in the business are two very different things. I drank more alcohol to cope with the stress of it all, which isn't one of my recommendations.

To really shift this behaviour, I was sick and tired of feeling sick and tired all of the time. Alcohol was a huge contributor to that so enough was enough. The biggest shift was in my mindset and actually taking the time to ask myself, "How do I want to show up?", "How do I want to feel today?", "How do I want to feel by the time my head hits the pillow?"

The "Hustle" Medal

"Work Hard, Play Hard" I have heard a lot over the years and I would like to really rephrase this to "Work Smart and Play". One thing I never did enough of in my early days of business was to stop and reflect on my hard work, to actually appreciate the steps I took to get the results in my business. I didn't look up to be present, to stop and breathe and actually enjoy the process. I was too focused on the destination, then moving quickly onto the next goal.

To get a different result, you have to accept that you have to adopt a different mindset and have a different approach. With this comes the process of learning something new and growing with it. Play is one of my favourite core values in life, health and in business.

Change is hard and sometimes painful, but not impossible and not for too long either. What makes change much easier is actually enjoying it, smiling and having fun with it. The amount of times I had a miserable face like a wet fish when making changes in health and in business, and not stopping to enjoy it actually made the process of change harder to stick to and establish.

In fact, pause reading and write down some wins right now. Have some fun and celebrate however you feel like. I give you permission to do so.

I remember coming home from a long day of clients and running the business, entering the living room where both of my parents sat watching the telly. My mum could tell I was completely exhausted and burnt out. She asked me how my day was to which I replied with two words, "Yeah fine". I had many days where by the end of it, I just didn't want to talk to anyone because I had given so much of myself to my business.

I had very little left for the people who loved and cared about me, and even less for myself. I'll never forget this one sentence my mum said to me that very evening, "You work so much we hardly ever see you, we get like 10% of you". My dad wasn't a man to say many words, but I felt his silence. This hit me deeply. It was the truth and at the time this is what I felt I had to do to be successful - work as much as possible, make sacrifices and then enjoy the rewards later. I couldn't have been more wrong.

Celebrating toxic success needs to stop and what I mean by this is the following:

- Not seeing or spending quality time with family and friends
- Not exercising at all
- Exercising every single day with no recovery time
- Not eating properly
- Not sleeping properly
- Being part of the 5am club
- Waking up early and going to bed quite late
- Not taking good care of yourself

I could go on and on, but the reality is that having no balance is not success. Failing to acknowledge areas where you have neglected your own needs actually requires self-awareness, self-responsibility and a different course of action, not some sort of hustle medal. Hustle at the detriment of your health is not success. It is a failure of the worst kind.

The Toxic Pattern
The moment you become out of balance with your self-care, how you take care of yourself physically, emotionally and mentally, there is trouble. I call this the toxic pattern, of which I have experienced many times on different levels throughout my entrepreneurial journey.

I thought it would be easier to illustrate what I meant by The Toxic Pattern and how it all works. So here we go, watch the flow…

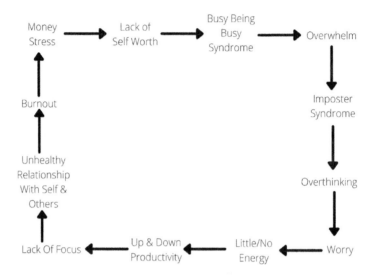

I began noticing this pattern when I started doing more self-development work. When my health started to take a turn for the worse, I noticed that a majority of my stress stemmed from money worries, which was always the starting point for a toxic build up. When I didn't manage this stress pattern properly, or even acknowledge it, I questioned my own self-worth. I had attached my worth to the numbers in my bank account. One lesson I truly learnt from this was that the numbers in my bank account were never disappointed in me. It was me that was disappointed in the numbers.

Take the emotions out of numbers and they remain numbers.

The lack of self-worth created the 'busy being busy' meaning through underlying panic. I was multitasking. Juggling health, business, people that mattered to me and trying to have some time off and exploring new ideas to create more business and so on. I wore all the hats you could think of. This created a lack of balance between work and life. I pretty much juggled everything most days, and got very overwhelmed. Then the imposter syndrome kicked in. My experience of imposter syndrome was that as much of my own behaviour and reactions. It was also other people's behaviours, insecurities that they were more than happy to project and dump on you rather than dealing with it. I experienced a lot of jealousy and envy from people very early on in my business journey, which triggered and stirred their own insecurities to which they made sure I knew about too. What I experienced was name calling, the cold shoulder, fake smiles, unsupportiveness, talking behind my back. Gaslighting and immature, narcissistic, toxic behaviour, which, if we are not careful, is so easy to internalise.

I started to doubt myself, thinking "What did I do to piss them off?" I compared myself to others and tried to do the things they would to keep the peace. Remember, it's not you, it's them. People's opinions of you have got nothing to do with you at all.

The moment you start to compare yourself to other peoples' results, the more the worry creeps in. The times to worry most were always when I laid down to rest, resulting in no or very little quality sleep. Having not enough sleep caused all sorts of disruption to my body and my hormones, which affected my mood, low in energy, poor decision making, poor focus and how I interacted with other people. It also affected my productivity day to day, causing a bit of a yo-yo effect on my energy levels and crashing by the afternoon.

Sleep is always a must!

This vicious toxic pattern over time started to create an unhealthy relationship with myself and therefore created an unhealthy relationship with others too. As a result, I actually burnt out completely. My body forced me to stop and rest.

Unless you disrupt the pattern at any point in this toxic pattern, it will continue just going round and round and round. Each time it went round for me, it got louder and louder and started to show up as pain in my body. The wicked thing about stress is that even though I had stepped away from running the business because I had a great team in place, I still had to deal with the damage it had left me with. It did not go away, it only got worse because I didn't do anything about it.

There's Trouble Ahead...
Having the attitude of, "It will sort itself out!" did land my health in hot water many times. I ignored the symptoms and pain. I pushed through during my business career, which led me down the path of creating my second business, The Gut Intuition.

The year 2018 was when everything changed for me.

I moved on from my first business to figure out what I wanted to do with my business career. I was on a discovery of what lit me up and what I actually felt passionate about to wake up to every day. I remember feeling like I wanted to take my time on this and have a breather for once. The stress of the last six years of my life had affected my emotions, my physicality and mental health. Amidst this time, life threw a curveball at me as I lost my father in June that same year. It was a sad, confusing and complex time for me. I remember feeling my head and my heart were so up and down all of the time.

It was a difficult reality to accept straight away that my dad was no longer here anymore, that I wasn't going to see his smile, hear his laughter, his voice or even give him a hug ever again. Grief is a funny old thing, there is no instruction manual that tells you how to grieve, how long for and what to expect. It's different for every single person and the journey of it is very unique too.

Before Christmas that same year, my health was at an all-time low. I wasn't able to sleep most nights without the excruciating pain in my stomach. Anything that I did eat wasn't digesting and I reacted to most foods with the uneasy, queasy feeling after every meal. I also put on a lot of weight because I craved sugary foods most days which I felt was so out of character for me. My energy levels and my focus on tasks were questionable sometimes and I got very easily distracted. To add to the mess, I was riddled with pain pretty much all over my body in my neck, hip, knees, stomach, back as well as headaches waking up some days. I was a walking, talking mess!

I had a gut feeling (pardon the pun!) that something wasn't right and a quick fix wasn't the answer here, I needed help. With the right help and the right tests, I found out that I had been carrying a rather nasty gut infection for a few years.

"How the hell did this happen right under my nose?" I thought. How did I not even notice an infection that literally got under my skin? Was I completely blind to this or plain ignorant of what my body was telling me for so long?

Either way, I started to make some serious changes to my health and how I use to approach it day by day. I'm not going to lie and say it was easy, it bloody wasn't! It was hard to break down old habits, eat foods I wasn't used to and actually look after myself for once.

Looking back at this now, I realised how much I allowed stress to take over. Not managing it cost me a huge amount and I'm not just talking about money here. I'm talking about my emotional and mental wellbeing here too. I gave a home in my mind to negative thoughts to live rent free. There were days I didn't want to show up or be present because I didn't have the energy to. In this chaos, I had to find some kindness and compassion towards myself too. Understanding my gut health was a very profound experience, one of which led me down the path of gut health, stress management and burnout for entrepreneurs and business owners. I continue to pursue gut health to this day.

Understanding gut bacteria and the role it played in how I felt, my mood, my behaviour was astonishing to learn about and implement in daily life. Looking beyond how many calories I was eating, how many reps I did at the gym was now surface level of health. I now had the hunger, the desire to go down the rabbit hole of health much deeper than I had imagined I ever would and I'm so glad I did.

The changes I made were the following:

- I ate my vegetables like an adult
- I got plenty of good quality fats, proteins and carbohydrates
- I went to bed on time and adopted a better sleep routine
- I moved every day with walking and gradually built it up to exercise
- I removed caffeine and alcohol
- I drank sufficient water
- I monitored my blood sugar levels
- I managed my stress levels better with some simple tools
- I worked on my environment and made changes where it was necessary

- I showed myself kindness and compassion
- I made my self-care a PRIORITY

It all starts with you!

You have to be aware of the toxicity around you as no one else can do this for you. Your body is the best thing that can tell you where there is a misalignment. It's now time to actually listen to it as all the clues are there right under your nose.

The Anatomy Of An Improved You
My biggest belief in life, health and business is that there is always another way, always.

It soon became my mission to help business owners and entrepreneurs go from Stressed to Success in health and in business. This was so that they could move on forward with their vision, mission and leave a legacy without burnout.

When you start to master how your body works is when you can master your business and how that works. When you feed and fuel your body and your brain with the good stuff, it becomes clear as day the positive changes that come with it. You can see what I mean with my lovely stick person that I spent hours drawing up in the diagram (kidding, I delegated it to my team). When I gave my body the attention it needed and the right fuel to function, it was liberating.

My focus shot up; I noticed all sorts of opportur   ·· ·- ·my
business. I kept showing up every day without
myself and learnt the art of patience. The resul
created one of the biggest collaborations I have e
- the Queens In Business Club. To add to this
finalist of the National Business Women's Awar

featured in Business Woman Today, and many other well-known publications.

I took aligned actions. Ideas were flowing and my heart was bursting with passion. The best feeling was that I was able to handle whatever life and business threw at me by listening to my intuition and trusting it, and looking after myself without sacrificing my own needs first.

I felt the best way to keep toxicity at arms-length, was to understand and listen to my own intuition. Intuition is the most natural, powerful asset you have from birth. Business and health require a healthy balance between intuition and logic, not one or the other. There have been countless times where I didn't use my intuition, or there was a subtle sign coming up to tell me to trust my gut feelings about a person, a situation, an opportunity both professionally and personally.

Sometimes, intuition can get suppressed by what you feed your body. If you consume food and drink that leave you feeling sluggish, then expect sluggish results in some way. Intuition has no time for sluggishness, it's razor sharp, assertive and a knowledgeable protector when you know how to use it.

Strive to achieve a balance between your own reasoning and your intuition every day, then you my friend, are onto a WINNER! I actually don't believe in the work-life balance jargon that most of society chases. Why? I realised there was one thing I kept forgetting about every time I was trying to fit in or compare or find a balance and that was me. If there is one thing I would love for you to get from understanding my journey, it's always look at yourself first when you feel there is a misalignment, however that is showing up for you.

So, what does success mean to me now? It's simple and explained in two powerful words, SELF CARE. You are a unique individual and an original, always! Looking after yourself physically, emotionally and mentally and immersing yourself in a supportive environment with people who want to see you win and love you unconditionally is true success. Everything else is a cherry on top.

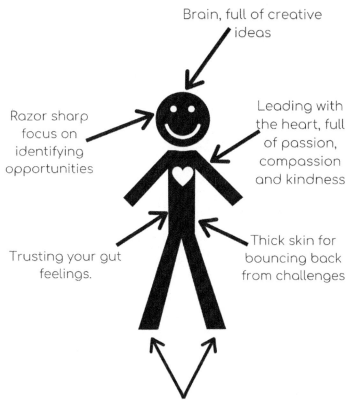

Brain, full of creative ideas

Razor sharp focus on identifying opportunities

Leading with the heart, full of passion, compassion and kindness

Trusting your gut feelings.

Thick skin for bouncing back from challenges

Happy feet to celebrate the epic wins.

About Me

I am the Founder of The Gut Intuition and Co-Founder and Project Manager of the Queens In Business Club, helping business owners and entrepreneurs go from stressed to success in health and in business. I've had the pleasure of being featured on many well-known publications like Business Woman Today, CBS News, Fox, NBC, ABC to really spread my message and my vision about health for the future of entrepreneurs all over the world.

Born and bred in East London, learning and being curious about the human body and the mind always intrigued me and the deeper the rabbit hole I went down, the more it got interesting. I came away from University with two degrees both in Sports Rehabilitation and from here I worked in gyms and leisure centres until I really got myself on the right path of the entrepreneurial journey.

Being part of this book with so many incredibly strong female entrepreneurs is an absolute true honour and one that I will never forget. It's not about being superior to anyone, it's about being an equal team player through the wins and the lessons towards yourself and to others. The entrepreneurial world can certainly start off a lonely journey. However, the more you work on yourself inside out, you'll soon end with a family of empowering individuals who always have your back.

I dedicate this chapter to you and me. Whatever happens, just keep going and working towards your true success.

Taking the 'Dis' Out Of Disadvantaged

Sunna Coleman

Founder and Editor in Chief

Inspired in the City

"You can't find your passion thinking about it." --- Marie Forleo

I remember the first time I saw my name published in print.

As a young child, I was an avid magazine reader, collecting boxes upon boxes of fashion mags, music mags, and celebrity mags - much to my mother's dismay. Tracing my finger down the masthead, I took in the different roles involved in putting these glossy pages together - from the Editor in Chief and Features Writers to the Art Directors and Designers. I dreamed of one day seeing my name among the list.

Then, there it was: Assistant Editor, Sunna Naseer (my maiden name).

I'd had my name published online plenty of times before, but not in print. Not until that day. There was something far more luxurious about holding the pages in my hands, seeing the jet-black ink printed onto the page. I felt like I had finally made it, and the promise to my younger self was fulfilled.

I've had several pinch-me moments like this throughout my career where I've stopped and thought, "How did I get so fortunate?" It happened the first time I actually got paid for submitting a piece of my journalism. It happened when restaurants would allow me to eat for free in return for my opinion. It happened when I sat front row at London Fashion Week as a catwalk show reporter. It happened when I was sent on an all-expenses-paid press trip to Mexico.

But why did I keep putting all this down to luck? Had I not worked to get this far?

I'm the Founder and Editor in Chief of lifestyle and career blog, Inspired in the City. I also mentor people to improve their confidence with writing. I've collaborated with global brands including the likes of Revlon, Ted Baker, Boohoo, Hotel Chocolat and Desenio. I'm also currently working on my first fiction novel.

I'm also one of the Co-Founders of the Queens In Business Club, without which you wouldn't be holding this book. And I've been doing all this, while juggling a full-time job to work my way up in the journalism and marketing industry.

But the truth is, for a very long time I felt like I ended up here by accident, as if I'd cheated the system. I didn't actually study journalism like all my peers around me. I didn't even study English. I came from a completely different background in fashion design. I wasn't really a "proper" journalist. At least, that's how I perceived myself.

Having not gone down the traditional route, my journey was not smooth. There were many moments where I felt like I would never make it because I was unable to get the right opportunities. With every adversity, the thought kept creeping back in – I'm not a "proper" journalist. I didn't have the professional training that all the other candidates had. If it wasn't for the burning ambition that I had to have my name published in a magazine, I may have given up. But I couldn't break the promise I had made to that young girl who had so much hope for the possibilities of the future.

I've been in the industry for almost a decade and have started working with budding writers, sharing my own advice on how to improve their work. It is only now that I'm finally beginning to acknowledge that maybe I do know what I'm talking about…

Hands up if you've ever felt the same.

That niggling feeling that you're the only one who doesn't belong in the field that you're in - that you're almost faking it. Well, chances are you're already far more of an expert than you realise. And you'd be aware of that if you could only see how many of you readers just raised your hands.

This phenomenon has a name. Some of you may already know it - it's called imposter syndrome. You may even read about it in other chapters of this book. Imposter syndrome can affect anyone, especially entrepreneurs. And although both men and women fall prey to it, numerous research has found that female entrepreneurs are far more likely to let this feeling hinder them in their business.

For me, it wasn't until I learned that this was an actual "thing", that I started to work through these feelings and put more belief in my ability. Knowing that I wasn't the only one made me less scared of it. So for anyone else who may not have heard that this thing has a name, you're not alone, welcome to the club.

It's important to note here that imposter syndrome isn't something that you can make disappear. It rears its ugly head at various points throughout your journey, most often when you're being brave enough to take on a new challenge. It's something that you learn how to manage, tackle and overcome - and you get better at it every time.

When No One Gives You The Opportunity, Create Your Own

After four gruelling years of university working very long hours, I finally graduated with a degree in Fashion Design. I had the notion of "designers don't get to sleep or have a social life" drilled into my brain from tutors which I experienced first-hand throughout the course of my degree. It's fair to say that I was no longer excited about my career path. With many outside interests, a buzzing social life and a love of sleep, the idea of becoming a slave to the industry did not seem to align with my values. Add to that the fact that they get paid peanuts and you've got a pretty miserable outlook.

With this in mind, I turned to another passion of mine: writing. Since I didn't want my degree to go to waste, and since I still admired the work of many designers in the industry (even more so now that I knew what they go through), I reasoned that I could begin my career working as a fashion intern at a magazine - and, I'd get to check off my childhood dream along the way.

Win-win.

As I started to browse available roles online, it dawned on me that this may not be as straightforward as I had imagined. With each click, I was beginning to lose hope. It looked something like this:

Job role: Editorial Assistant (Entry Level)

Desirable criteria:

- A passion for writing - ✓
- Creative ideas and fashion knowledge - ✓
- Brilliant research skills and grammar - ✓

Essential criteria:

- Degree in Journalism or English - ✗
- Previous experience of over six months at a magazine - ✗
- Must have been published in a glossy mag before - ✗

I was stuck. I had the desires but not the essentials.

I didn't want to give my life up to fashion design, but it was looking like I couldn't get into journalism without the credentials to back me up. But how was I supposed to get experience without someone taking a chance on me?

Hoping that the rules were flexible and that my CV would land in front of an editor on a good day, I sent off hundreds of applications and crossed my fingers.

Then, radio silence.

Weeks went by and not a word from anyone. Not even a "sorry, you don't meet the requirements".

Feeling dejected, I turned to the internet for help, researching other ways into journalism. During this search, I kept coming across copywriting roles for fashion brands, and these didn't seem to require a particular degree, simply good English. The job involved writing up product and web page descriptions - pretty boring I thought. But at least this would get my foot in the door, and perhaps I'd eventually be given longer writing tasks like contributing to company news articles.

Thinking ahead to my end goal, I once again wondered how anyone would trust me with more writing responsibility without relevant proof. I'd already learned this the hard way when I failed to receive a single response from my applications.

That's when I decided to take matters into my own hands.

There was a growing trend for blogging at the time, particularly in personal travel diaries and outfit inspiration. While I was at university, many friends used to ask me what the point of high fashion was, and how it related to what we end up wearing in everyday life. What if I set up my own blog to answer common queries like these, and help other young women understand fashion better? I could also dive into some of the issues I was passionate about, such as diversity on the catwalk.

Not only did this sound like a fun pastime for me, but it would be a great way to build up the portfolio of writing examples that I needed. Sure, it didn't hold as much weight as a third party publishing me, but it could be enough to get me into some of the entry level roles I was applying to.

Sensing a glimmer of hope, I researched how to set up a blog and started playing around with themes, colours and imagery to make my site look the part (the designer in me couldn't help it). I then dove into the technicalities of how to actually structure the site with menus, posts and interactive elements such as comment boxes.

This was a whole new world to me but I was determined to learn fast and get my posts out there. I was brimming with ideas and there was so much to get my head around in terms of getting my blog to function the right way. I must have spent hours and hours down this rabbit hole. But by the end of it, I had the makings of my very first blog and more importantly, I had an action plan.

Waking up both weary eyed yet full of drive the next day, I was eager to get posting. Scanning my ideas from the night before, I chose one and got to work. What should only take a couple of hours, took me the whole day but I knew it would eventually become second nature to me.

After deliberating over every word and every image in my post, I was ready to share it with the world. But in my excitement the night before, I had completely forgotten to factor in this one daunting aspect - what would my friends think?

Who was I to share my thoughts on fashion? Yes, I had a degree but I wasn't a writer and I wasn't a fashion expert with a glamorous job. I was just a graduate with no title forcing my opinions onto others. But at the same time, I was proud of what I had just put together. And once my friends realised that my blog wasn't just an excuse for me to post photos of myself in different outfits - something that many fashion blogs were at the time - they may find value in what I was sharing.

Keeping the reason for starting my blog at the forefront of my mind, pushing away any self-conscious negativity, I hovered over the "publish" button. Heart beginning to race, I closed my eyes and clicked...

It was the best decision I ever made for my career.

In contrast to all my fears, my friends were so enthusiastic about what I was posting - even sharing it further to their friends and family. The feeling of being in control of my own articles was so liberating and allowed me to explore any idea that I wanted to, while honing my skill for writing and eye for valuable content. Not only that, but I learned how to write headings in an interesting way. How to take eye-catching photos to encourage readers to my site. I learned how to manage my time better in order to fit blogging around my schedule. I learned how to plan editorial calendars to create timely content that taps into global themes and events. I learned how to network online to connect with my readers. I connected with other bloggers and eventually with brands for collaboration. I created for myself all of the skills and experience that were valuable to a career in journalism.

That's how I started standing out from other applicants. Throughout my career, employers have loved my blog. Instead of focusing on who had the right degree at a credible university, they saw the benefits of someone who demonstrated a real passion for writing and the industry. They saw that I was someone who cared enough to practise it in my spare time. Browsing my blog, employers could see the evidence of my writing style and ideas. More importantly, they could see that I was serious, driven and disciplined.

To my surprise, it only took a few clicks of "publish" before brands wanted to work with me. I hadn't been blogging for even a year yet. There were so many well-known fashion bloggers out there with a huge reader base. So why me?

I hadn't given in to the pressure to follow the formula to become a popular fashion blogger. Wanting to be a good journalist, I created my blog to help people understand fashion, not just to inspire them with style ideas. There was a deeper level to it with more value for the reader. In the end, that's why I stood out. Brands wanted that added value. They wanted me to dive into their stories. I had the ability to share what's unique about them. I took my time to write a considered review - not just snap a photo of me using their product.

I was going against the grain to stay authentic to myself rather than following in the footsteps of what a "successful fashion blogger" looks like. This meant that I was recognised for my unique value in the market. It also meant that I was happier and more fulfilled in what I was doing.

If You're Scared, You're Doing It Wrong, You May Be Onto Something

I'm sure you've felt it before.

When you want to be successful in what you do, you tend to look at others who have gone before you, wondering how they "made it". Analysing their website, videos or social media pages, you pick up on cues, noticing what brilliant ideas they've had and how they draw their audience to invest in them. You play with the idea of doing the same because that must be how it's done, right?

This feeling is especially strong in competitive markets where there tends to be a number of people doing the same thing to achieve similar results. Take the fashion blogger example from my own experience, seeing the adoration of online fans and fellow fashion bloggers commenting on each other's posey pictures. It was difficult not to fall into the trap of thinking this is how a fashion blog must be run in order to be a success. Although I didn't end up giving in to the temptation of following in their footsteps for a fast track to fame, there were certainly moments where I felt like I must be doing it wrong, that I should pack in my vision for the tried and tested method.

Moments like these are usually down to impatience. It's thinking you're "supposed to be" at a certain stage already when you're still a few steps behind that. But who says you're supposed to be there? This is your journey, and you're supposed to be exactly where you currently are. It doesn't mean you're going to remain stuck there. You know you won't let yourself do that. Don't panic.

The worst that can happen is that you realise there is a better way to achieve what you're trying to do and you evolve. You evolve to learn how to connect with your audience in a better way. You learn from your experiences and you adapt. But don't change for the sake of copying someone else's version of success. Why morph into your competitors when you can stand out and be yourself?

Whenever I notice imposter syndrome feelings creep up again, I take the time to reflect on how far I have come. I see what my audience and those that work with me think of my blog. When we keep note of all our little wins, reading back through them can remind us that we are getting somewhere. It's easy to forget all that we've done and all that we've learned so far. I keep a friendly reminder in the notes app on my phone so it's always handy whenever I have moments of doubt.

In the same way, listen to your audience and collaborators. Do they tend to give you positive feedback? What suggestions have they made that you could take into account? If the majority of people who interact with you have a positive experience, then there is a value in what you are providing. Then it is worth it to keep going for those that need to hear/see/experience what you have to offer. If you do receive criticism, look at it as a chance to reflect and improve your craft, not as a signal that you should quit.

For me, thinking back to the support of my friends, family and the comments from readers helps to counter doubt. The lovely feedback received from collaborators on the style, genuine feel and quality of my blog is enough to remind me that I am doing something right. I just had to be patient and continue to learn and evolve in order to push myself and my blog even further.

Take Advantage Of What's In Your Power

Cut to a few years down the line. My very first site had transformed from fashion-focused, to a full lifestyle and career blog offering inspiring content across style, beauty, food, art, travel, culture, sustainability and well-being.

The blog evolved with me as I grew in my career, working across different magazines and brands. I upskilled, using my blog to my advantage again to explore new topics I was interested in, building up my portfolio further across different genres. Just like before, this opened up more doors for me and gave me a whole new set of skills.

Once I'd mastered covering all sorts of lifestyle topics - on my blog as well as in my career - I came to realise that I now had another selling point as a blogger. I am an industry-trained professional. This is something that's quite rare in the saturated blogging market made up of hobbyists and self-taught content creators.

That's not to say that what they're doing isn't great. However, I had an advantage for brands looking for someone who has been trained in how to sell with words, and as a result, sell their products.

I used my industry skills to help me reach out to dream brands, far bigger than any I had ever worked with before. Sharing my content ideas and showing them that I understand how to promote them in a genuine way that connects with readers propelled my business.

I used my unique skill set and experience to land me the collaborations I was striving for, rather than trying to portray myself as the typical version of what a "successful" blogger looks like. These days success is often characterised as a social media following of over 10k - minimum.

With an Instagram following at a 10th of that size, I still get to work with global brands. By positioning my strengths, I'm achieving what "successful bloggers" are able to achieve, without the ridiculously high commitment to social media. That may be something that many others enjoy, but for me, spending hours of my time trying to grow a social media audience was hours of time taken away from my actual passion - writing.

Now, with several years of experience behind me and proof that you can stay true to who you are and still be successful, I want to help others achieve the same.

I am particularly passionate about this, having not followed the traditional route into my career. I was also fed up of seeing young bloggers posting content that was clearly influenced by copying the stereotypical "blogger" template. Where were their unique qualities and personalities? The stuff that makes us all interesting as individuals? I wanted to help people become unique content creators.

At the same time, I couldn't blame them. In the blogging world particularly, the competition is very high which has led to somewhat of a secret society. No one wants to share classified information on how they got to where they are for fear that they will increase their own competition.

I struggled with this when I first started, reaching out to bigger bloggers in the hopes that they would be willing to share advice. All I got were fluffy answers, nothing that could actually help me out.

Throughout my journey so far, I have disregarded the norm and the rulebooks. Believing in my unique value, I wasn't scared of copycats. Audiences are smart and they can see through inauthenticity anyway. We shouldn't be hiding our knowledge out of fear. Being secretive and selfish isn't going to get you very far. Besides, everyone has something to offer and you never know - someone who you help may be open to helping you in return someday.

Wanting to break some of these bad habits in the blogging industry, I founded Bloggers Inspired, a collective for up and coming bloggers to collaborate and share advice. Taking on the experiences of others is a far more efficient way to learn than making all the mistakes yourself. Plus, having the support and power of a group to break through the competition is much easier than one voice trying to be heard among a massive, noisy crowd.

Outside of the blogging community, I also started to run workshops with university students in creative degrees such as graphic design, fine art, languages and dance, teaching them the ways in which a blog can be used as a powerful portfolio. Contrary to popular belief, blogs aren't reserved for writers.

They can be used as a creative hub of expression, sharing your work, ideas, inspirations and thoughts on the industry. All you need to do is write in your natural voice, as if you were talking to a friend. It's far more interesting to read than the formal style of writing we're taught in school.

The more eyes I opened, and the more connections I made with others who were going through similar feelings that I once had, the more I wanted to help. Having the opportunity and privilege to grow with an amazing community of female entrepreneurs is also the reason I co-founded the Queens In Business Club.

Too many times, I have heard stories about people who desperately want to follow their dream but can't because they just didn't study the right course or weren't naturally gifted in a particular skill. There may be some professions where this can be a blocker, such as medicine where you need to invest the years in training. But in most cases I hear about, it isn't something that can't be overcome.

I seek to help people to achieve their goals no matter their background. We have the world at our fingertips. There is so much to explore and learn online, in any format that suits you, from written articles to visual diagrams to video tutorials or online courses. You can learn how to upcycle furniture, sew your own clothes, DJ, cook like a master chef, manage your finances, understand politics, use a professional camera, take care of your houseplants so they stop dying (not just me, right?).

The point is, you can learn the basics to almost anything for free online. And once you have the basics, you have the incentive and confidence to invest in more training.

Just because you have a family and a full-time job to pay your mortgage, doesn't mean you don't have some time to work towards your dream. We all find time to scroll aimlessly through social media, don't we?

Remember, there is no right way and there is no "normal" time-frame that you should be adhering to. Make it work for you and make it work around your other commitments. You'll be further along than you ever thought you'd be in no time. That's when you realise your dream is closer than it ever has been before. Isn't that an exciting feeling?

Going Backwards And Feeling Uncomfortable

As a young child, I was an avid magazine reader, collecting boxes upon boxes of fashion mags, music mags, and celebrity mags, much to my mother's dismay. You know the story already.

Having idolised the magazine world for so many years, it was no surprise that there came a time in my journey where I shaped my blog around these influences. I was at a point where I wanted to level up. I wanted Inspired in the City to be bigger and better than it was at that moment in time. So I looked up to the inspirations of my childhood, all those magazines that were now available in digital formats on the web. Clicking through the glossy sites of the glossy magazines, I decided I wanted my blog to feel like this - professional, slick and stylish.

But to become a magazine brand I needed to change the way I was writing my posts. I needed to alter my voice from first-person to third-person, removing the "blogger" aspect of my site and talking from my brand's perspective: "in this post we share our tips" rather than "in this post I share my tips", for example.

Painstakingly reworking all of my current posts (there were hundreds), I removed the personal elements from the introductions and replaced them with the "brand voice". I was confident that this was the way I was going to drive Inspired in the City to new levels of success.

A month or so in, I was left scratching my head. My website's traffic was dropping, and my content wasn't receiving the same level of enthusiasm as it once had. But why? Seeing as this drop directly related to the changes on my website, it was pretty clear that this move to becoming a "brand" hadn't gone down well. It may be the right option for traditional magazines, but it certainly didn't seem to be what my audience had signed up for.

I decided to put some feelers out, asking followers of the blog for their thoughts. They told me what should have been obvious to me from the start - I'd lost my voice. I'd lost my warm personal connection with the audience. I'd become a big cold brand.

Spending years staying authentic to myself had brought me my initial success. Now that I had it, I threw it aside without thinking, drawn in by the shiny proposition of becoming a magazine brand, just like those I had admired. Worse than that, I'd gone against my own advice - don't try to emulate another's success.

The reason these websites work for glossy magazines is because they're purpose built for that goal from the start. There's a huge team running these sites, contributing to them daily, drawing in a certain type of audience with fast, clickable content.

My site was not built for that and my audience isn't with me for that type of content. They champion honest opinions and useful content that can inspire them to live a more sustainable, creative and empowered life - that is my tag line after all.

I'm not saying that I won't have a team of writers one day, and that I can never be a brand, but my version may need to look different to the glossy magazine model. And ultimately, that's a good thing. It'll align better with my values and my personal mission, and it'll offer something different to what is already out there.

Realising this, I took a brave step backwards. I undid my big brand transformation and reinjected my personality into my posts. Rather than being embarrassed of having made a wrong move for my business, I was content in the lesson that I had learned. Without trying and failing, how would I have known that this wasn't right for me? It's better to experiment and test your ideas than to never try and therefore hinder your growth.

Stepping backwards is sometimes the right way to step forwards.

Don't let the fear of making the wrong decision stop you from ever moving forward. Even if you have to step back in the end, at least you now know for certain what you don't want to do - which can be just as useful to know as what you do want to do.

In fact, that uncomfortable feeling of stepping into the unknown is a sign of growth. You're breaking free of your comfort zone and heading into the growth zone. Ask any entrepreneur and they'll tell you that feeling completely ready for the next step is a myth. So don't wait around for a time that feels right. Chances are that time will never come.

When I first signed up as a Co-Founder of the Queens In Business Club, I knew that it would involve plenty of live sessions and video recording. This is something that I'd always been afraid of as I'd never done it before and thought I'd be no good. But I took my own advice and figured that I'd learn and improve along the way.

To my surprise, it was so much easier than I had ever imagined. I wasn't perfect the first few times I tried it. But when things are left to our imagination, we often make them out to be far worse than the reality is. So despite tripping over a few of my words, I was still left buzzing off the fact that I actually did it. It was more painless than I thought it would be.

Overcoming something that was once a fear is also one of the biggest drivers. It's proof that you can achieve more than you thought you were capable of. You can overcome challenges along the way. It's a great confidence booster.

It's about being brave enough to take the leap and grounded enough to know that you can always come back to your comfort zone, should you need to. You can step back in order to re-evaluate before you gear up to take another leap.

It's this resilience, paired with the ability to take criticism and failure on board in a way that fuels you, that separates the successful from the unsuccessful. You already stand out from your competition if you've taken a few knocks and you're still getting back up again.

This is a sentiment described well in one of my favourite quotes, taken from Being Boss by Emily Thompson and Kathleen Shannon: "If you're not falling down, you're not trying to stand up."

The truth is there are millions of people with great business ideas. But only a handful that choose not to give up when they inevitably stumble at the first hurdle. And there will always be hurdles.

It's how you deal with them and process them that counts.

If the reason for your business is built upon a true passion of yours, then keeping that drive and fire burning is more achievable. That is why it's so important to align it with your personal values, not mould it on someone else's. It takes effort and it's not easy, but it's certainly worth it.

So don't give up. Learn and adapt. Don't wait for opportunities to land in your lap. Take advantage of what is in your control. Don't think it's too late or it can't work for you. Pick up new skills and find solutions that do work for you. It's ok if you don't end up where you thought you wanted to go. Stay intuitive to your current values and be open to change.

Whatever you do, do it your way, on your terms. And have fun with it!

About Me

I'd like to dedicate this chapter to my younger sister, Zara, who first inspired me to lead by example.

Being part of this book among so many brilliant female entrepreneurs is a feeling like no other. Too often in business, the focus is on beating our competition in any way we can. But I've never quite agreed with this school of thought. The world is full of variety and there is something that each and every one of us can offer that is valuable to others. As the saying goes, 'someone else's success is not your failure'.

My background is in the fashion, magazine and blogging world. For what sounds like a glamorous industry, I have experienced a lot of ugliness. Sly undercuts, psychological games or blatantly trampling over each other. Some peers were ruthless in their pursuit of success.

But I've never played that game. It may have meant that I didn't rise up the ranks as quickly as I could have, but I've kept my integrity intact. More importantly, I've encouraged others to do the same. Banding together, sharing advice, helping each other up -

that's where true success comes from. And once you have the power of many behind you, there's no stopping your momentum.

In my own business, I am Founder and Editor in Chief of lifestyle and career blog, Inspired in the City, helping you live more sustainably, creatively and empowered. Within the Queens In Business Club, I help female entrepreneurs break down their writing fears and increase their confidence.

Passionate about community over competition, I love helping creatives and entrepreneurs understand the power of writing and blogging in building your personal brand or business. In 2020, I became the first blogger to deliver guest talks at London's University of Roehampton.

Through all my endeavours, I hope to empower others to be able to communicate their ideas and take control of their own career paths.

Be Ready To Listen!

Tanya Grant

Founder & CCI

The TNG Designs Group Limited

"It takes patience and time to set the right foundation – don't rush it." --- Coral Chung

Getting Comfortable With Uncomfortable

Before you get into the crux of who I am by way of this chapter and what you're about to read, please note that I am not a writer, nor do I journal. What I do is speak from the heart. So grab yourself a nice beveraaaage (drink), a highlighter, a pen or pencil to make your notes and let's get stuck in!

So this is me. I'm a Brand Specialist and a woman in business who hails from a 'TRONG' Jamaican lineage. I was born in Saudi and currently reside in "Sunny" England (ha-ha that's an inside joke to anyone who lives in the UK).

In my early twenties, if you'd have said to me…

"Tan, when you graduate from Uni, the job you believe you're going to get straight away, because your tutor said "Oh yeah you'll be fine", isn't going to happen. Oh, and that permanent role you'll keep on looking for won't land for another 13+ years. Oh, and the freelancing roles you will get, will poop all over the structure and certainty you once had for knowing what's going to be landing in your bank account each month. Your experiences will test you beyond your patience and knowledge, BUT you'll be ok. You'll learn to turn your frustrations and mental blocks into your power which will become your V.O.I.C.E." - Visionary, Openness, Integrity, Creative and Educate/Enjoyment.

If you'd have said all of that I might have looked at you sideways, but I would have said to you... BRING IT ON!

Back then, I had an attitude that was, I'd like to say, a healthy mix of stubbornness and sheer determination. To a certain extent it always pushed me to prove 'you' otherwise. In fact, if I'm honest, that part hasn't actually changed about me. When I am told "no you can't..." or "no it won't work..." that alone is enough to add extra fuel to my fire, to push and make sure that the very thing in question DOES work.

Now don't get me wrong, although I may be a little head strong, I'm not a cocky person. Believe me when I say that I count every single blessing thrown my way daily. What I have grown to believe in, FINALLY, is me. Was I always this bold and forthcoming? NOPE. I wrote that word 'finally' for a reason.

Did I always have a clear-cut direction in what I was doing and where I was going with it? DEFINITELY NOT! Did it take time to get to where I am now? YUP, and my journey's still going!

But here's the thing, I've learnt to accept that my 'speed' is what it is, and it won't be the same as my peers. Theirs won't be the same as mine either. I learnt to become OK with that. I had to for my own sanity. The experiences I've had throughout my journey are what they are. I went through them because I had to. All so that they could prepare me for the here, now and all of what's to come.

I'm a strong believer in my ability to get things done, and if it's not right the first try then I get it right on the next try. I won't give up until I've exhausted all avenues. I'm a natural problem solver, it's just what I do. And it's what I install into my career.

From Zoned-Out To Zen

I graduated from Uni in 2003, after partying with De La Soul at my end of year summer ball, and set my sights on conquering the big bad world of design. I was on a high. I was pumped. I was READY!

I applied for every Junior Designer role I came across. I equally got rejected from every Junior Designer role I came across. It got to the point where I was getting used to it after a while. I felt deflated. It was a kind of frustration that annoyed the hell out of me. Especially when I heard about all my other classmates landing roles in their "dream" jobs. I mean, I was happy for them and all. But I hated hearing about it all the same. I often zoned out of the conversation and entered into my Zen happy place.

Have you ever been in a situation where you reunite with someone after having not seen them for a while, and then were presented with that loaded question, "So how are things going?"

Can you feel that knot and churning sensation in your stomach? You know it's now your turn to share the goods of what's been going on with you, and the reality of that is far from matching theirs. Do you feel it now? That was me every time.

Ha-ha, now I can safely say that I have no problem with that question, regardless of my answer these days. Back then, I used to dread that question. I didn't want to hear of yet another person "making it". I would hear stories of how someone sent their CV into a prospective job printed on a pair of orange under pants, and landed their role. Creativity or no creativity, I couldn't understand who would want to hire someone who did that. I would then hear of another person getting scooped up, and hired shortly after graduation. Of others starting their own businesses and landing major clients too.

Meanwhile little old me - former year group leader and all round get on and doer - was jobless. I didn't get it. I understood others got those opportunities early on because they were all deserving of them, but so was I. It was the latter that I couldn't see the reasoning behind. It made me question my tutors who told me I'd be fine. It made me think that perhaps I wasn't actually as "good" as I believed myself to be. I felt inferior and lost. I felt like a failure before I'd even started my journey. Can you relate to this at any time in your life?

At this time in my life, I was wallowing in inconsistency of 'why this and why not that'. It felt like an eternity of self-loathing. But little did I know, it was all actually leading me to my first big break!

Be Ready For Opportunities

Fast forward one year to the summer of 2004. You would have witnessed me with the biggest grin on my face, head up, shoulders back, strutting down the busy paths of Oxford Street. I had a new bounce in my step. I'd landed my first freelancing Graphic Designer role in the marketing department for one of London's leading women's retail agencies, TOPSHOP.

Working with this internationally known agency is what kick started my career. I built up such a rapport with them that I went on to gain repeated contracts with TOPMAN, Dorothy Perkins and Miss Selfridges, during the Arcadia reign.

Sometimes we go along kicking and screaming thinking that we're doomed. At times that's all we can see and focus on. I'm here to tell you guys that it's ok to feel this way about your situation, but don't stay feeling like that. It doesn't serve you, so why allow it?

As I'm sitting here writing this chapter for you, I'm beginning to realise that time of uncertainty was where that 'healthy mix of stubbornness and sheer determination' really started to take shape.

Toing And Froing

That's pretty much the life of a freelancer... well at least for me it was. Toing and froing, working here, there and everywhere.

What initially started out as a temporary way for me to get my foot in the door for a full-time role spiralled into something else. I was now a fully-fledged, freelancing graphic designer bouncing from company to company.

Thankfully my contracts were long with each placement. I had repeated call backs from those I worked with. I was comfortable with that. Even to the point when seeing their design teams grow without my being considered for a permanent role, apart from one case, didn't even phase me. I'd gotten used to my new lifestyle.

I actually quite liked it. I gained a world of experience. I liked the freedom I had, to go off and travel when I wanted. Aside from the occasional freak out moments where I'd realise that I hadn't put enough aside to pay my taxes, the money was good. Knowing that my contracts had an 'end' was an added bonus at times too. Especially when the jobs were working for people who didn't align with my beliefs (and that's me putting it nicely!). It gave me an easy out.

I was happy just cruising. But all of that was the surface part of it.

The reality of freelancing as a graphic designer for some of those larger retail marketing companies meant that my level of creativity had to be parked to one side. It wasn't all the time, but it was enough for that uneasy feeling of frustration to start to rear its ugly head again. It was almost as if I was their genie in the lamp that my contractors would rub anytime they needed my help. They'd ask for their three wishes and send me right back into said lamp until they were ready for me again.

I remember going through a period where I used to sit there staring at my computer after being handed another load of senseless, mundane artwork to get through. It was mind numbing, really mind numbing! Imagine for a quick minute, because I want you to experience this little moment with me. Imagine that you're staring at a plain wall. On that wall is the most boring colour that you can think of, and you have to watch…it…dry…all...day...long. Day in, day out. Do you feel the mix of numbness and frustration bubbling up inside of you? That anger of knowing that you have more to offer here, but knowing that you won't be taken any notice of because you're here for that job and that job alone. They made it clear that I was to offer nothing else. I felt devalued and silenced because of it. I used to sit and question, "Why the hell am I here and furthermore what the hell am I doing?"

I was in an environment hearing of many people getting on with what I felt I should be doing. Some even had their side hustles. I had an abundance of ideas, but I could not seem to do anything with them. I didn't have the confidence any more to create my side hustle while paying my dues at the boring jobs.

Take yourself back to watching the paint dry moment. Now add on to that… imagine you've turned around and can see a HUGE glass building. Happening inside is all of the action you want to get involved in. But you don't have access to get in there. And there it is again, it's that angry, bubbly feeling gearing up for a good old outburst!

When you're creatively minded, and feel like you're watching everyone else get on with what you feel you should be getting involved with, it does something to a person's psyche. At some point, something has to give. When you think about it, at a point like this you have two choices. You either shut up, quit the moaning and keep going along a path that you know deep down doesn't serve you. Or you can step out to step back in again and make your move.

I chose to shut up…just joking!

Of course, I didn't.

I chose to step out, so that I could reassess what I needed to do in order to step back into my creativity again.

Step Out To Step Back In
Earlier I told you about my freelancing hang ups. What I should have added was that, although the money was good, it was a bit of a yo-yo income. What I mean by that, is those good money moments came along with those bad money moments. My getting in any new big contracts were at times few and far between. I found it tiring being always on the lookout again and again, never 'settled'. I wanted to set my sights on something a little more secure.

And so in February of 2016, my stepping out led me to finding a full time Senior Designer role at a medium sized company, near Waterloo Station. That extra bounce in my step I had as a new freelancer walking down Oxford Street came back again, and at this point I felt that this was it. I did it! I finally got my full-time role! Quite literally 13 years later, reluctantly I might add, but I got it.

I'd finally been recognised for my creative talents at a level I thought I was worthy of then. I'd be overseeing a small team of Junior Designers. At times I'd even get to do a little travelling in between - to the main office in West Yorkshire that is, but hey it was travelling all the same!

It's funny that although I was in a full-time role, I'd forgotten that I had to change my mentality around that. I was still working with the mind of a freelancer. The rules I had to abide by were different. I mean, who would have known that it wasn't ok to go ahead and book up a few short breaks here and there, without having triple checked it with the world of people!

I had to fix up in that department and at the same time that's when I realised that "My time" was no longer mine anymore. Although I didn't like that, if I wanted to stay, I had to adjust.

As time went on, my experience at this company led me to working with other brands such as New Look, Missguided and one of the European leading giants in retail in its own right, Primark. This should have been the "big opportunity" I'd been working towards for all these years.

Be Aware Of Your Side Steps
It was great until the point when it wasn't anymore. My role evolved and subtly, slowly separated me from my passion of design.

We were gearing up to move premises to a location now closer to London Bridge. Two colleagues and I turned it into a bad-ass splinter group that managed the office move. It meant that I'd be taking a sidestep into doing something else other than the role I was hired for.

I became an office space surveyor, interior decorator, office furniture finder and furniture designer. How did designing a high-seated breakfast bar area become my purpose? As much as I actually enjoyed doing that, I should have seen the warning signs.

I remember telling my friend's husband about the new shenanigans going on. He asked me "Tan, if you're doing all of that, who's doing your design work?" The long and short of that answer was, no one. Yes, the Junior Designers had their artwork bits to get on with but even that wasn't much.

You see, that little sidestep in my role was taking up all of my time. We weren't working on any other projects. So what did that actually mean?

I should add that this was all around the time that Brexit was picking up momentum. Suppliers were panicking and hiking up prices, or pulling out of deals within certain industries. Especially in the retail and design industry.

Fast forward to the new year where by now, the confusion of Brexit and what it entailed was picking up pace even more. The uncertainty about suppliers and outsourcing became common.

By now, I was nearing a full year into my role and the entire London team had moved into the new office successfully. We were all completely settled into the new groove of things and I have to say, the office was a pretty cool, light, airy and creative place overlooking an equally open park complete with tennis court area.

I remember looking out a window watching what looked to be a prissy dog fight about to go down. The Creative Director and Senior Manager called the entire London team and I to meet them in the boardroom. I had a sneaky suspicion about what this was going to be as the workplace 'tom-tom drums' had been pounding big time. Not to mention the day before this meeting one of our teammates had been let go.

"Due to recent events…" kick started the typical spiel of bad news, and it ended with a warning that there were going to be a few "…team re-structures". The day ended. We all went home with that now playing out in the back of our minds.

A new day came and with it the summons of yet another meeting. But this time rather than the calamity of everyone trying to pack into the room, it was only me with my Creative Director.

"Here we go," I said to myself. However, the result wasn't what I had thought it to be. I was told that although my Senior role no longer existed, they positioned a new Graphic Designer opportunity to me - which came along with a hefty pay cut. I was given one week to decide what I wanted to do. My mental patience was wearing thin with this company. However, I decided to stay and continue to build on my experience.

The next few months would bring about a whole new meaning to "overworked and underpaid". I was actually doing a hell of a lot more than in my Senior role. There were at least 10 other redundancies during that time. Morale was at an all-time low. Everyone was over the bull crap the company was spewing out, but we continued to accept it. After all, something was better than nothing, right? When the final round of June 2017 redundancies came about, that included me. It didn't actually surprise me. As a matter of fact, for me, I couldn't have received better news!

Side Hustle While In Your Day Job
You see, during this time I was still holding on to my little side businesses that would help start-up companies get on their way. In

that same year, I realised the only way to actually do the creative designing that I was born to do, was to make it happen.

My plans I had in mind were shouting louder and louder at me to get on and do it. When I was made redundant, where I typically would have had that bubble of anger and frustration kick in again, it didn't.

I had to fight myself from smiling during that meeting. I was so thrilled. I mean, yes, I did feel let down and disappointed at losing a job. But there was a shift in me and I also felt ridiculously happy. The sun was out that day, shining brighter than it ever had.

I was now free! It was time for me to step back out so that I could step back in again.

Ears Wide Open!
A few weeks after having been made redundant, I made my move. I tapped into my old contacts at TOPSHOP and TOPMAN. I got back into the world of freelancing again!

This new journey took me to 2019 where I set my sights on making what I do work better for myself. It was the "how can I…." part, that I was ready to pay attention to. Now at the time when I raised that question to God, I was amazed to see what answers actually fired back at me.

I was ready to listen; I mean truly listen to the answer. Like ears wide open, ready to receive and take action with the answers to my question, kind of listening. I continue to practice this to this day.

I was also ready to shout proudly about who I had become. The minute I did that, I started knowing and doing better. I had to start from scratch and be OK with that, especially if I wanted to 'make what I do work better for myself'.

I sought out amazing mentorship. I began putting the "fun back into re-investing" in and re-educating myself. I pretty much re-built what I initially thought was a reasonably ok "business".

I created systems which add game-changing value to the clients I work with. They get to select packages that help them level up even more than before.

And so, using the tools I learnt, I took myself from a freelancer to a Brand Specialist. I'm now the Founder & CCI of a multi-disciplined company called The TNG Designs Group Limited. CCI or 'Chief Creative Innovator' by the way, is my unique role in my company. Have a think on what your unique role could be in your company.

Another thing I had to re-establish was my purpose for doing what I do and why I do it. Where branding was concerned, I examined what my annoyances and frustrations were towards those who paid no attention to the idea of having a brand.

It annoys the hell out of me to see so many small to medium business owners neglect the one big thing in their business that can help to stop them from drowning amongst their competition. If they knew that by having a noteworthy brand backing who they are, could equally help them to not only make better connections with the audience they actually want to work with and ultimately sell without selling they'd give it A LOT more credit! They would capture the sales they may not be aware that they are losing out on. I want to help them to pay a hell of a lot more attention to it! OK, ok! Rant over, but you get the gist.

I also went below surface level and dug a little deeper to find out key questions that I'd like you to consider for yourself. I examined my values and my beliefs. Here's a little insight for your added reference:

My main three values are: Guide. Grounding. Growth.

My purpose or ethos for doing what I do as a whole is:

> To guide and help others to create a solid grounding that allows them to grow and be empowered, so that they can do the same for those they encounter as well.

So now it's your turn.

What's yours?

Use the following questions to help as an added prompt to get you going:

- What are your values (pick your top 3-5 to get yourself started)?
- What is your why or the true reason behind you doing what you do?
- What do you stand for? What are your personal beliefs?
- What are your beliefs based around your product or services – why is it any good?
- What are your annoyances in your industry?

If you know the answer to these already then brilliant! Get out there and use those to your advantage! If you don't know the answers to these questions, then no worries at all. Take a little time to think about it. Write it out either now or after you finish reading this chapter.

Figure out what those things could be for you. If you're saying that you don't have the time to figure this out right now, then re-read what I wrote for my frustration. Find the time now. The things we are avoiding in our business are often the things we need to focus on the most.

I was also presented with the opportunity to show up regularly in like-minded online communities to share value with my advice.

Learning and rediscovering what matters most to me gave me the courage to show up. I found certainty. I can now speak confidently about what I do and why I do it.

This was a special reason that we six Queens In Business Club Co-Founders bonded. There's power in good relationships, especially when you have aligned your values. The only way to know that is to show up and listen. I mean truly listen - ears wide open ready to receive and take action.

The long and short of it all…the crux of my message: be ready to listen, and welcome the answers coming to you.

I know that sometimes as we work through the rigmarole of getting our businesses together it gets overwhelming. Whatever stage we're at in our journeys is ok. The time it takes to get to where you feel you need to be will take as long as it needs to. So be OK in being patient with that.

Believe you me when I say that in the beginning, I had to dig reeeaaallly deep to find that patience. But I found it. It took time for me to get to where I am now, but I made it here. There's now certainty and clarity. I've still got some more moves to make though, so I'm not done quite yet. I will continue to innovate to provide more and more for my clients.

We're forever trying to sprint during a marathon, so again be OK with tackling one thing at a time. Don't tire or burn yourself out doing it. I've been there, done that, got the t-shirt and the masterclass! (QIB Club joke)

All in all, if there's anything that you take away from this chapter it's having tenacity, being resilient and staying persistent will help you to stay on track. When you feel stuck, don't feel that you have to stay still. Try until you set yourself free.

Move around, wriggle a little and work out the tactics that will pull you out or cut you lose!

Wishing you all the best!

About Me

'When you know better you do better!' ...a little snippet from one of my favourite quotes by Maya Angelou. This powerful and oh so very true thought is part of why I do what I do.

I am a Brand Specialist living in UK London, who is a natural solution-based collaborator, inspirational entrepreneur, course creator, empowering friend, fabulous aunty, Co-Founder of the

74

Queens In Business Club and the Founder & CCI of a multi-disciplined company called The TNG Designs Group Limited.

It's a mouthful but I love it all the same. As you get to find out more about what I do, you'll realise that I love helping, educating and empowering others, so that they don't feel lost in who they are or what they're doing in life and in business.

I used to feel lost in what I was doing so I know how much of an annoying, uneasy, foggy-minded kind of feeling it can be.

It causes you to lose focus and at times blurs the vision of you not only recognising your 'inner coolness' or talents, but also causes you to stop wanting to achieve certain positive things. Sometimes it even leads to you giving up in the process.

But really… when you think about it, we only feel like that because we're blocked and don't have the answers to our questions…yet!

So, in order to get those answers, it's a case of learning how to put those right questions out there and to be Ready To Listen to what gets fired back at us. Then we can know and do better. I did it and that's how I became known as the Brand Specialist of The TNG Designs Group Limited.

These answers came to me by way of my brilliant mentors, my loving supportive ever patient family and friends, the Queens who I work with and support, my clients and peers, my faith in God and my faith in myself.

I love and truly thank you all!

Do What Makes You Happy

Carrie Griffiths

Voice and Transformational Performance Coach

"True beauty is knowing who you are and what you want and never apologising for it." --- Pink

You have no idea how amazing you are.

It is my mission to help you to use your voice. Not just to be heard, but also to speak your truth. Because both are crucial to your happiness.

Years ago, in the early 2000s, I overheard a conversation that would shape the rest of my life. Travelling on the top deck of one of London's red buses in the early summer, a teenage girl and her mother were talking about their upcoming shopping trip:

"Well, I don't really know what I want." the young girl commented. Her mother replied, "Oh! That's very bad. You must always know what you want."

Of course, her mother wasn't merely alluding to the shopping trip, but to hopes, dreams and goals. I refer back to this conversation often and raised my daughter similarly.

I want to make something very clear: you can do whatever you want - as long as you know what it is, remain focused, and never give up. You don't have to conform to societal norms. You don't have to please people that don't pay your bills, much less those who don't even care whether you're able to.

Born To Do It?

It would be easy to brush over the humble beginnings of my singing career, but I want to dispel the myth that successful singers start young and are "born to do it". Because that is definitely not my story!

I grew up on the council estates of West London. I was a dancer as a child and teenager, winning a number of talent and dance competitions, and performing at street festivals and local carnivals. I signed my first autograph at the age of ten after I joined my mum's band on stage performing a self-choreographed routine. I stopped dancing when I was 16 and never really thought about performing after leaving school.

At the age of 23, I was married after a very short whirlwind romance and I was deeply in love with my then husband. We bought a starter home in a little town in Kent. There had been a few problems, but that was normal. I had always been a misfit, but here I was, finally living a "normal" life. I took my marriage vows seriously and I didn't want to end up another young divorcee.

A year and a half into our marriage, I'd performed with a local Musical Theatre group and enjoyed another taste of the world of entertainment. I thought back to my days as a dancer and I knew that this was what I wanted to do. But although my husband had given me my first singing lessons for Christmas, as a traditionalist, he didn't support my ambitions of becoming a singer. Very quickly, things became very difficult at home.

There may be times when you have to make difficult decisions in order to do what you love.

I'd be lying if I said it was easy when I left my husband. People I had known for years, and some who didn't know me from Jack, said I was a selfish mother. They decided that I should be at home with my daughter, rather than "living the high life".

The high life – yeah, right! Interesting that none of them had said the same thing when I was working nights at the casino…

Travelling through the wind, rain, hail and snow, loading in and out of venues, up and down flights of stairs, getting ready in the toilet, being treated like dirt and fighting to get paid after a full week at work, is definitely not "the high life". That 90 minutes or so on stage is the culmination of years of training, study, practise, planning, organisation, hustle and grind. I spent many days and nights wondering if I was doing the right thing, but I knew that "normal" wasn't for me and I had to show my daughter that it's ok to go against the grain and go after what you truly want.

Like other industries, the main reason most musicians struggle financially is that they aren't trained in business. There is a large section of society that believes that art shouldn't be sold. People who are not themselves artists constantly tell artists that they shouldn't be in it for the money. Paradoxically, these are some of the same people who happily pay art dealers thousands for a painting or pay a promoter for VIP tickets to see their favourite band.

Successful creatives understand that art can be a business and treat their art as a set of assets – viable products and services that they can monetise and profit from. Just like other entrepreneurs.

Networking is fundamental to your success in any industry. I didn't consider myself particularly good at networking at the time. But looking back, I built up a long list of contacts in various towns, cities, and countries, and in different genres.

By 2008, I'd played hundreds of gigs in pubs, clubs and small venues up and down the UK. OK, up and down England! I had recorded with producers in Europe and the US, done voiceover work in the Caribbean, and was making a modest amount of money – enough to pay my rent, topped up by my job with a large bookmaker. I'd worked tirelessly, building a reputation as a reliable and versatile singer and had worked with countless musicians, bands, songwriters, and producers of all genres. With ambitions to eventually teach in colleges and help young musicians, I started my degree at ICMP (Institute of Contemporary Music Performance) having failed three auditions previously. Here, I was around other ambitious and successful musicians. I honed my craft and learned even more about the business of music.

It's really important to be around people who have similar ambitions to yours, and to spend time learning from people who are doing or have done what you want to do. All of my teachers at ICMP were successful musicians in their own right and had many years of experience under their belts. Aside from formal education, there are lots of communities online, and a plethora of face-to-face groups and masterminds that you can meet up with in person for support and encouragement, to talk through the difficult times and share wins with.

I continued gigging, writing and performing, and in 2012 I was invited to go on tour with a rock 'n' roll band. They already had a following in Germany and I was excited to be part of it. I performed, recorded, and toured with them for five years.

We did the whole thing – sharing the stage with the biggest names in punk, ska, and hardcore, headlining large festivals, selling out our own shows. We built a huge following in the European punk and ska scene, even selling a number one album. There were newspaper and magazine articles, interviews, radio broadcasts and

TV appearances. We spent half of the week in a van, or in airplanes, driving for hours between gigs. We were performing to thousands of fans and meeting musicians I had grown up listening to! This be the stuff of dreams – and I was living it!

All of the sacrifices had paid off – I was a bona fide "singer".

During that time, I racked up performances in over thirty countries. I sang alongside countless leaders in the ska and punk scenes that have been heroes of mine for many years and my daughter even joined us for a weekend festival tour in 2015 and joined us on stage! Who knew, when I was planning world domination back in my two-up, two-down in Gillingham, that this would be my reality?

On a large festival stage early one summer evening, sweating under the lights, as I held up a beer saying "Cheers" to a crowd of thousands of people who were chanting our name, I thought back to the day I ended my marriage and left my home to become a singer, smiled to myself and thought, "I did it!".

The Growth Spurt
In 2016, I inadvertently heard of something called a paradigm. I finally understood the root of the personal demons that I had been battling behind the scenes and started working on freeing myself from them. My self-worth grew and I wanted to establish a level of equality within the band. With this change in dynamics, communication with some of my colleagues broke down and we realised it was time for me to move on.

As you progress and reach new levels, it's likely that you outgrow your original goals, and decide to do something different. It might take three years, it could take sixteen – as it had in my case, or it may never happen. If and when it does, it could be a bolt out of the blue, or a foreseeable change. However it occurs, don't fight it. Accept that this is your path and know that it's ok to move on, even if you don't feel ready.

I parted ways with Buster Shuffle, my former band, in 2017. It wasn't exactly amicable, but it wasn't the hostile split I had anticipated. Moving on can be both liberating and scary, especially when you've been in a bubble for a significant amount of time.

I still loved singing and performing but the thought of getting a group of people together in a room, travelling through the wind and rain to spend hours in a rehearsal room with no natural light, didn't fill me with the excitement it once had. I'd had a great time doing what I loved, but after seventeen years I was ready to branch out and make my mark in something other than singing. I had already been teaching singing, music and performance for fourteen years in colleges, youth programs, and training organisations. I focused on my job as Music Lecturer and Course Leader for Music Performance at a college in South London. I never planned on starting a business.

The Side Hustle
As the roller-skating hooker says in the Julia Roberts film Pretty Woman, "You gotta have a plan." I don't mind telling you that despite having been a musician for so many years, I had NO clue how to run a teaching business! To be honest, it didn't even click that I had a business.

You don't necessarily need a huge set up, or a large cash injection to start your business. Start where you are and get resourceful.

Because I had no plan, I had no strategy. I didn't even have a separate bank account, and I certainly didn't have a bookkeeper, as

Robert Kiyosaki repeatedly advised when I saw him speak in 2019. That was my first mistake.

I started teaching privately primarily to have some sense of purpose. I needed a reason to not party every weekend as if I was still on tour – a reason to get up on a Saturday morning rather than lay in bed nursing a hangover. My first advert cost £6 to place and I made it back fivefold with my first booking. I could smell success and pictured myself as the CEO of a top international vocal school. "This is easy" I thought. Little did I know what was to come.

After a few months I was fully booked at weekends and on weekday evenings with a growing waiting list. Having landed a dream job as a Vocal Director for an entertainment company, I was earning loads but I was tired and had no time to enjoy it. Then suddenly that job came to an end. That's when I started to take things seriously.

Once the lightbulb was flicked and I knew I had to make this work, I began to research business strategies. I built a website and set up a Facebook page and an Instagram account. I even did a Social Media Marketing training weekend and put out a couple of adverts, only to be met by tumbleweed! There was no response from the paid Facebook and Instagram adverts.

Fortunately, students found me via tutoring websites, platforms and apps and classified ads, so at the end of that year I was still fully booked. I knew I needed more training and so I registered for a business and marketing course and approached Christmas optimistic about the coming year. I was going to learn how to build a six-figure business. My life was about to change.

That business and marketing program did change the course of my life. But it was to take longer than I thought.

After Christmas, things suddenly changed. There was a period of dark times. Hardly any of my students rebooked and people on my waiting list weren't answering my calls. I put it down to the usual post-Christmas slump. But it didn't pick up in February, nor in March.

Getting Down To Business

The first and biggest challenge was shifting my mindset. I'd built up so many patterns and beliefs over the years – how singing lessons are sold, who to teach, how to attract clients and how to take money. I had worked out how to get paid in advance and minimise cancellations, but like most singing teachers I was charging by the hour. I didn't think there was any other way.

The second biggest challenge was marketing. I was like a fish out of water when it came to that part. I created a program, increased my prices, and proudly marketed a new sparkly version of my business.

Then nothing. No more students.

Riding The Rollercoaster

It felt like I cried every day that year. I felt like giving up and getting a full-time job. Most of the students I had didn't want to pay for more than one lesson at a time, and found cheaper, more traditional teachers. I had a core of just three students and kept my business ticking over, just about propped with my college salary. But with so few students and poor marketing skills, I couldn't see how I could possibly keep going. Considering I'd never intended to even start a business, I couldn't see the point of continuing.

Implementing what I'd learned on the business and marketing program, I created a free online course to get leads and I got them. But only one person out of those 300 leads bought my £7 upsell.

One. My only online sale from months and months of training and hard work.

I felt like a failure. I had focused on that lonely sale and measured my lack of success based on what I hadn't yet achieved. What I hadn't taken into consideration was the 300 leads I acquired that I could now speak to whenever I wanted. That is what they call The Long Game.

Start where you are. Yes, you need to consider the bigger picture, but what is your next step? Ask yourself these questions before you start shelling out any cash:

- Do you need to spend money on social media advertising, even if it only costs £2 a day? Could that money be better spent on a VA for a few hours a month, so that you can focus on what you do well?

- If you're going into debt to buy a course, do you have a plan to pay it back? I've sat in the audience being told by a mentor or guru how rubbish I am for not taking on debt to pay for their program. I know many people who put those courses on credit cards, took out loans, or borrowed from family, and lived to regret it. Some business coaches are so good at sales that they can literally smell the desperation when they tell you why you need THEIR program.

I'm not saying you shouldn't borrow money to make money, but it's important to know what you're buying, before you put your hand in your pocket.

The truth was that I wasn't ready to build a full-time business. My personal life was a joke. My relationship was in a mess, my mum was ill, and I was renting a room from a friend. To build a profitable business you have to have your sh*t together in the background. That might mean that you build a team who can carry the business forward when you're unable to, or, if you're going solo, that your personal life is stable. Both of these were missing in my case.

Fortunately, I had invested in honest mentors and coaches who genuinely want to see their delegates succeed.

Business can be lonely. So, when you find a supportive community of like-minded people, my advice is to use it at every opportunity. There will be someone who has come through something similar and can at the very least be a listening ear, and possibly even help you through it.

It's important to balance light with dark. Maybe if I'd been more open about what I was going through I would have gotten the help I really needed. Instead, I continued the performances of my touring days, made "awesome" videos that attracted three views and zero clients, and kept quiet. I kept plugging away. I meditated, I studied, and I doggedly attended business and marketing training, even when I felt like there was no business to market. As my life slowly became more stable, I was able to start making real plans.

I set up my first private group course through my business in the winter months of 2019. Things really started to pick up and my monthly group Taster sessions were really building momentum. I had a steady stream of new students again, and I was looking forward to the biggest year in my business.

Then COVID-19 hit.

The first UK lockdown started in March 2020. I had already been teaching online and so the transition was simple. But despite the recent upturn I had very little confidence in my business skills.

I spent the first month of lockdown busily trying to do what my mentors and coaches recommended and get new business in. Truth be told I was in a daze. I started leading daily vocal warm-ups on Facebook, which I later dubbed Wake Up and Warm Up. This would keep me sane over the next three months while I tried to work out how to keep building my business.

Use Your Voice
I said at the top of the chapter that I'm obsessed with your voice. And I am, for this reason: most people who are able to speak take their voice for granted. They don't pay attention to it while it's there and try to work out how to get it back quickly when they lose it or start to have problems. Maybe you're the same.

Being around so many speakers and coaches, I hear a lot of people overuse their voices, expecting to be able to keep pushing it day after day, week after week. If you keep doing this, you're eventually going to cause serious damage – and by then it might be too late.

Most entrepreneurs and business owners use our voices for work, even if we're not speakers or coaches. If you speak for hours at a time, if you want to project your voice regularly, or if you have problems with your voice, it's important to remember these three things:

1. Your vocal cords are strong but delicate. It doesn't take much to strain them and cause long term damage.

2. Your whole body is an instrument, not just your larynx.
3. The only way to control your voice is to work with it rather than against it.

Learning to work with your voice isn't something that you can learn overnight, or in one conversation from a voice coach at a networking event. I have helped to save a certain multi award-winning International Speaker's voice at an event, but if you want to save your voice long term, it takes time, practice, and patience.

The number one tip I can give you here is to avoid any tension around your throat, larynx and abdomen when you speak. I have worked with so many people who have heard about "speaking from the diaphragm" and tried to implement this without the guidance of a qualified and experienced voice coach only to end up causing more problems that take longer to unravel and resolve.

Whether you think you have issues with your voice or not, if you rely on it for work, I implore you to check in with a voice coach to make sure that you are not inadvertently establishing problems that could take longer to fix than they did to create.

And if you're reading this and thinking, "actually, my voice does get wobbly/weak/quiet/croaky when I speak at length/project/present/get nervous" then book an appointment with a reputable voice coach as soon as possible. Minimise damage and start to use your voice properly so that you can increase the lifespan of your professional voice.

Bonus Tip: Keep your voice hydrated.

You Never Know Who Is Watching...

Question: What do you do when you get a text on a Saturday afternoon inviting you to go into business with one of the people you respect the most in the world?

Answer: YOU TAKE THE OPPORTUNITY!

Being asked to be a Co-Founder of the Queens In Business Club is a defining moment in my career. It was the moment when I realised that all of the hard work had been noticed.

I didn't see constant likes and comments on my social media but I am consistent (even if I consistently made mistakes at first!), I was authentic, and I was ready for the opportunity. I'm not sure I'll ever fully understand why I was chosen but what I do know is that, when I make a decision about something, I give it 110%. My aim is to leave people, places, and things better than I found them. And with the QIB Club I truly believe that our pillars – Education, Empowerment, and Execution – are fundamental to doing exactly that.

I had absolutely no idea what I was letting myself in for!

At the time of writing, we're just six months into the business. It's been an absolute whirlwind, and we're only getting started.

Our membership speaks for the impact of the Queens In Business Club. We are a group of women who absolutely LOVE what we do. We've made mistakes. We have down days. We even have days when we don't believe in ourselves – just like you do. But with strong values, and a belief that together we can make a REAL difference, we are building something that has the potential to impact generations after we've gone.

Lessons Learned

By now it's clear that when I started out in business, I had no idea what I was doing. It's only now that I can see what I did, what I failed to do, and what I shouldn't have done, and piece the puzzle together.

The one thing I wish I knew when I first started out is this: pay someone. In fact, pay as many people as you can! Stay in your zone of genius. You can't be a bookkeeper, an accountant, a web designer, a graphic designer, a copywriter, a marketer, a sales expert and video creator. Ok, I know one lady who is. But most of us are really good at one or two things; the rest you should pay someone to do everything else.

I'm guilty of hanging onto things and trying to do them myself but I've learned the hard way that it's a false economy. It's a cliché because it's true. Stick to what you're good at. Outsource the rest.

I'm a fan of lists, so I have put together a checklist that I recommend for all start-ups. I'm sure that most of these appear on the majority of checklists for entrepreneurs. But that just goes to show how true they are.

1. Get a coach and a mentor.
2. Get a coach and a mentor.
3. Get a coach and a mentor.

Are you getting the message?

It's vital that you get the right guidance and have accountability from people who have been on a similar journey to you. They have made the mistakes that you're making, and they know how to guide you through the ups and downs. And there will be downs.

4. Have your clients pay upfront as much as possible, especially if you're a service provider.

5. Celebrate your wins. Even the tiniest ones. Even when it feels silly. There may be no one around who understands how hard you've worked but if you celebrate yourself and your business, other people will too.

6. Get around people who want you to succeed. They will do everything in their power to help you – believe me, I know.

Just keep going. I'll never forget something one of my coaches told me, two years into my entrepreneurship. I think I knew it all along, but it took someone else to point it out. And it's this: success has a lag effect. All of the work you're putting in right now takes time to come into fruition. It's like planting strawberry seeds: you feed and water it them through the cold season. When you can't see any growth, you might be tempted to give up and throw the whole thing in the bin. But if you just keep feeding and watering it a little longer, you'll enjoy the delicious fruits when it gets warmer.

Time To Expand

You may recall that I also said at the beginning of the chapter that speaking your truth is vital for your happiness.

For many years, despite living my dreams of becoming a singer, I was caught in a cycle of toxic relationships. Looking back, it made sense. Growing up where I did, I had been around some very toxic adults and had seen and heard some very inappropriate behaviour. I was attracted to the drama of toxic relationships.

Since learning about paradigms and studying NLP I am on the cusp of launching a program to help women and people from minority genders to break free from the cycle of toxic relationships so that they can speak their truth, say yes to themselves more often and live the lives they deserve, doing what makes them happy. It's something I've wanted to do for a long time and feels like a natural progression for me.

As I said before, growth often means moving forward and transitioning. Some of the people around you won't understand why you're making certain decisions, but they can't see what you see.

As Bob Proctor says, everything is created twice, once in our heads, and again in real life. As entrepreneurs, we are the creators.

Speak your truth and surround yourself with people who speak theirs. Your coaches and mentors will help you to create what you see in your mind's eye, and if they don't, they are probably not the right people for you.

"Cool Story Bro..."

You can do whatever you want to do. I decided a long time ago that I wouldn't be held back by background. I didn't want to be another statistic from a broken council estate home.

I wanted to be a singer, and I DID IT! Carrie Griffiths Voice Training is growing month by month, and the Queens In Business Club is reaching women globally.

Yes, I have made sacrifices. Yes, there were bad times. But I'd do all of it again in a heartbeat.

Whatever it is that you have set your heart on, as long as it's legal and doesn't hurt anyone, bloody well get off your butt and get it! Because if I can do it, I promise you that you can too!

Do what makes you happy.

About Me

I am a voice coach and singing teacher and Co-Founder of the Queens In Business Club. I help voice workers including singers, speakers, and coaches to utilise their voices without causing damage, and help to fix vocal issues. My clients include celebrated entrepreneurs such as Jenny Woo and Jessen James.

I grew up on the council estates of West London and attended university as a mature student, leaving with BMus in Music Performance, Music Teaching Licentiate and Level 7 PGCE at the Institute of Education.

As a singer, I have performed in over thirty countries, selling top ten albums including a European Number One. I have been featured in countless U.K. and international music and lifestyle publications including Street Sounds, Vive Le Rock, Q Magazine, Scootering Magazine, CBS, NBC and Fox and on U.K and international Radio stations including Radio X, Radio 6 Music and Radio Eins, Berlin.

At the time of writing, I am the Music Lecturer and Course Leader for Music Performance at South Thames College, London. I am transitioning into full-time entrepreneurship with the launch of my Transformational Performance Coaching business.

I am truly honoured to be a part of this book alongside these awesome female entrepreneurs. We are here to show you that it is possible to live your dreams and that you don't have to do it alone.

Special acknowledgements to Chloë Bisson, and my mum, Zana Griffiths, for always believing me and encouraging me to follow my dreams. My daughter Teah Smith who constantly inspires me to be better every day and allows me to shamelessly plaster her name wherever I go!

I dedicate this book to anyone who ever dares to follow their dreams.

Stay hydrated.

Release Your Wings

Marjah Simon-Meinefeld, Esquire

Publishing Results Expert

Author Writer's Academy

"One of the hardest things in life to learn are which bridges to cross and which bridges to burn." --- Oprah Winfrey

The Devil I Knew

I was trying to ignore the quiet, still, calling inside of me. I'm a writer. I'm a speaker. I love words. As an attorney, I was using words daily, but not in a way that actually served my soul. I was in my last job for seven years. For most of those years, my soul knew the truth - I didn't belong there. But I ignored it, trying to do what society said was the right thing to do. Keep working in your job no matter what. I ignored that inner voice like so many of us do. I became physically sick and emotionally spent. It was mentally draining. But I was good at my job, I knew it well. So I just kept at it. Health issues began compounding. My doctors kept warning me to quit my job, I ignored them for as long as I could. Night after night, unable to sleep, I'd feel like I was going a bit insane.

Sunday nights consisted of crying in my bed, because waking up meant another day in mental anguish. I'd drive the 60 minutes to work and cry in the parking lot. Once I gathered the strength to walk inside, I'd trudge up to my second-floor office. By lunch, I'd sometimes crawl under my desk into a ball. I felt unstable, unwell and in pain. All because I was ignoring the truth. The truth was this job was not why I'm here on earth. But by society's standards I was "successful". Earning six figures, office with a window, a professional title and the respect of my colleagues – what's there to complain about? The first two years were ok, but each of the five progressive years became harder to bear.

There was a voice inside telling me to get out while I still had some health left. But the other voice of doubt and fear paralysed me. "Stay. Do your job. The pain will eventually pass. You'll be ok." And it was confirmed by my husband. He meant well. He wanted the assurances that came with two steady pay checks brought to our family. But I don't think he understood how much life was draining out of me day by day. So I ignored the signs. After all, I worked hard and sacrificed a lot to become an attorney. I beat the odds, overcame the stereotypes by those that said I couldn't do it. So how could I just let it go?

Almost every one to two years, a new senior supervisor rotated in. As the only female, non-white attorney, it seemed that I had to prove to each supervisor that I belonged there. They'd assume that the white men knew their jobs. But they'd want to closely check my work, the same work that I'd been doing successfully for years. I was criticised, reprimanded and scrutinised on a regular basis. But if I pushed back, I'd be seen as the "angry black woman", "the emotional chick", confirming their preconceptions. So I smiled, stayed friendly and tried to show up as a "team player". All that got me was more work piled on top until I couldn't breathe.

As I watched my colleagues get awards for the same work that I did without recognition, it was salt in the wound. When none of the attorneys or even my supervisors showed up for my 15-year award, the commander postponed it. After repeated times of reasons why they couldn't show, she finally presented it to me in front of her employees. I felt so lonely. But I internalised the anger as usual.

The Moment Of Decision
Many believe that it takes a long time to make the decision to do something different. One of my coaches, Tony Robbins, said it only

takes a heartbeat to get to the moment of decision. And that moment came during an office phone call.

One day, the security manager told me that accidentally plugging my mobile into my work computer, for five seconds, triggered a security breach. This meant that my computer would be taken and examined to be sure that I didn't do anything wrong. I was already drained and tired, so I didn't care. It was inconvenient, but since I didn't do anything wrong, I wasn't worried. Then he said to get my computer back, it would have to be approved by a General in the US. I didn't care. After a decade in the military JACG Corps, high-ranking people didn't intimidate me. Then he said "Oh, and you won't be allowed to work from home ever again." I told him that the two days I got to work from home were medically authorised to help manage my increasing health issues. He callously replied that it didn't matter because that's the rule. He said if I begged, perhaps the General would grant it back to me in time. If I begged?! Moment of decision.

I took a deep breath, hung up the phone and walked out of my office. Before I realised, I was sitting in the personnel office crying. I couldn't do this anymore.

It was at that moment of giving up, of giving in, of saying, "Enough!" that my courage opened up to begin a new life chapter. It took months of paperwork to extradite myself from 'the system'. During those months, there was so much doubt. Did I do the right thing? Would I be able to replace my income? What would my husband say? But I leaned into the faith that God had a better plan for me. Then I waited and listened for a new call on my life.

A Different Chapter
With my first book, Fork Disease, Go Vegan, that I published several years prior to leaving my job, I had so much pain

throughout the process. It was the pain that most people experience who say they want to write a book. I was unsure of myself, I didn't know the process, I didn't know what to do and I didn't know if I was doing it correctly. I was continuously editing and re-editing and writing. A year passed, two years passed, three years, seven years, eight years, and it continued on and on. Then finally, I pulled the trigger. I said, "Enough! Whatever it is, it's done. I'm publishing it and putting it out."

Just to get my first book out was about 10 years of agony. It felt so heavy, but it should not have felt like a burden. I believe that sharing wisdom should be a joy. It's love, it's a light, it's hope. But doing it the way "everyone else does it" didn't feel like that. I published that book with a traditional publisher; and experienced even more pain. The publisher took most of the royalties. I still haven't seen anything from it in as many years and as much work as I put into it, as much money as I put into it. And, with all the money that I poured into it they didn't even market my book.

They said, "Oh, you want us to market it? You'll have to pay us more." "Excuse me?" "You have to pay us more." So, of course, I didn't do that. And a book that's not marketed is unfortunately, in this noisy environment, a book that nobody knows exists.

Then I was doing my own marketing. My sister and I were running a business at the time, selling our book along with our business services. So, all of these little things, pain points of trying to figure it out, to figure out how to get the cover we want, how to keep our royalties, how to keep our rights, how to get it published, how to do it quickly, how to not edit ourselves into a decade of not writing—all of these little pain points I saw. I understand what entrepreneurs, with the desire and contrasting fears, are experiencing.

My second book was an eBook cookbook with my sister, and I decided, "Okay, we're gonna do this ourselves, we're gonna publish it." And then I hit additional pain points, and I learned from that as well.

My third book, The One Law for Amazing Abundance In Every Area of Your Life, was a spiritual download of information that came through me. And I hid it away on my computer for two years. I was gun-shy about publishing another book. Plus, I was stuck in my ego, afraid of what I thought other people would think of what I wrote. But when I left my job, I heard a soft, quiet voice, "It's time." Instead of running away, I leaned in. I trusted that inner voice and let go of worry.

My attorney brain went to work. I looked at all of the publishing pieces that worked and didn't work. I saw a pattern, a framework and created a system. I said, "You know what, this is how it would work." I decided to use my AWA system to help entrepreneurs experience joy in becoming an author. When I stepped out on faith, the right people appeared. Little did I know that Chloë, an amazing woman I met at a speaking event, would become my business partner in the next chapter of my life!

The One Law became an international bestseller in the US, Germany and the UK. People were quoting my words!

I started getting messages from people because it was marketed out into the world. I have received the most beautiful messages:

"You've changed my life."
"Thank you so much."
"It's an amazing book."

It was incredible. This feeling that I felt - a sense of accomplishment, this lightness, this connection - I realised that it was something that I loved. I wanted other authors to feel that too. I wanted to take them out of that pain that I experienced with my first and second book. I want them to feel only that joy and that sense of completion experienced with my third book. Because my heart wanted to share the beautiful experience, Author Writer's Academy was born.

Lean Into Faith Even When You Fear The Fall

It wasn't an easy decision to walk away from what I had been doing for over a decade. But making the hard decisions when we know in our hearts that it's best, will free us. What are you holding onto from your past that is weighing you down, keeping you from soaring high? Do you have desires calling that you are hanging onto out of fear and self-doubt? That desire just may be your purpose, your mission to bring your unique gifts to the world. Go airborne. Your wings appear when you are willing to fly.

Now I'm on a special mission to create authors around the world, robbing the graveyard of wisdom in the process. I'm an entrepreneur, best-selling author, professional speaker, mindset coach, international attorney and prior military. I created Author Writer's Academy (AWA) to capture the wisdom of productive, successful entrepreneurs. Through their experiences and insights, they will positively impact millions of lives. The unique AWA system takes them from "One day I might write a book…" to "It's done!" in a fun, fast, easy way, without them having to write a word!

Because I'm an attorney, my brain thinks in a unique way. I can't stop it. I can't help it. It's just what it is. I'm sure you've known attorneys, and they're a little nutty. And fortunately for my clients, it works in their favour.

What I use are the skills that I developed in court when I was prosecuting - getting people's stories out of them, asking the right questions, hearing what's not being said, understanding where the holes are, where the disconnects are, and connecting those pieces. I'm able to use those and draw their story out of them, draw their words out of them, and reflect back to them in their authentic voice.

Most of my ideal clients never have to write a word. They don't want to write for various reasons. They don't have time. They feel they're not good writers. They have lots of different reasons for not writing. But I'm here, they don't have to write a word if they don't want to. And I love working with these clients. I'm able to use my skills that create an experience for them that's like having a conversation with a friend. I ask them questions, and they answer. They talk about their experiences, about their wisdom, about their ideas. I ask them another question. I draw them out even more. I lead them through the path in creating their book through an old ancient tradition. So many of our customs around the world started with oral storytelling long before we were able to write and read. And I bring it back to that moment, using my unique attorney skills. That's my X-Factor.

I'm able to hear it, see it, understand it. Then once all of these conversations are had, I put it together as a cohesive manuscript that flows, authentically representing that author in their unique voice, in their power.

As an international attorney, I represented the US government in foreign contracts and with foreign companies and governments. Because of that, I'm able to synthesise and think about lots of data, lots of words at one time. I understand how it best flows together, what fits and doesn't fit. I use those skills to bring all of those words together in a way that flows like no other. And then I have a wonderful, amazing team that I work with. Together we get our clients from "I have an idea" to "I'm a finished published author with a marketed book!" My team and I take them from start to finish, and we love what we're doing. I love that moment when the new author is holding their book in their hands and they're crying tears of joy, "Yes, it's done!" I take them from, "One day, I might write a book" to "It's done."

Doing Life On My Terms

As I grow my business on my terms with my amazing team, we get to serve amazing clients. I am now in alignment with who God made me to be. Are you searching for your flow, your alignment? There were many lessons I've learned that I'd love to share with you:

1. Look within every pain, obstacle, and problem - this is where your biggest opportunity lives.
2. Trust your instinct and inner heart/voice even when it makes no sense to anyone else, even if it doesn't make sense to your mind.
3. Learn to quickly master every aspect of your business before you delegate it out.
4. Just because you can do something, doesn't mean you should do it. Continuously narrow down what you do to your zone of genius. Let others operate in their zone of genius.
5. What's success without love and fun? If you're not having fun, you're doing it wrong!

Another lesson that I've learned is that this is not easy. It's simple, but it's not easy. There are so many different aspects of being in business that when you go into business for yourself you just don't know. Even if you've been in business before, when you do a different business, it's something else. You're dealing with entirely different elements of things, of people, of processes, of ideas, but mostly you're dealing with yourself.

One of the biggest lessons that I am learning every day is to be comfortable with being uncomfortable. Every day on this journey is uncomfortable for me. But if I'm comfortable, that means I'm not doing anything. That means I'm not growing. That means I'm not learning. That means I'm not paying attention. In contrast, when I'm uncomfortable, it's because I'm forcing myself to not sit back and rest on my laurels with the attitude of, "Oh, I've done this. I've succeeded." Uncomfortable is when you look forward and ask, "What else is there? How else can I serve? What else can I do? What else do I need to know? What don't I know? How can I learn? How can I grow? How can I help? Who do I need to become in order to be the person that can do this?"

Uncomfortable is the state that a lot of people, in my opinion, avoid. We must release something about who we are right now, and step into something that we are unsure about being. We must show up every day and do something that we haven't done before. We must be willing to be vulnerable. We must be willing to look stupid, look foolish, and ask questions that make us feel insecure. We must be willing to do that. All of that is uncomfortable. So the biggest lesson I would say is that I learned, am still learning, and reminding myself every day, to be comfortable with being uncomfortable.

Entrepreneurs go through a lot of emotional and mental stress due to constant uncertainties. I think the first thing is redefining stress. Stress is the name I think that we give to undesirable things. And we kind of expand that word for stress going from just things that are undesirable to anything that's new, anything that's uncomfortable, anything that's unfamiliar. We may often react in a way that goes into this thought process of "it's stressful."

For me, dealing with stress is stepping back, looking at it, and saying what it really is. I'm taking that pause, taking that breath, taking that time to examine what's actually happening. "Where's the opportunity in this?" Often, in "stress", there are opportunities. If we're willing to be uncomfortable, if we're willing to grow, if we're willing to step into and accept it, then the stress becomes excitement.

Also, what I noticed is that we become stressed when we're not willing to let go of what no longer exists. A lot of times we feel stressed when we are holding on to the way things used to be, or the way we think things should be or ought to be. Either they no longer exist, or they never existed. Operating like that is stressful. For me, every time I feel this level of stress, I ask myself, "What am I holding on to that I need to let go of? What am I trying to push into that doesn't yet exist or may never exist? What is the story that I'm telling myself here?" And then I start to shift that story, I start to let go of those resistances. Once we can say, "You know what? That was, and I'm grateful. This is what it is right now. This is today's reality." We step into today's reality, then suddenly, we can operate. "Okay, this is what I'm here to focus on."

I also find that stress happens when I'm focused on too many things at once. Kind of like taking 10 balls and trying to juggle them all at once. That's a lot. But if you instead say, "Okay, I have 10 balls, I need to handle, manage, juggle, in a different way." Take just the one, place it in front of you. If you're bouncing that one goal, up and down, it's easy, it's focused, it's concentrated. And so, blocking my mind and focusing specifically on what task is in front of me, helps to alleviate a lot of my stress.

Also, I plan for taking care of myself. One of the other things that I do in dealing with stress is I'm proactive with it. A lot of times stress happens because we're being reactive. We are dishonest with ourselves about what is happening. We wait as things are piling up, piling up, piling up, and then we try to deal with it. We try to handle it, manage it, and figure it all out.

Instead, I'm being proactive, taking care of my personal health. I'm doing the best I can to keep a flow with my life. I'm paying attention to the things that are actually important. Not just the things that appear to be urgent.

Stress is going to happen. It's just about how we prepare for it ahead of time. When people are surprised that stress is happening, it's like those people that are surprised that Christmas came on 25th December. "Oh, my goodness, it just snuck up on us this year." "Oh, wow, wish we could've planned for it, better rush the shopping!" It's the same every year.

The thing with stress, especially as an entrepreneur, if you're in business for yourself, there's going to be stressors. If you're not in business and you're doing something else, there's gonna be stressors. If we're breathing, if we're alive, if we're interacting with people, if we're handling multiple things, there's going to be stressors. So for me, I've learned over the years to be proactive, to pay attention, to listen, to ask myself the right questions, and to have some grace with myself.

And I think we're so hard on ourselves. We're beating ourselves up that we didn't get everything done, or we didn't do everything exactly perfectly. We're human. It's okay to be human. It's okay to give yourself a break, to forgive yourself and forgive others. This relieves a lot of stress right there. Learn, grow, move forward, acknowledge. Learn the lesson that needs to be learned, take it on board, and keep going forward.

If you are in a job that no longer serves you, but you don't know what else to do, lean in.

Lean into faith even when you fear the fall. Again, I urge you to go airborne. Your wings appear only when you are willing to fly. So how do you know what to lean into?

The thing that you can do day and night without even thinking about it, the thing that just seems second nature to you, don't overlook it because often, that is your purpose. That is why you're here.

Many of us think we don't know our purpose. You're just overlooking the thing that you do and flow so easily, that thing that you just want to know more and more about, that thing that keeps you up at night, late at night and gets you up early in the morning, that thing that you can talk about endlessly and tirelessly until people are rolling their eyes at you, that thing that lights you up and makes you smile, the thing that you would do until you're tired and dropping and you'll get up gladly and happily and do it again, the thing that rolls out of you effortlessly but yet you still put effort into it, the thing that people are often exclaiming, "Oh wow, how do you do that? You're amazing. Wow, that was incredible", that thing that you then shrug your shoulders and go, "No big deal".

I'm here to tell you that dismissal of that is wrong. It is a big deal. That's your purpose. That's why you're here. Don't overlook your purpose. Don't overlook what comes easy to you. Don't mistake easy for cheap. Develop that one. Develop, develop, develop the thing that comes easy to you. Put your effort, put your work into it. And if you have multiple things that come easy to you, pick one of those things, focus, go all in, get obsessed by it, and learn everything you can. That's how you create success in your life. That's the wind beneath your open wings.

About Me

I am Marjah Simon-Meinefeld, married to Marcus Meinefeld, based in Germany and the United States. I have two children - Alejandra, aged 14, Jada, aged 24; and blessed with a 2-year-old grandson, Alex.

I create authors of busy, successful entrepreneurs and professionals, without them having to write a word! I created the Author Writer's Academy (AWA) in order to capture the wisdom of these incredible minds and share it with the world. Most of what people know doesn't live beyond them. I am on a special mission to rob the graveyard of wisdom. I'm here to help people that have these amazing stories to share to bring out their amazing experiences that can transform, change, give hope and help people. My mission, my purpose in life, is to bring those messages out to the world.

I am so grateful that God allows me to be surrounded with amazing people in my life as I do this. My husband Marcus, who loves me no matter what, my wonderful children and my cuddly grandson make every day worthwhile. My mentor, coach, and friend Luke Wren and my Greatness Tribe and Mastermind family, who cheer me on and believe in me. My coach Tony Robbins and all of my loving Platinum Partner family, that cause me to dream bigger and lean in even more. My Unblinded coaches Sean Callagy and team, that teach me to live in my four energies every day, in my business and in life.

My Queens In Business Club family, a community I am proud to be a co-founder of with five of the most amazing women I have ever met. My Inner Heart of Bath crazy UK family, you remind me to always have fun. My dear sister by birth, Jasmine, and my dear sister by choice, Tracie, thank you for encouraging me. My Pastors, Bishop and Lady Blacknall – your constant prayers and guidance continue to be a blessing to me. My amazing clients – your passion, positivity, and powerful stories make what I do worthwhile. And I want to thank me – Marjah. I chose to lean into my faith, step through the fear, and into my moment of decision that allows me to fly. My wings are open. Let's fly together!

Radiate Your Superpowers by Crushing your Limiting Beliefs

Eva Martins

#1 International Best-Selling Author, Executive Leader in
Fortune 500 Company, Success Coach
Global Women Leadership Academy

"To me, power is to make things happen."' --- Beyonce

Wearing The Masculine Mask To Survive

Being every role you want to fulfil is extremely challenging nowadays. I get that. The pressure is high. The demand never stops, and we wish we could fulfil everybody's expectations. I, for one, felt like I was sacrificing myself almost all of the time. I was fulfilling everybody else's expectations but mine.

The environment is demanding. You feel you need to be at your best every day, but unfortunately it never feels enough. I felt this way too. And I almost lost myself along the way…

Born in Paris, a feministic country where women are encouraged to be strong and independent, I learned from a young age that I should have clear goals. Work hard to achieve them, without trusting too much in the people around me. I copied a model that equated "successful" with this strong force, having clear objectives and going for it no matter what the cost. It became a survival need in order to fit in.

I started my career in a male-dominated corporate industry where you soon understand that if you do not have power, you go nowhere. Women were few and quite competitive instead of supporting each other. And how did you get power? Your ideas

108

had to be heard, you had to be seen, look smart and work endless hours. You were not allowed to say no. You had to be at your best every waking day. A low day was not allowed.

First, I had to prove myself. I felt mandated to instil in their minds that I'm not only a beautiful face but I also have a brain. I had to prove that I had a voice; that I could also raise my voice if needed and that I was an expert. It was not easy. I even had a few senior leaders who tried to use their power to abuse me. Unfortunately, you soon understand that if you go against expectations, your career is done. They are much stronger, influential, especially when you live in a man's world.

I decided to ignore and pretend to be them. But staying silent wasn't the best option. With mustered courage, I put up limits and raised my voice. I might have showcased my confident and hautaine side, but it was my way to impose a certain distance in order to protect myself. Inside of me, I was definitely not that self-confident. I was living with constant anxiety, stress and in alert mode. I made my way up the ladder by working on my mindset, my leadership skills, and understanding ways I could co-create those behaviours on others.

But the few women in my office and I experienced that if you did not have a strong voice, you were not heard. That is, if you did not adopt a more masculine attitude you were blocked from exceling.

If we showed our passion and feminine drive, we were seen as too emotional. If we dressed too feminine, I mean anything other than a grey suit, we were criticised. So, we numbed ourselves, rejected our intuition and sensitive side. We allowed our masculine energy and assertiveness to take over as a way to survive. But without balance, most of the time it was too much. So, we were seen as being demanding and competitive, even towards each other. Does any of this sound familiar?

It took me more than 10 years of operating in many different leading roles to realise what was happening. I had a successful career, but I was sacrificing myself. Disconnecting from who I was, from my natural gifts as a way to fit in, in an attempt to be successful became the norm. In reality, I was trying to fulfil other expectations in order to feel valued and recognised. I was actually limiting my full potential.

Slowly but surely, I started to disconnect from my dreams, my wishes, my emotions. They were reminding me that I was not happy, not living my life, the one that I much deserve.

There was no feeling of connection anymore. I was doing more and more every day and it was never enough. Everything was a struggle.

Doing my best at work and feeling exhausted, coming back home to the kids and feeling more and more alone inside of myself. Not being able to express it, not feeling understood, not feeling heard either. All of this with constant arguments that it was not enough. Having to be a beautiful, smiley wife and always ready for him, for them. I was there for everyone, except for myself.

It took me many years until I understood that I was not living my life, but someone else's expectations of it.

My light was vanishing. My passion was gone. I was living for safety instead of fulfilment. I invented excuses, redefining my dreams, lowering my own expectations over life, pretending everything was all right. Yet inside of me, a feeling of dissatisfaction was growing bigger.

The universe pushed me so hard that I had to wake up or extinguish my soul.

Few situations forced me to open my eyes and to understand I was not happy, nor did I know what happiness was.

I lost a baby, had a big car crash, a cancer threat and many other dramatic situations. They all had the same flavour: loneliness. In all of them, I realised that I was alone, having to fight for myself, having to raise my voice, having to impose boundaries, and having to self-respect. Above all, I had to learn to love myself independently of other judgements and demands.

A turning point for me when I realised I was not the example I wanted to showcase to my kids. My divorce was extremely painful for all. I went through the suffering of believing I was destroying a family, destroying my kids roots and balance, destroying their happiness.

I had to face the fears of being alone with my kids as I could not count on their father. I had to start all over again. Something inside of me was telling me I had no choice, I had to run away from this situation for my kids.... but it was also for me.

When I look back, I truly believe with all my soul it was the best decision ever, a gift from the universe. I learnt so much about myself and others. I decided to be free no matter what and give this gift to my kids. I did it for them ultimately as my soul was dying.

Many years have passed, my kids are much more fulfilled, self-confident, positive, respecting themselves, free to express themselves, and with a different mental agility which will guide their lives.

A New Energy

Now, I am deeply grateful for all of those events, for the life lessons. For the strength I uncovered, for the clarity and awareness it gave me. It pushed me to a new journey of conscious self-discovery, uncovering mind programs, patterns and beliefs which were limiting instead of empowering me.

Now, I have the conviction that nothing happens by chance. Everything has a reason. I spent so many years trying to change my environment, pleasing people around me, sacrificing to fit in when all along the solution was inside of me.

The change comes from within!

I began to understand the misconceptions of the feminine and masculine powers. I understood the mechanism of self-sabotage through lack of wealth, playing small and keeping safe. I saw the effects of the rejection of our own power and sacrificing versus serving others. Then I knew how to lead people towards their own success and happiness.

Living and embodying our feminine self-identity, with all its beauty and sensitivity, is more powerful and fulfilling than always being in masculine energy. I discovered that in our feminine energy, we can still be this strong force of nature, taking action and moving forward.

I also understood that the solution was within myself. I uncovered hundreds of hundreds of inner limiting beliefs. I did not know I had it in my subconscious mind and yet they were there, having an impact in my daily life. Life was mirroring them back to me, as they attempted to tell me where I had to evolve and change, but I was not yet prepared to understand the message.

As I gained more self-confidence, as I released many subconscious limiting beliefs such as "I am not good enough, I do not deserve, I am not smart enough, my ideas are not good enough". All BS! As I trusted myself more, the environment was also showing it back to me.

I became a better leader, being able to build strong and high performing teams, and support other women along the journey. I still meet today male leaders who think they know what's best for us. Not to generalise, I do understand that it comes from a genuine intent to help. I would say the best is not to assume for others but ask them what they would love to achieve.

Not that long ago, I had a senior leader telling me that I should try to have a less risky job, a bit hidden as I was single at that time and had two kids to raise. It shocked me. I pushed back – I already had a dad in my life. I did not need another one in my corporate life! I realised that the more I was working on myself the more my life was changing for the better. Today I invest at least 10% of my income in personal growth.

Without knowing, we hold onto thousands of years of programming whether from our family, the society, our genetics or our past experience. All of them are registered in our subconscious mind. Those are the lenses influencing the way we live and see life.

Everything we experience in life is a reflection of our inner world, well hidden in our subconscious mind. So, the secret is to deep dive into our inner world, identifying those lies we believe as our own truth. Reframe them so they empower us instead of limiting us.

One of my passions in life is ensuring that I am growing and improving every day. I love acquiring new skills, new capabilities.

I studied until I came to understand the power of our brain and how it works so we can explore its full potential.

While driving a successful career as a female leader in the pharmaceutical industry at the local and global scale, I pursued my quest in understanding how we can use our brain to work in our favour. I understood that our environment is simply a reflection of our inner world. I trained with the best experts, travelled around the world with Tony Robbins for two years. I trained with Joe Dispenza; Mastering NLP with the founder John Grinder; and the geared experience I gained. It allowed me to become a better leader, create high performing teams, allowing them to flourish at their best and create much bigger impact!

I consider myself a change agent, sparking transformation and fulfilment in others.

Today my mission is to continue my corporate career in order to better serve our patients. We bring them back to life and focus on female empowerment through the creation of the Global Women Leadership Academy. My dream is to inspire as many women as I can to play a bigger role in life. I aim to allow them to express themselves and take the lead of their life, so they can live their full potential and spark a global impact.

And now you may ask me how can I achieve the same?

After so many years of coaching hundreds of women, I founded the Global Women Leadership Academy to serve women in different stages. They begin at the no-BS level, where we uncover the limiting beliefs, to take action through the THRIVE with no B.S. 7-week program. They then enter the Empower level where I give them constant support through mastermind and mentorship, but also train them with new skills so they can empower themselves.

Their next step is the Unleash, where they break through in their lives. I coach them to navigate much faster and confidently through their personal transformation journey, always with love, caring but also no B.S.

THRIVE with no B.S. 7-week program is designed to awaken the leader inside of you, transform your life from the inside. Know who you are underneath the masks, the labels, the expectations from others, reconnect with your soul, with your big why in life, your life mission, your purpose.

We go deep into your subconscious mind to uncover your foundational limiting beliefs, past traumas and change them in minutes. Then we deep dive into the relationships in your life and your career. Understand what is limiting you and transform those two big pillars of your life. I even have recently added a new module to go deep into the money issue, as women tend to reject money as a way to play small and minimise the impact we can have in the world. We finish by redesigning your new life blueprint.

I truly believe it is time for women to stand up, let go of the need to sacrifice for others, put themselves at the same level as they put others and start shining their own natural gifts. The world needs us more than ever!

Women leaders are needed more than ever in society today. The dynamics are changing. We see women governing countries, and they are starting to be recognised for it. Others are leading big corporations but it is still the exception. We congratulate ourselves when we achieve a top position and rightfully so, as most of the time it has required colossal effort. I am waiting for a time when we no longer need to congratulate ourselves for achieving this as a woman, because it is the norm.

Female leaders are showing new traits, caring for their teams, their people, their companies and their countries. They are leading from their heart and not only their head. They use their intuition as much as their smartness. Their empathy level is far more developed. They do not focus only on what needs to be done, but also on how it needs to be done in order to bring the highest impact. But of course, all of this is true if they are aligned with themselves, living authentically, in harmony with themselves.

I believe women and men are complementary, when in balance. Being a woman is a creation of many factors, going far beyond the physiological. Feminine radiance is feeling, sensitivity, openness, empathy, loving, intuition, nurturing, caring, and compassion. It is not about our body type, our sexuality, our hair style, or how we dress up. It is entirely about our inner self and how we project in life. The feminine is about "being" while the masculine is about "doing". Over the years, we were all trained, men and women alike, to reject our feminine side. In misunderstanding its openness, sensitivity, empathy as weakness, we thought we had to reject our emotions to be strong. But actually, it takes courage to be open. It takes strength to be in truth, and to speak the truth.

The pressure on women is high nowadays. We are supposed to be perfect wives, best mums, amazing friends, or successful career women. We are not taught to take care of ourselves but serve others, serve a higher cause. Most end up exhausted at some point as it is far too demanding.

I have worked with thousands of women through my coaching and training programs. The secret of unlocking your life is when you make a real deep inner change in your unconscious mind. I have seen amazing results. Women deciding to reset their life, divorcing in a couple of weeks, changing countries, finding a new love, getting three job offers from nowhere, increasing their business exponentially, others creating new flourishing businesses - all with more ease and effortlessness as they do not need to fight against their own fears anymore.

They do not need to sabotage themselves as a way to keep hidden. Above all, they feel reconnected with themselves, with their dreams, their goals, with more self-love, self-confidence, courage, knowing what they want, feeling complete, stronger, living a life with more passion and fulfilment and taking action, making things happen in their life. In a nutshell, living a life with a deeper meaning.

Supporting their transformation, seeing them open their wings, reconnecting with life, with dreams with a new inner sense of limitlessness is what fills me with love and passion. I am proud of my students and clients for having the courage to make this world a better place for all.

You might ask, why are you running a personal coaching business, while you already have a successful corporate career? Aren't you still doing too much? Yes I am, and I love it! I need to have many challenges running in parallel otherwise I get bored. I am conscious about it, but it is my drive, my passion. I want to live my life and feel that I have left something behind.

When I wrote my first International best-seller, <u>Stop Believing the B.S.</u>, my intention was to help one woman at least, to give her hope, to show her the path towards freedom. I was not expecting such a success. I have been coaching and training women for 20 years now and I love it, as much as I love the challenges my corporate world provides me.

I have a secret, a dream. Yes, I want to be successful, not because of money, not because of recognition, not because of other's admiration. I want to inspire all women in the world that they can achieve the same. They are allowed to go for their dreams, they are allowed to have it all. YES, they can serve but without sacrificing themselves along the way. I want them to understand that the world needs their own natural gifts, their love, their power! Only then we can change the face of the world.

I want my daughters to be proud of their mum. They must know they live in a world where women have equal chances. Ideal is that they are not asking permission to be happy and fulfilled, rather, where they live free in expressing their authentic self.

A big part of my motivation, passion and fuel comes with the dream of creating a community of women supporting each other globally. We've created an international foundation where we could partner with companies for young girls. In countries where they might not have access to education, neither have the freedom to dream high, we are shifting the paradigm.

In conclusion, you are right. I do a lot, but it is because I know why. We all have low days or weeks where we want to stop and quit whatever we are doing. Sometimes the challenges might feel too intense.

The life of a corporate leader and entrepreneur is not always easy, neither is the life of a mum, I get that. I have those moments, moments of doubts, moments where I feel overwhelmed with what I need to overcome. Most of the time fear of change, fear of being even more visible, fear of being an imposter, fear of being judged, fear of not being enough are also present. Have you ever felt like that? I bet you have, we all do and it is ok.

I know I do! Especially when I have to work 14 hours a day, things might not always happen the way I wished. We might wonder if it is all worth the effort. Not so long ago, I was spending 10 hours a day in online meetings in an aggressive environment, where you constantly need to watch your back.

In those moments, it is important to go back to our bigger why and reconnect with our inner motivation. I do it by asking myself the question.

Who am I betraying for not showing up?

Who am I leaving behind for not sharing my skills, my experience?

I might step back for a few days to resource myself, to reconnect with my intuition and motivation but it always comes back.

Those moments never last long. I remind myself of my WHY, my end goal, my dreams. How does it make me feel?

And often I ask myself how I would feel if I would not make the most of my life and give it a try...

Do you know your WHY, your dreams?
Do you have a clear goal you want to achieve?

If not, that's where you should start. It is not about having a family, a job, or a perfect husband. It is about YOU and how you feel when you have all of this. It is about the legacy you leave behind you. So, what is it for you?

What are your dreams?
What are your goals?
Ask your heart and it will show you.

Give it a try and ask yourself everyday how you can make your day count? I promise, after a while it will wake you up!

I often get asked the question, "Are you sure you have the ability to change my life?" No, I don't...but you do! By changing your inner beliefs, you literally change your life! I am here to guide, train and support you, but I cannot take action for you, neither do it for you.

After 20 years of research, self-development with the best experts in the world, I have mastered the power of reading your brain. I'm understanding why and how you limit yourself, which were the traumatic memories. More importantly, I have the ability to reframe your brain in minutes. It has the power to create big shifts in your life. I experienced it myself.

If you would have told me five years ago that I would change my entire life and become successful I would have smiled at you and seen it as a beautiful unrealistic dream...but all of this happened and in less than two years!

It does not mean it is a dream every day, but I know now that I co-create my life. I have the power to design it or change it! I do not run away from challenges anymore; I choose what I want to achieve, who I want in my life and make it happen. And when something less positive happens, I know there is a deeper meaning. I deep dive into my unconscious mind to understand in which ways I am co-creating the situation. I often find situations related to the past where, unconsciously, I made decisions for myself.

All of those beliefs will unconsciously try to prove themselves in your life by reaffirming themselves. So, you might attract situations to prove yourself you are more than good enough, but you will just reaffirm the opposite as it is what you believe unconsciously. I spent so much energy trying to get appreciated or acknowledged by others. It never worked because I was not believing it myself.

Those beliefs shape your behaviours, your actions, your life. By uncovering them I literally changed my life. Remember it is not about changing your external environment. Life is about growing, changing your inner world so the external can reflect it back to you. The funny thing is that when you do not need any more appreciation or love that's when you meet it... because you vibrate this new truth!

I see the same happening to my clients. 'M', she was feeling stuck in her career after maternity leave. So afraid of being like her mum that she was not allowing herself to live her motherhood. She thought she had to prove herself constantly to get seen and recognised. As we released all of those memories and beliefs, she attracted three job offers at the same time in a couple of weeks.

'I' was career driven, but sacrificing herself and her dreams for the family. She was so much attached to the perfect family image that she did not see any abusive dynamics around her. She even thought she had the perfect life, but if you would ask her if she was happy, she could not define what happiness was. She never knew what receiving love meant. She was living her life through others but not for herself as it is the way she learnt it at home.

A mum was supposed to sacrifice herself for her kids and husband. She opened her eyes from one week to the other, she understood she was seeking a life with more meaning, more love and less sacrifice. She decided to divorce, taking care of her kids, became good friends with her ex, moved countries and even got promoted.

It can be that easy when you work on your mindset and release past traumas, patterns and limiting beliefs.

'I' was struggling for many years, spending lots of money on training and self-development. Never taking a step forward in her own business, afraid of her own visibility and power. As we released her own fear in stepping up, in embracing her own feminine power she attracted the money she needed to pay for the 7-week program in two weeks. She is now launching her own training feeling empowered and self-confident. She moved from living in a constant drama to co-designing the life of her dreams, starting with manifesting the house she always wished for.

I have so many testimonials, all of them so inspiring. That's what gives me energy every day to pursue my mission. That's why I wake up with a smile in my heart every day.

If I had three pieces of advice to give you…

First of all, understand that your environment is a reflection of your story and your unconscious thoughts. It is not about blaming yourself but taking full responsibility for your life and taking the lead to upgrade it. And I know for some, increasing the level of responsibility feels scary. It is because often we have the wrong understanding of what responsibility means. Responsibility comes from response and ability.

You have the ability to give a response to a situation. It does not mean you need to fix it and be perfect. It does not mean you need to carry others on your shoulders. This comes from sacrifice instead. When I understood that life was all about testing and learning with no place for failure, it took a different dimension for me. I understood that instead of being a consequence of my environment, I had the choice to design it the way I wanted by releasing my fears, my inner limiting beliefs and co-creating the reality I wanted to live in.

Second, work on your mindset. Find a methodology, a coach, and training which allows you to uncover those limiting beliefs hindering you from upgrading. If there is something that I learned is that life is meant to be lived in fulfilment and not in pain, and it does not need to take years. Personal transformation can happen in minutes. We need to reach the root cause inside of our subconscious mind, release it and reframe it. I hope that through my personal story you start believing that the impossible is possible. We need to believe in it and say YES to life! And if you feel inspired, feel free to connect with me, I would be more than happy to welcome you in the GWLA to transform your life from the inside out!

Third, stop finding excuses. Stop playing small, stop procrastinating, stop putting that on others, stop feeding the B.S yourself. Life is too short to be in pain and suffering. Every day we replicate 95% of the same thoughts we had the day before. We constantly replicate the same life, the same challenges independent of your conscious actions. The secret lies in changing your deep unconscious to have a quick and big impact in your life. Your unconscious is responsible for 95% of your life! Take a decision today that will change your tomorrow. Otherwise, you will replicate the same patterns and stay in the same vicious circle.

You can make things happen but only if you have the courage to see beyond what's holding you back.

With love,
Eva Martins

About Me

I am the founder of the Global Women Leadership Academy, a #1 international best-selling author, international speaker, executive leader in Fortune 500 Company, and a business owner with a mission to empower women to skyrocket their lives.

My career began in a male-dominated corporate industry where I soon grasped that if you do not have power, you go nowhere. The message was clear - if you do not have a strong voice, you are not heard. If you do not adopt a more masculine attitude, you will be blocked from excelling. It took me more than 20 years of operating in many different leading roles to realise things needed to change.

I now dedicate my energy to empowering other women to step up in their lives through coaching and training offerings at the Global Women Leadership Academy, which has trained hundreds of women. My mission is to inspire women to spark their natural superpowers authentically and in freedom, drive gender equality at all levels of society and encourage women to raise their voices and dreams, inspire them that the impossible is possible when they believe in it. This is why my Leadership Academy to empower women was created.

This chapter is dedicated to all the women in the world, who are trying to be perfect on all fronts.

Working hard to find happiness while being afraid of judgement and afraid of not being heard or acknowledged.

For the ladies who want to unlock their true essence and skyrocket their lives and dreams, this one's for you!

Driving People To Freedom

Barbara Davis

Owner, Driving Instructor Trainer

Barbara's School of Motoring

"The potential for greatness lives within each of us."
--- Wilma Rudolph

The Formative Years

Who am I and what do I mean, 'Driving People to Freedom'?

I'm a driving instructor in the South East of England and have been teaching people to drive for the last 21 years. I also train others to become driving instructors and to take control of their own lives and finances. That's the quick version.

So how did I get here at the grand age of 65? Well that is a long story. I haven't always been a driving instructor. I've had many JOBs (Just Over Broke) before this.

I believe that each of us are unique because of our experiences since birth which are all different. Those experiences, both good and bad have shaped us into who we are and led us to where and who we are now. The story is still going on and we are developing every day into new versions of ourselves.

Growing up, I was the eldest of three children in a reasonably well-off middle-class family. My dad was a Solicitor and mum, who had trained as a Physiotherapist, was a stay at home mum. She supported and volunteered with a number of charities and causes dear to her heart. She was always there when we came back from school and took us to whatever activities we took part in until we were able to take ourselves. We always knew we loved and supported.

We were encouraged to try many activities and sports, including swimming, horse riding, tennis, badminton, skating, skiing and sailing. One memory from when I was about 12 is my dad taking me to the local lake with the scouts and trying to teach me to sail in a small tippy dinghy. I definitely did not like it, especially the fact that if it capsized, as it would inevitably do at some point and you have to swim round to climb on the centreboard. Then you'd have to pull the boat up and jump in as it comes upright. To this day, I haven't set foot in a sailing dinghy, nor ever will.

Subsequently, when I met my husband, he taught me to sail in a 'day keel boat', which he assured me would never capsize! It has a fixed heavy keel underneath to keep it upright.

We sailed in an International Tempest which, on the water, looks like a 7-metre-long overgrown dinghy with a trapeze which I had to hang from to balance the boat. Crucially, it may behave like a dinghy but when it goes over, it comes back all on its own! MAGIC.

We sailed together within the Tempest class for 29 years at world class level working our way through three tempests, each one newer than the last one which we got brand new in 1997. It had been built by the world champion for the world champion so we knew it was a good boat!

We were the top mixed crew in the world over many years. I was the first female to win a world championship race in the history of the class, also winning the Ladies prize on a number of occasions.

In return, I taught him to ski and we had many great ski holidays over the years, on our own and with other members of the family.

In fact, when we married in October 1981, we delayed our honeymoon until February of 1982 as we wanted to ski in America at Jackson Hole in Wyoming.

I was never particularly academic and hated the private junior school that I attended. The only highlight was the weekly swimming lessons at the local municipal pool, at which I excelled. I enjoyed the sports too, particularly netball. In my last year at the school, I used to help with reading to the younger years and knew from that early age that I wanted to teach, or help others in some similar capacity.

Swim Forward

Failing the 11+ exam meant that I could not go to any of the private secondary schools that my parents were looking at. They had given me a choice as to whether I wanted to go away to boarding school or stay at home and I chose home. In the end, I went to the local comprehensive school instead.

One of the best things was that the school had its own swimming pool. In the middle and upper years, the Deputy Head Teacher, who was interested in swimming and especially the Royal Life Saving Society's life-saving tests, encouraged me to work at these. Ultimately, I earned the Life-Saving Teacher's qualification.

In the 2nd year, a friend introduced me to the Leeds Ladies Swimming Club. From then on, Thursday nights were swimming nights. At age 16, the club sponsored me to do the Amateur Swimming Association Club Instructors course. I was then able to teach the younger members to swim which was something I loved. Also, after attaining the Life-Saving Teachers Certificate I was able to teach that as well as continuing to train and race at club level.

128

When I was in the 6th form, one of my regular duties was to help out at the local nursery school. Friday nights were Girl Guide Nights. I had been a Brownie and went on the Guides and then onto Ranger Guides, becoming a Guide leader as soon as I was able. As a Guide, I used to help with the Brownies as a Pack leader and as a Ranger, I helped with the Guide unit. During that time, I also achieved Queen's Guide and a small article in the local newspaper.

Looking back at that time, I feel that everything I was doing was leading me to a teaching career.

In the late 60s/early 70s, the constant cry from the careers department was to go into 'teaching', and so I went to teacher training college in Northumberland for three years.

Switching Lanes
I loved that aspect of my life at college but when it came to teaching practice, I came to realise that the classroom was NOT the environment I wanted to teach in.

Throughout those three years, I continued as a Guide Leader, running a local company with a college friend, gaining a camper's licence and various other qualifications along the way enabling me to take the girls away to camp (the highlight of the Guide year).

After leaving Teacher Training College, despite over 300 applications and just six interviews, there was no teaching job. I came to the conclusion that teaching in schools was not for me. I worked for six months as a nanny and for the civil service, not my desired career choices!

Whilst looking for a suitable career, someone suggested banking so I applied to and was interviewed at NatWest Bank. I was told they had no jobs available in Leeds but that there was an opening in North London, "Would I be interested?" "Yes".

Over the next 7-8 years I worked up to clerical grade three and did First Cashier, Securities, Foreign Desk and various other duties within the branch. I was also training others to do the duties I had learned. Throughout all my 'employed' careers, I always ended up in a teaching and training role helping others do the jobs I had become skilled at.

I was never happier than when I was teaching and coaching and helping others! When we started our family, I left the bank as having two small children in childcare was not cost effective.

Whilst the children were small, I got involved doing party planning, selling tupperware with a reasonable amount of success. Selling was not my 'thing' and after doing children's books and toys, I discovered Trichem Fabric Paints. This enabled me to start teaching people how to decorate their clothes and other household items selling them the products to achieve 'professional' results. I still have cupboards full of tupperware and paints!

As the children grew older and went to junior school, I needed to earn some reasonable money and looked for a part time job that would fit around school time. I went to work as a checkout operator at the local large supermarket. I found I enjoyed the company of the other staff and customers but it wasn't completely fulfilling my need to teach or help others in a significant way. When a Morning Supervisor vacancy came up, I applied and was awarded the job, still doing the hours that fitted round the children. It involved helping the checkout operators, and customers and also training checkout operators.

Why A Driving Instructor?

Come with me back to 1995. You find me standing, looking down the long line of 35 checkouts. The sun is streaming down through a huge triangular glass 'atrium' type roof bathing everything in bright light. Behind the checkouts is the store café. You can hear the chink of crockery and the ping of items being scanned as well as the happy sound of customer chatter. The smell of cooking bacon from the cafe permeates the air.

I'm holding a memo from Personnel. Not just at this store but from the head office in Leeds.

"We are excited to let you know of the major changes coming to your store very soon. We have been looking at the way the Company is working and how best to maximise profitability and utilise our staff most effectively. To that end, we will be re-structuring the staffing on the shop floor to integrate the supervisor roles back to the basic shop floor duties as we feel that all our colleagues are able to fulfil all the duties required".

Have you ever felt betrayed? Like the bottom has just dropped out of your world? I felt anger welling up in me and all I could do was cry. I didn't do anger well back then. Everything I had worked for over the last few years was being swept away in one fell swoop. As supervisors we were paid an extra 20p per hour. It was not a massive amount and that was being taken away as well! They were going to change the hours we worked too. My nice morning hours that fitted in with school would all change. What would I do?

You can imagine that it took some time to come to terms with this and even longer to completely get over the anger that kept bubbling up inside me at this 'betrayal'. I'm not an angry kind of person and didn't have a strategy for dealing with it.

Eventually, I came to terms with the new hours, then was given the role of 'Trainer' for the checkouts and front end. I would train new colleagues and also the rest of the shop floor on checkouts so they could come over at busy times. They were called 'Queue busters'. No extra pay and we had to fight it out for the overtime with the rest of the checkout colleagues. I was able to make the job 'my own'. Another Trainer was appointed to help and I enjoyed the job again.

Despite doing more and more overtime to cover training the evening and night colleagues (by now the store was 24 hours), I never quite managed to earn enough money and a few debts were mounting up.

Fast forward to 1997, two years later. I still had not sorted the money side of things and those debts would not go away. I decided that I would have to take steps to earn more and started to look for a management position within the company, Deputy Customer Service Manager. It was not likely to be in the same store as I had worked in up to now so I kept my eye on the vacancy boards in the store. A vacancy came up in High Wycombe which was 40 minutes travelling time from home so I applied. Not long after I was invited to an interview with the store manager and the store personnel (HR) manager.

I got the job and would start the following month. A new car was needed as I might well have to leave before my husband and the children who were now well into their teens. As a salaried member of staff, we were required to do 8-10 hour shifts plus over 40 minutes each way commuting. The store manager also decided that I would not need any training as was normally given to new managers.

Another aspect of the store was that it was dark. There were lights but there was no daylight. I had been used to massive amounts of daylight at my old store. I also found that I had badly miscalculated how much salary to ask for and the expenses that I would now be accumulating just to get there and back and also the cost of the loan for the new car.

There was also little or no support and encouragement from the senior management to do the job which was little more than the previous supervisor role had been but without the training aspect that I loved so much. I also had to work on the weekend which limited our sailing, something my husband was not happy about!

Before long, the strain was setting in and the job I had been looking forward to doing was not what I had imagined. I started dreading going to work. I didn't want to be there because I didn't enjoy working there. I wasn't able to see so much of my family.

I had badly misjudged the salary; I was getting less than I had been before so guess what? Those debts that I had been trying to pay weren't being paid and were getting more and more behind. I dreaded my phone ringing and what letters would come through the letterbox. And as can so easily happen, I buried my head in the sand and tried to ignore everything! That, of course, did not solve anything.

The store had recently gone to 24 hour trading so in February 1999 I filled in for two weeks on the Night shift in the hope of seeing more of my family. Going into nights was fine and there would be three days off at the end. I cannot say that I liked working nights but it was quiet and a lot of the time was spent stocking the shelves around the checkouts.

It was coming off nights that was the problem. My body clock was all messed up and I immediately came down with flu and laryngitis, losing my voice, all of which completely ruined my days off. I couldn't get out of bed.

It was the first and only time in my life that I'd ever had the flu and I would not wish that on my worst enemy! Once I had got over the infection and the flu, my voice did not come back. This is not a good thing when you're in a job that requires you to talk to staff and customers alike all day. It had got to a point where I knew something had to change. I couldn't carry on in this job but I didn't have a clue what I could do.

One month went by and still no voice... two months... three months and still no voice, just a croaky squeaky sound.

On every day off each week I would scour the local newspaper in the jobs section for something I could do. Nothing stood out until after three months a little unassuming ad at the top of the page caught my eye:

"BECOME A DRIVING INSTRUCTOR - WORK YOUR OWN HOURS - ALL TRAINING GIVEN - NO EXPERIENCE NECESSARY - CALL FOR AN APPOINTMENT TO FIND OUT MORE"

I enjoyed driving, and had taken an advanced driving test some years before. I knew I could teach, and was interested in road safety. So, I called and made an appointment for an interview which ended up being in Enfield. After a really good interview with the branch manager, I made the decision to follow this through. I signed and paid the first of three instalments for the training. And as if by magic the next time I opened my mouth to speak my voice was back!

That had to be a sign. Up to that point I hadn't considered stress to be a factor. At that point, it had to have been.

I didn't know how long the training would take and thought if I stayed in the job at that store, I would not have the time to fit in the training so I arranged to return to the old store as an hourly paid checkout operator and negotiated the hours I wanted to work, knowing I could do some overtime if I wished. I even got permission that if the requisite six-day course came up in December that I could attend. Normally, no holiday is allowed in December.

Becoming A Qualified Driving Instructor
To become a Qualified Driving Instructor, there are three exams to pass: a Theory test in which the pass mark is 85-90%; an advanced Practical Driving Test with no more than six minor faults; and a Test of Instructional Ability.

When I paid my first of three instalments for the training, I received a pack of books and course materials that I had to read and study. This was in June 1999. I had to go back to the Enfield branch three or four times to pass mock tests before being allowed to take the Theory test in July which I passed with 98%. It was a written test then and held at a venue in London. That was Part 1 done.

For Part 2, the Practical test, I was teamed up with another woman, Gill. It was late August before we had our first 4 hour (2 hours each) in car training session with our Trainer, Mike. Then we had a 4 hour training session every three or four weeks until early December. We had to practice in between those sessions so we teamed up for those and were also able to borrow our trainer's car. This went on into November before he allowed us to take the Part 2 Practical test, a one-and-a-half-hour drive, in early December, which we both passed.

Before we were allowed to be let loose on the paying public with a Trainee Licence, we had to attend a 6-day, 40-hour course. We both wanted to do this as soon as we possibly could. Ray, the branch manager at Enfield, found a course in Streatham, London that had vacancies for us in the week before Christmas week.

I was feeling very pleased with myself that I'd had the foresight to negotiate that time off work in December! The course started on a Friday and finished on the following Friday. Gill would drive to my place and I would drive into Streatham each morning. Old fashioned navigation with a map book!

Gill and I found we had lots in common and similar values and got on well. We became friends and still see each other regularly to this day, 22 years later.

There were six candidates attending this training which included some classroom work each morning. Then we were paired up to go out in the car with a trainer. Gill and I were put together for that with our trainer, Martin. This was where the fun began as we learned and practiced how we were supposed to teach learners and use the dual controls in the car.

During that week we had to put together a folder of Lesson Plans for all the topics that would need to teach learners. This was a bit of a tall order in just one week so we were able to borrow and copy Mike's plans.

One top tip from Martin that I still use is to have a notebook and record every lesson you do with each learner as when you're teaching many lessons each week then you'll remember what they were doing in the last lesson and how well, what they need to practice next time.

At the end of the week, both Gill and I passed and we were both able to go on and apply for our Pink Trainee licences ready to start working on a franchise with different branches into the New Year. That meant that we got a company car and pupils to practice with so we could go on to take the Part 3 Instructional Ability Test to finally qualify as fully registered Approved Driving Instructors. It took Gill two goes to pass and I passed at the third and final attempt in August 2000.

I found this to be the most challenging part of the whole course. It involved the examiner role playing a beginner for half an hour whilst being taught by me a pre-set topic, then another half hour 'lesson' on a pre-set topic as a partly trained student. I have never been a fan of role play. Even as a small child it would make me run a mile in the opposite direction.

By the time it came to the third and final attempt, I was a bag of nerves and stressed again! If I didn't pass this time everything I had worked for over the last year, and paid around £2,000 for would be for nothing. Finally, I passed! The relief from that stress caused me to burst into floods of tears on the way back to my car. It took about a half hour before I was fit to drive home.

I thoroughly enjoyed the work and had left my job back in February, when I had asked to change my hours and they would not. There was a new checkout manager and I don't believe that he thought I would leave. I handed in my months' notice at the end of January. My last day working in the store would be 14th February as I had a two-week holiday to take. That made me feel a bit smug, I have to confess.

Working As A Driving Instructor
Now I was able to swap my pink Trainee licence for a green registered Approved Driving Instructor (ADI) badge for a fee of

£300 and renewable every four years for £300. Sounds a lot but it works out at £75 a year.

The next hurdle was going to be a Check Test, which is supposed to be every four years. An examiner comes out on a lesson to watch you teaching a student to make sure you are maintaining the standards that they want you to adopt. This has changed over the years to a Standards Check in line with the new Client Centred learning coaching techniques that the DVSA (Driver and Vehicle Standards Agency) want us to adopt.

I carried on working with this company for about three years. I was into control and wanted to run my own diary. They had continued giving me students and I had a few of my own too. I would have to go into the office every day to update my diary. It was getting to the point where they would double book me and that was not a good thing. There were still weeks when the number of lessons was not paying the franchise fee and I would end up having to pay them. 20 lessons per week just paid the franchise! This is one of the reasons why many Instructors left them after a very short time.

Being a qualified Driving Instructor also meant that I could much more effectively teach my own two children to drive, thereby saving thousands of pounds. So, I decided to part company with BSM. I could lease a car and insure it for a lot less than the franchise fee and I kept the students, as they wanted to learn with me by that stage.

As a result, Barbara's School of Motoring was born.

Over the years, I have done various driving instructor related courses including Fleet trainer, ORDIT (Official Register of Driving Instructor Trainers) Train the Trainer, twice, and attended many meetings of Driving Instructors to further my Continuous

Professional Development (CPD). Also, an Accident Investigation course and worked as an Accident Investigator for a brief period.

In 2007, I started looking into training instructors liaising with a Driving School in the West Country who did the marketing for us and helped to produce my book. Unfortunately, this did not result in any Trainees coming forward for me, perhaps because I did not have a course that I felt confident to deliver.

After a period when a lot of my students passed their tests around 2011, there was not enough coming in to pay the lease and other expenses so I subcontracted out to another driving school who had a contract with the MOD. I did intensive courses, picking up two students from a military base on a Monday morning, teaching them all day every day that week with a view to them passing their tests on the Friday. That would pay a lump sum for each student passing their test.

Although those candidates received a normal full licence, the military had their own examiners and a completely different system for booking the tests.

Trailer training also became part of my skillset. I could borrow the other driving school's trailer and sometimes cars for that. I bought my own box trailer in 2015 also with our house move in 2016 in mind.

I never wanted to go more than about one to one and half hours from home as I could then fit my own students into the evenings. This carried on for about 3-4 years until the number of my own students increased to the point that I couldn't fit it in any more.

The focus since moving from Watford to Kent has been on developing the Driving School into an entity, by taking on and training instructors in and around Watford and in Kent. I still work in Watford on two days a week and don't actively market for students in Kent. Some still come to me.

If we had had a choice, we wouldn't have moved at all. My husband retired and the mortgage had to be paid off along with a number of accumulated debts so we needed to downsize. We chose to move to the Medway where house prices were cheaper and to be closer to our yacht that was moored there. He had great plans as to what we would do and where we could go with the yacht.

Sadly, he was not well when we moved and he was deteriorating all the time. He finally signed with and visited a doctor in July 2017. Told he had kidney failure, he was started on dialysis. His health never really improved and tragically he died suddenly and unexpectedly a year later. We never got to enjoy his retirement as he would have liked.

In time, I realised that the life changes leave me footloose and fancy free to do what I like, when I like, how I like, and with whom I like. And that's what I have done and will continue to do.

Things I Wish I Had Known or Done Before Starting My Business
Hindsight is a wonderful thing. Would I have done things any differently?

One thing that I wish I had done in the beginning was to check out the other driving school's Instructor Training courses. I heard from other instructors later about the various failings of the different driving schools when it came to training instructors. I just went with the first advert and first company. It was a known name and must be good. I think that perhaps Gill and I were lucky as we were paired with very good trainers for parts two and three. Inevitably,

140

they were constrained by the system within which they were working. It could have been so different and we could have had to spend a lot more money than we did if our trainers had not been as good as they were.

Another point is the way the course was structured. We had to pass the Theory before we could go on to the Practical training. Then we had to pass the Practical before going on to the Instructional ability and passing that. This extended the time between starting the course and qualifying. In my case over a year, never mind the complications trying to extend the 6-month trainee licence for over a month.

How much more efficient if a potential Trainee could meet their trainer at the start of a course that integrates all three parts from the beginning of a twelve or thirteen module structured programme that they could work through in their own timescale? The same trainer is available throughout for the trainee to ask questions and provide continuity. This could take as little as 24 weeks or less. During that time, they could take and pass parts 1 and 2 and then go on to pass part 3. Or do the 13th module that is required if they choose to take out a Trainee licence. Or do the whole course and then take the exams. It is completely flexible to the trainee's circumstances and wishes.

I don't think that this was around 20 years ago but since the advent of 'Client Centred' learning and Coaching, I have discovered this course which I am now confident to deliver and that has a much higher success rate than the traditional courses.

When I started my business back in 2000, I immediately set up a number of financial transfers to start saving for tax and national insurance and other things. I had not properly assessed how much would be coming in and had to quickly cancel them as there was not as much money coming in as I had hoped initially. My advice now would be to wait for a month or so to see how the finances develop and then sort out relevant transfers and savings plans. Look into potential pension plans in detail and carefully. Take proper professional financial advice. There are a lot more options now than there used to be. Take your time and do not rush into something you will regret later.

Do not assume a student is going to pay you until it's in your bank account! They are quite likely to cancel. Take block bookings if you can and payment in advance by internet or phone banking. They are much more committed and it is easier to make them pay if they cancel at the last minute.

Have a simple Terms and Conditions that you go over in the first lesson and get them to sign it. Give them a copy on their next lesson.

These are all things that I do now, having been caught out by not doing them in the past. I'm running a business not a charity and this is how it is run.

Know your worth!

Challenges And Wins

One of the challenges I face to this day is that my students do not always pay at regular times in the month so forecasting a fixed income is not always possible. I encourage them to pay for a block of lessons (usually 10 hours) and then it may be two and a half months before they pay again. Especially as I only work two days a week.

Some of the most challenging students are the ones from other countries, often Asian, African or even Eastern Bloc countries who have been driving for a long time there. Not everyone though. There are some who think it will be simple to drive in this country with our Highway Code full of the rules of the road.

It's challenging to get them to appreciate that driving in the UK is not a 'given'. Some think that they will have a little practice, 'cross the examiners palm with silver' and they'll get their full licence. They soon find out that this is not the case and they have to put a little work in!

One big win is that I have been in this industry for more than 20 years and have never had any desire to change or go back to being employed. My maxim that I am now unemployable stands as I would not have the discipline or desire to make someone else rich in that way!

Another big win was my very first student. She was a 68-year-old lady who needed to learn to drive so she could take her husband to hospital appointments. She had just passed her Theory test and was described as being partly trained. In fact, she barely knew how to change gear! Not what I would describe as partly trained.

She was a joy to teach and although it took her longer to pass and several attempts at the test, she never missed a lesson and did pass some 20 months later. I did tell her then that she was my very first student/lesson. At one point, we had done a mock test with another instructor who cheerfully told me that she would never pass. It just shows what a little persistence can achieve.

One other student of note was an Indian lady for whom English was definitely her second language. She came to me having taken and failed several tests previously. On looking at the test reports it was obvious that she was not ready.

It was quite a time before I was prepared to let her take another test. It still took her several goes before she passed but each one got better than the last until it was obvious that it was just her understanding that was holding her back. But again, with some persistence on both our parts she did eventually pass.

Values And Motto

I have always considered myself to be Patient, Friendly, Considerate, Responsible, and committed to anything I choose to do. The things I value above all else are Freedom and Helping others.

My motto is Driving to Freedom which is what I help my students and trainees to do.

I recently had the opportunity to discover my life purpose, which turns out to be to make a positive difference in people's lives. Teaching, and in particular the Driving Tuition, is the Vehicle (pardon the pun) I use to do that.

About Me

I was born in Leeds, Barbara Jeanne Slater on 25th August 1955 and adopted by John and Anne Hopps and became Barbara Jean Hopps. Very soon after they adopted me, they had two sons of their own. This is often known to happen when a couple adopts. I was never made to feel any different and we were all loved equally. My adoption was never any secret.

We grew up in relative prosperity and never wanted for anything. Dad was a Solicitor and would go to work in the week, early in the morning and come back late. He worked in Bradford.

When I was 3 1/2 years old and my youngest brother 10 weeks, we move house to a larger property. At the new house, I was given a brand-new purple tricycle. My 2-year-old brother and I were sent to a nanny for lunch while my parents sorted out the house. I remember screaming and crying when we had to get into a black car to go for lunch. I don't know why because we had a great time. Looking back, I think that maybe that was how I could never express my anger in any other way than crying.

Moving forward, my upbringing was relatively normal. I went to a private junior school which I hated and then to the local comprehensive school which I quite liked. I was never brilliantly academic but I got the 'O' levels and 'A' level that I needed to be able to go to the teacher training college that I wanted.

I understand now that I know my life purpose, why teaching in the classroom was not for me. As a child, I interpreted all the helping out at the nursery, Brownies and Guides, teaching at the swimming club as a calling to the teaching profession. We knew no different and these opportunities to find out were not there at that time.

Throughout my various jobs where teaching and helping others to learn was part of my duties I was never happier. The only time in my life when I suffered from stress was when I did not feel that I was fulfilling my life purpose of making a positive difference in peoples' lives.

In the last three years, I have had the opportunity to learn about property strategies and done a number of business and marketing courses.

I learned public speaking which in my earlier life would have completely terrified me. I have also taken the chance to become an NLP Practitioner and intend to go on to develop that further to Master Practitioner and maybe further still to Trainer.

Two years ago, I traced my birth family. Too late to meet my mother, but I intend to meet my half-sister in Canada and half-brother in Florida. Both places I have not visited yet.

I met Chloë two and a half years ago at the Business and Marketing Bootcamp and have followed her progress closely. I feel privileged to call her a friend along with many of the other founder members of the Queens In Business Club, some of whom I have worked with. I am also in Chloë's Get Featured Getaway Retreat. As such it seems fitting to share my story in the first Queens In Business book.

Born To Reign

Rumbi Jena

Founder

iReign Female Academy

"Nothing is impossible, the world itself says I'm possible."
--- Audrey Hepburn

Preface

I was in my mid-thirties when I started seriously considering that I did not want to be an employee for the rest of my life. It had crossed my mind a few times before that, but I had not given it the attention required to make the necessary changes.

I had a great career. I earned way above the average salary. Talking about my dissatisfaction was hard. As far as most people around me were concerned, I was doing better than most. In addition to that, change was daunting. However, that feeling, that nudge that I needed to try a different path stayed within me. I yearned for more freedom and time; for family, loved ones and causes that are dear to my heart. It took getting a 'no' at more than twenty interviews and a cycle of depression to make the change. I will expound on this story as the chapter continues. Open your heart and mind and let this story inspire you.

I trained as a nurse and manager in the healthcare industry, I worked hard to move up the ranks and get into management. It did not take long in my career to get to management level positions, because I was always up for a new challenge. I knew I would have a great career, and I knew that I wanted to get to the top management jobs in my chosen pathway. It was a no brainer.

I remember being in school and having it drummed into my head that I would be a success if I got the right education and got a great career. I always knew that I would have a great career because growing up, I got what society considers to be the right education. I am not here to put down education or great careers. I one hundred percent believe in getting a solid education, and I understand how important careers are. However, at that young age, I was not taught to believe that I could take a part of my career and turn it into a business. I was not even taught to believe that I could start, let alone run a business.

The actions I took over the next fifteen plus years were dictated by the knowledge I received at that young age. That knowledge is what shaped and helped structure my belief system. Had I known what I know now, the transition that I needed to make would have been so much easier. If I could speak to teenage Rumbi today, I would tell her, the world is your oyster, you can be and do anything you desire.

One thing I remember very well, is that even though I was excelling professionally, I could not see or seem to get a job that gave me the satisfaction, time, or freedom I was looking for. The competition for top managerial positions was steep. I soon realised that it would take a lot of hard work and longer than I imagined getting anywhere near my dream job. I always imagined myself being a Chief Executive Officer in a large organisation one day. After all, I believe in dreaming and dreaming big.

So many times, I have heard people say, "I am ordinary and if I made it, you can". Well, I am here to tell you that you are not ordinary! There is an inherent ability inside of each one of us to be and do anything we set our minds to do; but you must be intentional about you want. You can do it and be a success at it.

Unfortunately, a lot of times, people go through life without ever realising this. So, dream and dream big.

With the right tools and mindset, dreams can become reality. With the right tools and mindset, you can live out your full potential.

I remember the period where I attended more than twenty interviews, and did not get offered a single job like it was yesterday. I felt dejected, disappointed, hurt, and stressed. I recall the anger, the questions, the sadness. Why hadn't anyone told me this is what it was going to be like? I followed the system I knew. How come the plan was not working? It was not for lack of trying or hard work on my part. Around that same time, I also realised I was stuck in a cycle that was not giving me the life I desired; the flexibility, freedom, and time I wanted. Inevitably, it hit me hard and I found myself depressed.

Depression

As I talk about depression, I am not legally giving any healthcare advice but sharing my experience of dealing with depression.

Depression in simple terms is defined as low mood. It can last for anything from days, weeks to months or years. It can negatively impact feelings, thoughts, and actions. It is my belief that there is a huge difference between being low in mood for a few days and going through years or months of feeling depressed. When the feeling persists for a prolonged period, you can begin to feel deep unhappiness and hopelessness.

I recall struggling to get out of bed most days. Simple things like cooking, cleaning, or doing laundry were difficult. I burned my food on a regular basis. Everything was difficult. There was a time, I even felt scared to leave the house. My sleep pattern was erratic. My confidence plummeted. I would sit in the dark for hours doing nothing. Simply picking up the phone and talking to the next person was such an effort.

Talking to family or friends was a chore. Answering my phone was tough. Family and friends could not understand why I seldom answered my phone. Talking to other human beings was too much work. Depression had set in; as a healthcare professional, I recognised the signs but felt helpless at the same time. It was also challenging to talk about feeling depressed. That also made it a scary and very lonely place.

Symptoms of depression range from mild to severe. Clinical assessment classified the level of depression I felt as moderate. Being a Christian, I got help from a spiritual standpoint because I felt this was the best option for me. However, there are other treatment options available. It was not an overnight transformation; it took a lot of work, support and conscious effort. During that period, I also found myself thinking that there must be another way to turn my dreams to reality. I did not know where to start but I knew, there had to be another way. I suppose that inherent ability to be great inside of me would not let me rest. I was looking for that glimmer of hope, and as I continued to search for it, I found hope.

If you are reading this and are not sure where to start, that is ok, and you are not alone. As the chapter continues, I explain how I got started, not knowing where or how to start.

Gradually, some days I mustered the mental strength to do something. I would force myself to spend around an hour a day looking for free training events around London. I was not sure what I was looking for at first, but I wanted and needed to get some inspiration. I soon discovered that there were loads of free training days in London offered by people who had started and were successful at running their own businesses. From property, coaching, running healthcare agencies to trading and running online businesses amongst many others. I started consciously looking for free events to attend. At the beginning, I attended all sorts of business seminars, until I narrowed it down to what made me feel passion and motivation. It would take me a lot of effort to get out of my bed and go to an event but once I got there, I found myself inspired. The more I got out, the more I got inspired.

Bit by bit, I began to see glimpses of light at the end of the tunnel. I started reading different books written by successful entrepreneurs in addition to attending business events. I understood that having the right mindset was key. Therefore, I started analysing the difference between how employees and entrepreneurs think. I discovered that entrepreneurs tend to mastermind their own ventures rather than get paid for performance. They are continually learning and engaging in activities that help build a resilient mindset. Being employed, I was used to getting paid for performance and never ever saw or imagined how I could construct a plan to start and run a business.

I also learned that the right mindset always accommodates growth. This means that you can control your abilities and are capable of learning anything. I used to believe that you needed to have a lot of money and time in order to start a business. As I educated myself, I later discovered that when you have the right mindset, you will find that the time and resources you need to start and grow your business will gravitate towards you.

My Reality Of Being An Employee

Growing up, I never once considered I would be anything other than employed. I knew that I would work for someone one day and be successful at it. My tertiary education even drummed this in some more. I appreciate the education I have, and I strongly believe the level of critical reasoning I attained through tertiary education contributed a great deal in helping me get to where I am today. But I also believe that it is important to train young adults to see beyond being employed and open their minds to other possibilities.

For example, you can get business ideas from your career. I started coaching as a hobby not knowing what it was. It was because I enjoyed mentoring and coaching staff in the workplace. That is a skill I learned in my job that I am now expanding into a business.

To this day, I enjoy being a part of the healthcare industry. And I intend to continue making a difference in the industry and beyond but on my own terms. I get to help people through exceedingly difficult journeys, and make a real difference in the lives of people. I wanted to help and make a significant difference to others. I needed to know how do it in a different way.

In my personal network, I was already considered a success. I earned way above the average income in England. Therefore, most people did not understand why I struggled with the idea of staying employed as I moved up the ranks. It became more and more difficult to voice my feelings. By the time I was in my early thirties, I was beginning to feel depressed. Getting rejected in over twenty interviews was the tipping point.

What happened in my mid-thirties was a domino effect of events in the preceding three years or so.

On reflection, I am grateful for my journey. I am who I am today because of the challenges and the difficulties. The pain forced me to step out of my comfort zone and open my eyes and mind to the realm of possibilities. Once I made the decision to make the necessary changes and started being intentional about turning my dream into reality, I saw growth and found more joy.

The Making Of iReign Female Academy

I started in business not knowing exactly where to start. The only two things I was certain of were that I wanted to do something I was passionate about, and I had to be helping people in some way. I continued to attend free training or networking programs, including enrolling in a two-day coaching program. During this course, I discovered that I was already mentoring and coaching people without using the terms. Since 2013, I had been speaking at programs on progressing professionally and financially.

It had never occurred to me that I could turn my passion for mentoring and coaching into a business until 2019. At the same two-day course, I also realised that my mindset was holding me back. I had so many doubts that affected and influenced my beliefs around starting and running a business. As I attended more networking and training seminars, it become clearer to me how entrepreneurship was a mindset. So, I consciously set out to change my thinking.

Change must be intentional. It takes conscious effort. For most, stepping out of that comfort zone can be daunting and difficult but little to no growth takes place within that comfort zone. I had to do the necessary to see the possibilities.

As I made a conscious effort to manage my mind better, my mental eyes opened to possibilities. As my mentality changed, I started analysing my skillset, my passion, my vision, and purpose. Make no mistake, the process was not overnight. There were periods I felt like giving up. There were days the feeling that I was not cut out for business crept it. I had to keep pushing through the doubts and negative thoughts. I had to learn to manage my mind better.

As I continued to do the necessary, I grew personally, emotionally, and spiritually in two years more than I had in the preceding five years.

Finally, I got to a point where I believed I had something to give as a business owner. I believed I could help someone in a similar position out there. I and my business are a work in progress because the world we live in is dynamic and there will always be opportunities to improve oneself. I make strides to better myself daily. There are moments doubts still arise but I consciously remind myself that I can do it.

One of the key things that has made a great difference in my journey is being mentored. I believe in mentorship and already had a great spiritual mentor. Therefore, early in the journey I set out to find a business mentor; someone who was successful in starting an online business and could teach me how to do the same. I invested in learning because I wanted to learn how to run a business the right way. I was not too sure where to start but I knew I wanted it to be online and include life coaching.

Mentorship is what made the difference. It helped me shape the idea, it made me responsible and accountable for my actions. It taught me the value of discipline and the right mindset. When the going gets tough, discipline helps you to keep going.

I started my business in February 2020. Before that, I spent roughly two years wondering if I could do it and working on my mind until I had enough self-belief to take that step. Remember, earlier I mentioned that we all have the inherent ability in us to be great? I knew I was born to reign. I reigned as a professional smashing goal after goal! I needed to apply that same faith when it came to starting a business. I needed to reign living out my purpose. The question is, is what you are doing enabling you to live out your purpose to the full?

Make note, starting iReign Female Academy was hard work. Ladies, this is why I say, 'mindset is key'. I had to discipline myself to follow through with the work. I learned to design online products, how to use the systems I needed to run the business amongst other things. When the work became too overwhelming and stressful, I turned to and still turn to my mentor for advice and support. I also have a network of like-minded women who are creating their own paths and running their own businesses. This is how I manage the challenges and stress that comes with being an entrepreneur.

In November 2020, I launched my 1st online product. iReign Female Academy went live! It was definitely a proud moment. The voice that used to whisper 'you can't' had been silenced. From that moment, I knew I could. It was that simple. The product was a Self-Coaching Toolkit designed to help women transition from Employee to Entrepreneur Mindset. This process took me at least two years.

I am in the process of working on phase 2.

I designed the toolkit to help women transform their mindset like I did but in a much shorter space of time. These are lessons I learned in my journey and how l got the results I desired. You may be wondering "why women?". I know what it like to be woman climbing that professional ladder to get to the top. The reality of being an employee for the majority in any industry is sobering. Society tells us that if you are a woman, you are at an even greater disadvantage when it comes to earning power.

This is the reason why I am passionate about helping women. I want to see women succeed and break barriers, ceilings and limits that society has placed. This is why iReign Female Academy is strictly for women. I am here to tell you that, you can, and you were born to reign. Make a conscious effort to transform your mindset. Cross the line to the arena of possibilities. Dare to believe that you can, and I can help you with that.

At iReign Female Academy, we empower and equip you with the right tools and mindset to help you establish yourself as a female entrepreneur.

Mindset
I started the journey of transforming my mindset by learning about the mind and how it works. My spiritual mentor was the first person to teach about the mind. As I did the work on mind management, I began to understand the power that the mind holds. It may sound too simple or almost fairy tale like, but the reality is your mind is powerful. I had learned the concept of mind management a few years back but, I could see clearly that I had not considered how important having the right mindset was.

In simple terms, mindset refers to a mental state, beliefs, inclination and/or attitude. It determines how you think and process information and situations that influence and/or affect your day-to-day living. These thoughts and habits affect what you do and how you feel. Your mind is responsible for interpreting images and pictures you see. If your mind holds the power of your beliefs, thoughts, and imagination, this means that your mind carries power. It is therefore important to understand the power of your mind.

You can consciously use your mind as a tool to create that life that you desire. You can use it to actualise your dream. This means you can train or re-train your mind to think a certain way. I was over 30 years old when I started re-training my mind regarding entrepreneurship. So, whichever stage you are in your life, it is possible to create a new mindset that supports your dreams.

There are several activities you can do to help start cultivating the right mindset for business. One activity I personally believe in is the power of positive affirmations. These are phrases that help you affect your subconscious and conscious mind. It is important to understand that your subconscious mind stores your previous experiences, memories, and beliefs. This includes things you heard and learned growing up that may influence your life as an adult today regardless of your awareness of their impact. Your conscious mind on the other hand is your thinking mind. It consists of everything inside your awareness – perceptions, feelings, sensations, fantasises etc.

Using affirmations, you can challenge thoughts and actions that influence both your past and present experiences.

Below are twenty affirmations I use that have helped me transform my mindset. I started working on transforming my mind to think like an entrepreneur, but I found that the work positively impacted other areas of my life. Remember it is not about how you feel or what you see right now. It is about creating that picture you want to see. It may feel forced at the beginning but the more you do this exercise the easier it becomes.

To get the best results, take a few minutes to say the affirmations out to yourself loud enough to hear what you are saying.

- Money flows to me effortlessly every single day.
- I am open to receiving wealth.

- I only think thoughts of abundance.

- Everything around me is in perfect harmony.

- I live in peace and prosperity.

- I believe in myself, and I know I can accomplish my goals.

- I am confident, able, and focused.

- I am smart enough to learn and master anything I do not know.

- My experiences enable me to help someone else.

- I can start and run a successful business.

- I am a solution centre and make progress daily.

- I deserve success and will honour my dreams.

- My business is getting bigger and better each day.

- I have million-dollar ideas.

- I was born to reign!

- I am reigning in life.

- My passion about my purpose shows up in everything I do.

- Opportunities come my way every day.

- I am one hundred percent dedicated to turning my dream into reality.

- I create avenues for my personal growth and that of others.

Wow! Powerful exercise, right? Affirmations helped me to create the right conditions for my transition from employee to entrepreneur mindset. They helped heal from past mistakes, pain, and channel my mind to think the right thoughts. This is an exercise I continue to do because the work on my mindset is an ongoing process. Affirmations will help keep you motivated, stay on track with your goals and influence your subconscious mind to access new beliefs.

Purpose

As I educated myself, I also discovered the importance of purpose. To me, purpose refers to the reason for existence. The reason you were born and what you are meant to achieve with your life. I believe everyone was born for a purpose. It is therefore important to discover your purpose in life and build on that. It takes conscious effort. It gives you that passion and drive to remain focused even when the going gets tough. You align your inner self with your outer self.

This means you begin to know exactly who and what you are and why you are who you are. Purpose enables you to live a value-based life. Once I got clear on my purpose, I got clarity on what was important and what was not. Consider this, is what you are doing helping you to fulfil the reason for your existence?

Closing Thoughts

As my journey continues, I continue to discover and bring out the greatness in me. What I am sure of is that it can and will only be upwards and forwards. There are challenges in starting and running a business, but you can choose to see them as a springboard to help you leap to the next stage. This is a conscious choice I make daily. For me, purpose + value = profit trumps purpose + value = salary any day.

Now that you are at the end of the chapter, my hope is that you have been inspired to take action. You have the inherent ability to be great inside of you. You have a story that will inspire someone else. Your business may even lie within that story. In the stories you find resilience, mental strength, potential, and ambition.

Your story is your strength. Work on your mindset, do the necessary and see the possibilities. Turn your story, passion, or skillset into something that gives you a profit.

What are your next steps?

My hope is you have begun making or will start making the necessary changes to manage your mind effectively. Once you master the concept of mind management, you open yourself to endless possibilities. Remember you are beautiful, worthy, and more than capable. Girl, you were born to reign!

About Me

My name is Rumbi. I founded iReign Female Academy in 2020 to help women like me who are looking for change, whether it is time for family, oneself, or the freedom to focus on the causes that are dear to you. I started helping women transform their mindset in 2013.

My background is Nursing and Management in Healthcare. Around five years into my career, I stepped into management and worked in several management positions over the next eight years. Despite the success I quickly attained, there was a part of me that yearned for more time and freedom for my loved ones and causes that are important to me. Although I knew almost five years ago that I wanted to embark on a different path, it took me years to cultivate the right mindset to make the change. For a long time, I did not believe that I could start a business, let alone run one. Through research over a couple of years, I finally discovered the key to moving from employee to entrepreneur – MINDSET!

Mind management, not necessarily having enough money or time was the key. It however still took me another year or so to start making some real changes. Therefore, I decided to start the academy and creates tools and programs to help other women make that transformation much faster than I did. The right mindset opens the arena of possibilities. The money and time you need to start and grow a business will gravitate towards you.

My aim is to empower and equip you with the right tools and mindset so that you are positioned to turn that dream into reality. The right positioning will help you start and or establish yourself as a female business owner. Girl, it is your time to reign.

Dedication
To the One who Was and Is to Come.

It Starts With You

Judy Hamilton

Co-Founder, Director and Coach

Hamilton Coaching

"Anything is possible when you have the right people there to support you." --- Misty Copeland

My Vision...

I see a world where women are catalysts for change, women who truly know themselves, confident women who believe in themselves.

I see women drawing strength from within, intentionally living out their self-identified purpose, knowing they will make a difference. I see women empowering their families - strengthening, modelling, influencing and championing them, as unique individuals.

I see strong, connected families who acknowledge, accept, listen and love, living purposefully, believing the best in others and making impact in communities. I see women influencing change in our world as they recognise the power of valuing the individual, and their unique contribution regardless of gender, age or race.

It starts with you...You are valuable, You matter.

I'm Judy and I am a life coach. I have a passion to see women connected to themselves and into communities. My mission is to equip and empower women to live their lives with purpose and intention, walking with them on a journey of discovery. This mission is paramount to my work.

I believe that when you 'Discover the Real You' is when you find balance and fulfilment. That is when everything starts to make sense and fall into place, and you have the freedom to be yourself. This is my journey, so I know its power…but it hasn't always been this way.

I rolled over and looked at the clock… 3am Argh! Why can't I sleep more than 4 hours?! My mind started racing, I need to sleep!

I started processing the previous day and everything I didn't get done. Why do I take on all this stuff? Why do I say yes? I always end up doing everything for everyone else…but I'm getting nowhere! I can't keep going like this. I don't think anyone even realises I'm drowning. Do they even notice me? I wish I had the courage to say no. I wish I could have some time for me. I don't even know what I would do. I don't even know who I am anymore. I don't have time to think about me or what I want, I need to get through each day.

I feel so lonely, I haven't got time for friends… I don't fit in anyway.

At least when I'm working, I feel valuable, but what difference am I making? I want to do something meaningful.

I buried my head in the pillow and tried not to focus on the fact I had to get up in 2 hours.

This is a snapshot of the former me. Can you relate? This was a typical conversation in my head. I was feeling exhausted, overwhelmed, out of balance, running fast in lots of different directions but feeling like I was getting nowhere. I was left wondering who am I, what's my purpose and why do I feel so empty? Feeling like I had to work so hard to belong anywhere. Doing lots of 'stuff' for others, always being connected with people but feeling lonely and disconnected, like I didn't belong. Making others' happy but never feeling happy within myself. This habit started early in my life. I was always a bit of a "people pleaser".

'The Good Girl'

I grew up in a family of five in the Blue Mountains in New South Wales, Australia. I was the only girl in the middle of two brothers, so I quickly learned to hold my own. I loved life and I loved spending time with people, old and young. I was always keen to help out and make people happy. I hated being out of favour and I hated it when my parents fought. I always strived to be 'the good girl'.

I couldn't wait to get to school. I thrived in the structure of that learning environment, and the affirmation from teachers when I was 'a good girl'. I noticed everybody and prided myself on the fact that I knew the names of everyone in our small school. I was good at making friends, especially with the new kids. I connected most with the ones that seemed to be on the edge, 'the fringe dwellers' - I didn't like that they looked scared and lonely. This extended to other situations too, like church. I remember sitting next to the elderly ladies who didn't have husbands anymore, so they didn't have to be alone. I wanted to make them happy.

Although I loved freely, I worked out quickly at school that everyone didn't love me, especially when I got to high school. I valued achievement and I tried my best, but this didn't make any impact with my peers, they called me 'goody two shoes' and other names or overlooked me completely. I grew up thinking that maybe I wasn't as good as other people - not pretty enough, smart enough, not cool enough, not good enough... I didn't quite 'make the cut', I often felt like I didn't belong. I felt like the 'fringe dweller'.

As a result, I developed this learned behaviour of downplaying my own achievements, being proud inside but not speaking it out. This habit followed me into my adult years. I also learned that I did things for people so that they'd noticed me and were happy with me. I worked out this was the best way to be recognised, affirmed, stay out of trouble and feel happy about myself. It was all about what I could do for others, it was about saying 'yes'. It was always about being 'the good girl'.

Belonging To Others

There is a beautiful quote from Maya Angelou, "You are only free when you realise you belong no place, you belong every place, no place at all. The price is high. The reward is great".

As a teenager, I slipped further into the habit of not telling people what I really thought. I didn't want to be rejected. I longed to be included and be a part of the group. It seemed like a constant battle. I started thinking that others' thoughts and opinions were more important than mine, so I took on their values as my own. I fell into the trap of ignoring myself and my own needs. Instead, I found "fulfilment" in doing things for others, living up to their expectations and focusing on avoiding conflict.

What I didn't know at the time, and what I've learned in my later journey, is that to be in a good relationship with other people, you have to be in a good relationship with yourself first. It's about accepting yourself and operating from that foundation of strength.

Brené Brown, who also speaks a lot about belonging, takes Maya Angelou's quote further by saying, "We confuse belonging with fitting in, but the truth is that belonging is just in our heart, and when we belong to ourselves and believe in ourselves above all else, we belong everywhere and nowhere."

It was about fitting in for me and I felt like a square peg in a round hole. My first realisation of this came when I attended a church youth camp when I was about 16. I was struggling with my identity (as were many girls my age) so the weekend focus of 'Knowing who you are' was perfect. I was confronted, challenged, and given a glimmer of hope. We listened to some talks about 'loving yourself', all I could think was 'I hate myself; I want to be loved and accepted'.

As I reflected, I could see that what I was doing was worthwhile, but when it came to focusing on me, I could only see my flaws and failings. I didn't think that I measured up. I remember talking to one of the leaders. She held space for me, she acknowledged my pain and loneliness and held me when I cried. She talked about how I was created by God and how important I was to Him. She gave me a poem called 'Learning' which resonated deeply. I remember it started like this:

> "I've been learning to love myself,
> By learning that God loves me.
> And though it seems I always need His help,
> Well, I'm finally beginning to see.
> That God loves me the way I am,
> Though at times it's hard to understand!
> But I will walk by faith and not by sight
> Cause He's given me His hand."
> --- Unknown Author

This caused a shift in my thinking as I started to see and understand that I had my own value, by just being me. This message faded after the camp, but was to come back time and again, over the next few years. I would remember this lesson when I found myself struggling, under the weight of expectation and people pleasing.

This attitude of knowing my own value was especially hard as a wife, a mother, a teacher, and as a part of the local community so many people were dependent upon me. I wanted the people in my life to be happy and healthy, to set them up well for the future. I would say 'yes' to anyone and take on anything. I wanted others to be happy and I wanted to feel like I was contributing and serving.

I found myself putting all my energy and resources into others. I was always giving out. Although these were all 'good things', I couldn't help wondering if I was doing the 'right thing'. It felt like something was missing. Was this my purpose? I felt good when I was doing stuff for others, but I was exhausted, overwhelmed and often depleted. I recognised that something had to change.

Belonging To Self - Discover The Real Me

Looking back, I can see that I was only happy when I was helping others. I would fill up on their happiness but still didn't recognise my own value. I would be quick to put myself aside, thinking others were not interested or that they were more important - even though I knew in my head that this wasn't true. Although I didn't focus on my own value, I could definitely see and champion this in others. As a teacher, this was one of my outstanding qualities, the way I valued the individual. I cared about each child, seeing their uniqueness, and believing in their potential. I wanted them to recognise their own gifts as special.

It wasn't until many years later that I was challenged, once again, to apply this lens to myself…to take a look at my own uniqueness. I had been invited to participate in a course focused on being a 'Significant Woman'. I resonated with the concept but didn't realise at the time just how much this would change my life. As a person of faith, I believe we are all unique individuals, created in God's

167

image and that God has a purpose for us in this world. But I had never thought deeply about this from my own perspective.

The concepts were confronting, I was so used to avoiding myself that when I did look at myself, I could only see my faults. I felt guilty focusing on myself, like I was big-noting myself. I also had to face those old tapes in my head that said, "You don't matter", "You're not good enough" and "You don't belong". Again, I felt a shift in me. I remembered thinking...

"How can I tell others that they are valuable and significant, especially my own children, when I don't believe it myself?"

For the first time during this course, I unpacked my thinking about what was valuable to me and about me, not what I thought I should say or what others expected me to say, but what was in my heart, and I believed it! I understood 'my Truth'.

The other thing that was so liberating was articulating my purpose. What an amazing feeling to know I actually had one! And I was already living it out! My purpose wasn't to do anything, my purpose is to be me - the unique individual that God created me to be and to live in alignment with 'the Truth' in my heart.

The Journey - Discover My Purpose
This realisation took me on a deeper journey of self-discovery, and over the next few years I started to dive down the layers of me. I dug deep with the help of some wonderful people, who held the space I needed and spoke my value and truth back to me. I began to move through the layers of self-doubt and the negative self-talk and uncover the 'real me', the me who has her own value and worth.

There is an analogy about an oyster shell which illustrates this process beautifully…

It starts by observing the shell from the outside – they are fairly bland looking, brown or grey. They might be chipped and cracked, a bit rough and may be covered in sea moss. They don't look much but that's their purpose; they are designed to blend into the environment in a way that they don't draw attention to themselves. Their role is to protect the soft body that's encased within, so when a threat is perceived the shell clamps shut.

Now think about what the oyster shell looks like on the inside – they are so different, comparing the two is like night and day. On the inside, they are smooth and white, coated with a substance called Nacre which provides a beautiful sheen, a rainbow-like effect. They are so beautiful that people make jewellery from them – but this beauty is not obvious until the shell is opened.

We are like the oyster shell; we come into this world with our own uniqueness - all our gifts, skills and abilities wrapped up in a beautiful bundle within us. We are then exposed to the world. Like the oyster, we might test the water by opening 'our shell' but at the first sign of a threat or danger, we quickly close it until it feels safe. This process might happen again and again. If we experience a life with exposure to lots of hurt and trauma, it becomes an automatic response to keep 'the shell' closed and stop trying to open it - so much so, that we may not even remember the beauty and light inside anymore. Then we may blend into the environment, as a form of self-protection, thus allowing it to be buried deep, under layers of sediment (the hard stuff in life). Often, we have to dig deep to even find 'the shell'.

And that is a part of the journey of 'discovering the real you'. Digging down through all those layers – finding then opening yourself, in a safe environment, allowing that natural beauty to shine out. This is our place of strength; this is us at our deepest core.

The analogy also goes a little further; in some of those oyster shells there is a pearl, though not in every oyster. Pearls are actually formed from an irritant, a grain of sand (or something similar) that gets in and disturbs the environment. When this happens, the shell goes to work and coats the irritant with layer upon layer of Nacre, until it's perfectly smooth and one with the shell. It not only becomes part of the shell, but it also stands out as a shining beauty! What a beautiful picture to hold onto, the challenges in our life can end up being the things that make us shine even brighter.

When I finally understood the enormity of all this, it blew me away and started some new patterns of thinking:

→ Instead of berating and pulling myself down, I started affirming and seeing my qualities.

→ Instead of living to others values and expectations, I started valuing my own thoughts and opinions.

→ Instead of letting others make decisions for me I began to make my own.

→ I started taking risks.

→ I started believing in myself.

→ I started trusting myself.

I finally felt like I could say "I know who I am and I love myself."

I realised from this point that this was a gift that I wanted to give others, especially women like me. I wanted them to know the power and freedom that could be theirs. By discovering themselves, unveiling 'their truth' and living in alignment with it.

This was my purpose to come alongside people, to support and encourage them to grow in Truth and the understanding of their own value and worth. I think I always knew my purpose, deep inside, but once I could articulate it, I had immediate clarity about my direction. I knew with certainty what I was here to do. It wasn't about having a particular job or doing a particular thing, it was living out that purpose wherever I was, in whatever I was doing.

The Journey - Discover My Direction
And that's exactly what I did! I had energy and motivation, I felt like I was on a mission, whatever I was doing. Whether it was teaching in the classroom being a wife or mum at home, talking to my friends at playgroup, kids sport or dance, being involved with church or in community groups, I was seeking out opportunities to come alongside people, speaking their own value and truth back to them in simple ways that they could understand.

Fast forward to 2014. My husband and I had been working in a non-profit organisation where we had the opportunity to work with a coaching company on some leadership development. After this work, we were invited to train as coaches, launch our own business and join the team. We were particularly focusing on a youth leadership program. This was exciting for me! It felt like the opportunity of a lifetime, so many boxes ticked; my experience, skills, qualities, values, passions and purpose all rolled into one. I also have a particular passion for community. This was a community-based program working with high schools, local businesses and clubs in the local community. This seemed like an amazing way to make a difference!

The experience was fantastic, it gave me a lot of confidence as a coach, as a facilitator and as program manager. I also had exposure to a variety of different coaching opportunities. My favourite was being in a family program where I was coaching mums of children with special needs. I recognised a particular passion for working with women again and what a perfect vehicle coaching was for living out my purpose.

The first real challenge came when my husband decided to move on from coaching and go in a different direction. The opportunities with the coaching company also changed around this time. So, I had to decide about what I was going to do going forward.

It is times like this where it's so important to have your purpose identified and your foundation to come back to. As scary as it was, I knew with certainty that I wanted to continue with coaching and based on my experience I knew I wanted to do this with women. I didn't know what it was going to look like, I hadn't done it by myself before so I was stepping out of my comfort zone. I came back to my foundation, reminding myself of what I did know, what was in my oyster shell. I opened up my own strengths, qualities, skills, experiences and natural abilities, realising that I actually had everything that I needed.

There were probably two key things that were holding me back. The first challenge was the fear of the unknown or the unfamiliar. I was exploring the idea of launching coaching from an online perspective, and I wasn't familiar with that space at all although I knew it was the only way I would free up enough time to make this a profitable business.

The second challenge was belief in myself. I needed courage to take a risk, to step out and do it by myself. If there was one thing, I wish that I knew about myself back then it would be that I'm consistent, hard-working and capable. I know my stuff and the message I have to share makes a real difference in the lives of women. The thing that was so helpful to me in overcoming these fears was plugging into a network of people who were on the same journey. I got to know some amazing peers and mentors. Many of them I still connect with today as friends and colleagues. It's vital to have those networks around you especially when you're on your own in a small business.

Another piece of helpful advice that I received early on was to prioritise income first. Once you gain that momentum, it's easier to keep going. You can develop programs and the like later. I took this advice and joined a program where this was the focus.

That first sale was amazing!

I couldn't believe that I did it! Somebody valued what I had, so much that they wanted to pay me for it. That gave me the confidence and the courage to keep going.

Seven years on in business, and three of those on my own, I still feel like I'm on a learning curve. I've seen many others come and go in my industry and I'm still here. I'm proud of myself for my consistency, for sticking it out and not giving up, especially in those early days when everything was new. My message to you, if you are a small business owner just starting out: trust yourself, listen to that inner voice, come back to your foundation.

Remember, 'What you seek is within'.

Be Free To Be Me
Real freedom comes when you know who you are, when you identify your purpose, when you are clear about your direction, and then live your life in alignment with it. This is my own journey.

I know its power and value and this is the same journey I walk through with the women I work with.

There are two levels of freedom from my perspective:

- Freedom with-in
- Freedom with-out

Freedom with-in is that place of inner strength, tapping into who you are. This may not be new information but it's being able to see all of your qualities together, in one place at one time. It is a powerful way to look at yourself.

Freedom with-out is applying those inner qualities with purpose and intention in every area of your life. This application brings clarity, energy and focus to your dreams and goals.

The key is to keep coming back to your foundation, providing a solid base on which to build, allowing balance in your life when it is lived in the framework of your life purpose. We all know that balance is important. We desire it but it seems to be the one thing that gets out of control. I believe when we get our inner balance sorted then everything else will start to flow.

It reminds me of when I was learning to ride a bike. My dad was holding the back of the bike as I was riding (we didn't have training wheels back then). I felt safe and supported because he was there. But as I gained confidence and momentum, he let go. I was pedaling and chatting away not realising he was back down the street. Then I fell off...Ha-ha. That was also part of the journey, a learning opportunity.

That is what I like to do as a coach; walk with somebody closely at first, helping them to gain balance, and encouraging them every step of the way. Help them establish those good habits and thinking patterns, then pull back step by step, until they have the confidence to move off and do it on their own, maintaining their own balance and momentum. As Albert Einstein says…'Life is like riding a bicycle. To keep your balance, you must keep moving'.

Below is the diagram I use for describing balance, it's actually a bicycle wheel. As the 'hub' on a bike wheel governs the integrity of the wheel, your 'hub' (foundation) governs the integrity of your life balance.

When your 'hub' is serviced, lubed, and aligned, the rest of the wheel has balance, flow and efficiency. Whenever you do any work on the 'hub', it will positively impact all areas of your life.

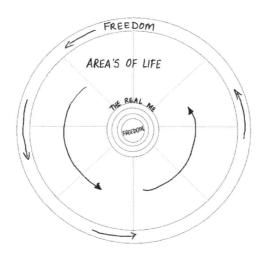

Make A Difference

The journey of discovering yourself is so key to allowing that balance and flow in life. Being authentic is so important to me and

I want this to be the mark of who I am. As I said earlier, when I recognised and articulated my purpose it gave me the freedom to be myself, whatever I was doing.

Coaching for me is a perfect vehicle for living out my purpose. It allows me to be my authentic self and to make a difference at the same time. My vision and mission for my coaching practice is built on the same model as my personal journey. It starts with empowering the individual:

Empowered women, Empowering families, Empowering communities.

Women from every family, in every community, living lives of purpose and intention. I believe that this can be world changing. It starts by equipping and empowering that individual with their own value and worth. Then seeing this ripple out into their families and their communities.

I also have a heart for community both local and global. I believe when like-minded people are living and working in a community, amazing things can happen. We as humans were created to be in community. It's through this that we bring out the best in each other. We each have our differences, our strengths and our uniqueness. We can't be individually strong in everything, but when we come together in community it can have exciting outcomes. It's like all the different parts of a body working together.

I love the support that comes from community. If you think about our physical bodies, when one part is hurting or injured the other parts support it and are stronger, while the injured part recovers. This is my picture of ideal community. This sort of connected community also allows its members to shine, to stand out and use their gifts while being supported and encouraged by other like-minded individuals.

With this understanding of ideal community, I had a dream to create an online community to support and be an extension of my coaching space. This would be a place where like-minded women could gather, connect, engage, share, support and shine out their own uniqueness.

This community called 'Be Free to Be Me' was launched in 2019 with a small group of 10 to 20 like-minded women, who had worked with me and have very similar values. I wanted to develop a strong nucleus and provide a solid foundation moving forward. I was so excited for these beautiful women to meet each other, lean into real relationships and do life with one another. They immediately started supporting and caring for each other, and it developed into a community with a strong core. As it strengthened, more people were invited into it. I wanted it to be like people joining a moving train, feeling the momentum, like something exciting was happening in the space. Inviting them to be a part of a journey that they could jump into and feel immediately comfortable.

Today, this community is still growing and it's everything I was hoping that it would be. There is still that nucleus of super supportive ladies that love and care in a solid way. When one is hurting, they reach out with support. We have even moved this into the offline space with physical meetups. It's so amazing that a group of ladies that haven't yet met in person can meet at a coffee shop and experience immediate connection, like friends or sisters. It is a beautiful community that warms my heart.

You Are Valuable…You Matter

I want to leave you with a story, which is a beautiful expression of why I do what I do. It is my hope that it will inspire you to align with your passion and purpose, 'the real you' and never give up.

Once upon a time, there was an old man who used to go to the ocean to do his writing. He had a habit of walking on the beach every morning before he began his work. Early one morning, he was walking along the shore after a big storm had passed and found the vast beach littered with starfish as far as the eye could see, stretching in both directions. Off in the distance, the old man noticed a small boy approaching.

As the boy walked, he paused every so often and as he grew closer, the man could see that he was occasionally bending down to pick up an object and throwing it into the sea. The boy came closer still and the man called out, "Good morning! May I ask what it is that you are doing?"

The young boy paused, looked up, and replied "Throwing starfish into the ocean. The tide has washed them up onto the beach and they can't return to the sea by themselves. When the sun gets high, they will die, unless I throw them back into the water."

The old man replied, "But there must be tens of thousands of starfish on this beach. I'm afraid you won't be able to make much of a difference." The boy bent down, picked up yet another starfish and threw it as far as he could into the ocean. Then he turned, smiled and said, "It made a difference to that one!"

Adapted from The Star Thrower by Loren Eiseley (1907 – 1977)

About Me

I am excited and honoured to be the Australian representative of this collective. I live in the beautiful Blue Mountains of New South Wales, with my husband Darren. I am the mother of two adult children and have a menagerie of animals, including my daily walking companions - two red Siberian Huskies. I love nature, especially beautiful sunrises, and holidays at the beach; my happy place.

I am passionate about connecting with and building into women. I value the individual and believe that everyone deserves to have someone to listen to, affirm and encourage them.

I have had my own struggles with self-worth, finding it difficult to see my own value. This experience led me on a journey to discover my own identity and purpose. In time, this resulted in a deep sense of knowing my own worth and significance, having a clear purpose and the confidence to live this out. I passionately believe that knowing 'the real you' is key to experiencing both inner and outer freedom - the solid foundation on which our lives must be built, both personal and business. I believe this is a gift to share with others, and I have been doing this, through various roles, for the past three decades.

Today I achieve this as Co-Founder, Director and Coach at Hamilton Coaching. I have coached hundreds of women, from around the world. These women have a common issue; their struggle with Identity, Purpose and Direction. I have the daily privilege of walking with them on a journey to Freedom, being spurred on by my vision to see Empowered women, Empowering families, Empowering communities.

This book is another opportunity for me to share this gift. It is my hope that my words and those of the other inspiring authors, will be the start of a beautiful journey for you.

I am dedicating this chapter to my husband Darren for always believing in me, even when I struggle to believe in myself.

To Wayne, for giving me the opportunity to turn my dream into reality. And, to my beautiful Community for inspiring me to live out my purpose every day.

The Phoenix Rising From The Ashes

Angie Parry

Specialist Podiatrist, Clinical Director, Business Owner &

Entrepreneur

Podiatry & Chiropody Clinic

"Make bold choices and make mistakes. It's all those things that add up to the person you become." --- Angelina Jolie

The Beginning

From adults around me at an early age, I frequently heard the expressions "life is what you make it and you get what you settle for." It put the responsibility of my life firmly in my lap; it brought out the hedonist in me and the commitment-phobe, qualities that drove and shaped my life along its varied and interesting path of constantly trying new and wonderful experiences. Life is certainly for living!

Growing up in the 1970s and the constraints of an egalitarian society, the future seemed quite dismal. "A job for life" was another coined phrase of the era, working hard in one profession, saving relentlessly and only in retirement would I get to do what I wanted. This seemed unfathomable. The messages I was receiving contradicted each other.

How could I decide at a young age what I was going to do for the rest of my life? The options did not seem interesting enough. Thankfully, the 1980s burst in with full colour and with that big change: dynamism, yuppies, high earners, capitalism, a work hard play hard mentality, and everything started to align with those early mantras.

The suffocating shackles of the previous decade, where perception was that only the rich got what they wanted to do, started to fall away and a new culture was emerging. Travel was my passion; fortunately, I was born to parents whose idea of a summer holiday was camping in Spain rather than Southend and therefore I was delightfully exposed to foreign countries and cultures whilst at primary school. To stifle that desire and wait until I was sixty before I could travel the world seemed intolerable and so at eighteen, I cut to the chase and set off to discover the University of Life with an around the world ticket!

I was brought up to be an independent child with the ethos of "having to get on with it" and "there's no word as 'can't' in the dictionary" passed down through the generations from my mother and her mother, and their mothers before them. I had no choice but to do things, however challenging they may have felt previously, and only having time afterwards to reflect whether I found them difficult or not.

"Fortune favours the brave" is my one clear message and this approach set me in good stead as a temp worker in London when my mother told me at sixteen to get a job, any job. I had flunked my exams and emerged from a good school with little more than three O levels and scraped another two more in retakes. At least I had my English and Maths, she said as that was the benchmark. The subject English had been the bane of my life, ironic when ten years later I became a TEFL teacher in Germany and in the process taught myself whilst teaching others the mysteries of the English language.

Everything that I have experienced and endured in my life has got me where I am today. Have I made the most of life? I have most definitely tried. Have I got what I settled for? I do not need to, as I change things and move on when the time is right.

East Meets West

I am a fifty-two-year-old specialist podiatrist and co-director of a limited company called A&M Podmedics, trading as Podiatry and Chiropody Clinic in East Sussex, a business I set up with my husband Martin Parry eleven years ago.

We have developed our two clinics into specialist foot, ankle, and orthotic centres, offering solutions to people with foot health and foot function problems, especially foot drop and osteoarthritis of the ankle. The St Leonards' clinic has come a long way in the last eleven years from when we started off with just the two of us, alternating who did the work whilst the other sat on reception.

In 2018, we expanded and employed another podiatrist who enables us to go away and keeps the business open. We have three other staff members, two receptionists and a personal assistant.

When I look back, our systems were archaic for 2010, but that was all we could afford and that was how we had to operate until we organically grew. We worked from a paper diary, using a pencil and rubber and did not have a computer until the end of the first year, which was only a laptop. All our money had gone into buying the clinics, the equipment needed and paying back the business loan. It has only been since 2018 that we invested in a computerised diary system that covers the two locations. Our predecessors had both practiced for eighteen years and had invested virtually nothing into the properties or their businesses and it showed, installing debit card machines seemed futuristic to our client base at the time.

The Rye clinic was our first acquisition and a year later, the St Leonards clinic landed in our laps. We never intended on buying two clinics, it just happened that way. We were newly married and instead of children coming along quickly at our age, clinics did instead.

I had met Martin, an ex-Royal Navy Fleet Air Arm international triathlete on my podiatry degree at Brighton University in 2006. He had always held podiatrists in high esteem as they were the ones who had helped him overcome his injuries in the Navy. Whereas at thirty-seven, I had not been re-appointed for a job I enjoyed when I had to reapply for it. I felt I needed a degree to progress, a vocational degree and after being rejected by the physiotherapy department, I pursued a place on the podiatry course which I secured. It was meant to be, as I took to podiatry like a duck to water. We were in clinic every day treating patients, something that was not unfamiliar to me as I had been a holistic therapist working for myself for six years and had many clients.

My treatments had included Aromatherapy Massage, Indian Head Massage, Light Touch Spinal Therapy, Reflexology and Reiki.

There is an epic story behind why I transitioned out of holistic therapies and into wanting to do a podiatry degree. The emotionally painful problems I was experiencing with a significant other, significant for all the wrong reasons and the way he was making me feel were creating the perfect storm. The frustrations I endured by not progressing financially, the self-loathing I developed for supposedly being in love with someone who was hell bent on crushing my confidence, was horrendous. It was a dark time in my life that I tackled with good humour and a nervous laugh.

I just wanted everything to work out, but the Universe had 'cruel to be kind' intentions for me. The story involves packing up my flat in Brighton and moving to Ibiza to escape the stalking ex, who despite not wanting to be with me followed me out there. Ensues a story of cutting the ties with the help of new friends sheltering me, to finding out weeks later that the ties were being knitted back together when I shockingly discovered I was pregnant at thirteen weeks.

The life events I consequently endured were lack of acceptance from family members, heart-breaking loss when the baby was born prematurely in Tenerife at twenty-six weeks and died three days later, overwhelming grief, feeling like second-hand goods and ultimately desolation that my dream of having a family, was very unlikely if I were ever to do things 'properly'. I was thirty-five and had been through so much, I had nothing to give with my hands-on healing work. I was told to put myself first which I had to learn to do with difficulty.

Martin And The Brainchild

After leaving the Royal Navy, Martin had been a personal trainer specialising in rehabilitation corrective exercises and worked for himself. We had a common interest whereby we had both been sole traders to our own little businesses. Every business, big or small, has the same processes and in the case of sole traders they don many hats.

Not only do you practice what you are trained to do, you must also keep on top of patient records, admin, you need to market and advertise yourself, do the accounts, submit tax returns, network, order stock, have stationery and so the list goes on. Before you know it, you are running and organising a business and on the verge of exhausting yourself in the process.

During the last year of the degree, there was a module whereby we had to write our own aims and objectives, this module could cover any topic. My aim after the degree was to work in the NHS, however I had a moment of concern in case I did not secure a job. I needed a contingency plan and used the module to discover private practice opportunities in the Hastings and Rother area. I decided it would be good to find out what it was like to be a business owner of a private podiatry practice, so I compiled a list of questions, consulted the Yellow Pages and Thompson Directory, (as it was before Google) and set about phoning them up.

My mum, known as ma, had been brought up in a house with a shop front that was a hairdresser, her mother being the business owner and hairdresser in the 1940s until she retired in 1968. My ma had drummed into me as a child that when you work for yourself you never leave the job behind, you are married to it. She used to say that she woke up to the sound of the till roll and went to bed to the sound of the till roll.

When I reflect on that now, it sounds like business was booming, but my ma gave the impression that it was a slog. Hence, I went into the project of phoning the local podiatry business owners with the view that running a practice had a high price to pay and it might not be for me.

I found the podiatrists very keen to talk, telling me all about their businesses and how much they charged. It was fascinating and sounded lucrative. They gave the impression that they did not get much opportunity to talk about their businesses and one invited me to his practice to observe him.

Word got around that I was doing research on private practices, and someone brought to my attention that a business owner was looking to sell her practice in Rye. I contacted the owner who was in shock that someone had come along so quickly. She had advertised in her society's magazine, that had only come out the day before.

After a meeting, it was agreed that once I qualified, I would work in the practice one day a week as a trial. If things worked out, I had the option to buy the practice. We were both elated.

That week, I found out that I had got a part-time job in the NHS as well as in the private practice. The NHS had offered me a full-time job, but after hearing how depressingly low the salary was, I asked for the part-time job which I had originally applied for, which they agreed to. I could not believe how well everything was working out. They offered Martin the full-time job. We were the first students of the cohort to secure employment, and this was still four months before we graduated.

Martin and I were in an amazing whirlwind. We were finishing our degrees, getting married, graduating, honeymooning and starting our new jobs in a matter of only weeks apart. Goodness, it was non-stop celebrations! One of the things I keep hearing from business mentors is persevere, keep chipping away. I believe even if you do not realise you are doing it, you most probably are. Individually, Martin and I never gave up on meeting the right person for ourselves. I could write a page-turning tragic-comedy on my disastrous relationships whereas Martin was more reticent about his relationship history. But oh boy, did I and all our wedding guests hear a fantastically entertaining synopsis of Martin's unsuccessful relationships in the best man speech – thank you Al!

I had always felt embarrassed that I was attracted to disastrous men, especially when people said that the problem was within me. I was the common denominator. If you want to improve anything in your life, you must change what you are doing or thinking.

I thought about where I was going wrong, why I was going wrong and resisted old behavioural patterns that were not serving me, regardless of how difficult I found it. I can imagine it is like being in recovery from alcohol and drugs - you must be strong and the longer you stay strong and resist temptation, the easier it gets until it becomes the norm and then your prize is Mr. Fantastic!

I had not worked on my values then like I have now, but I used to think, "Can you honestly imagine this person sitting around the table for my family Christmas dinner, being quizzed by my interrogating sister, would they be able to hold their own, feel comfortable and not display erratic, nerve wracking behaviour?" This was the benchmark. Martin passed with flying colours. Since then, I have sought clarity on my values and align my business decisions with them, making life a whole lot easier.

A Day In The Life Of

I am an advocate for the humble foot, a stalwart of a bodily part that is literally down-trodden, nearly flattened in some cases, shoved into ill-fitting footwear, taken for granted and rarely cared for until it starts to hurt. What other bodily part would put up with so much? When feet go wrong, my goodness do they hurt, hinder mobility and then all hell lets loose and a quick resolution is needed – emergency stations!!

Moving people out of their foot pain and enabling them to continue their jobs, hobbies and sport is what the job is all about. In the past, chiropody had the reputation of little old ladies having their toenails cut and their corns removed. What happened to the men? Did they die off before they contemplated having their feet done? The profession was stuck in this image for a long time, more so only recently has it begun to move on. Nowadays with social media, many podiatrists including myself are trying to raise the profile of podiatry, create foot health awareness and attract people into this extremely small profession.

Podiatry in the UK definitely needs to be sexed up, in line with America and Australia and out of the dark ages. It is annoying to admit that in society you need things to be attractive to attract attention. If all the high-profile footballers and sports people like Andy Murray came out and said I wear orthotics to improve my foot function, once everyone had Googled the word orthotic, they would be rushing to their nearest podiatrist for a bespoke pair.

Being a podiatrist is being a doctor of the foot. There are eleven systems of the body all affecting the feet. Assessments of the feet and nails can indicate a lot about one's health. I could listen to the pulses in your feet to tell you if you had atrial fibrillation or test the nerves for an upper or lower motor neuron lesion. I believe people only do something about their feet once they go wrong, they do not know what else podiatrists do, which is a broad scope of practice. People's health psychology fascinates me, with many people putting up with pain and problems until they get unbearable before they will do something about it. Some people are also frightened of the cost and are surprised that treatments are relatively inexpensive.

Podiatry is one of the only jobs I can think of where you can be assessing someone, and they tell you in a short period of time loads about themselves, their life, job, and family. It is one of the best aspects of the job; you would never get to hear so many interesting and intimate details about a person within thirty minutes in any other job. There is the sad side too where you hear of people's tragedies. In the early days of being a podiatrist, I used to call it 'a tragedy a day'. It is a people-person job that keeps life very real. There is also a lot of responsibility and high expectations to move someone out of pain as quickly as you can. If I cannot help the person who will?

Becoming The Governor

I have explained how I found the clinics we bought from the research I did. With the Rye clinic, the proprietor was not prepared to leave immediately as she had imagined it would take a couple of years to sell the clinic and devised a plan for us to overlap. I bought the business for £29K, in 2010. She wanted £30k but did not have a proper lease on the space she rented from the building owners who were her friends. I managed to negotiate her down by £1,000. I gave her a £5,000 deposit and agreed to pay £500 a month for four years. She agreed to give me another day in the clinic, which meant I worked there for two days a week whilst I carried on working in the NHS. I was hoping to start a family if it was not too late as I was forty and did not want to work in the clinic full time to start with.

When I first worked in the clinic as an associate, the proprietor took 17% of my earnings which was extremely low. In other practices, it was between 40-50%. Once I had agreed to buy the clinic, her accountant who later became my accountant said that officially I needed to become the proprietor and that the old proprietor, and an associate needed to pay me 17% instead and I would have to pay the overheads. At that time, they were low, she had been paying a pepper-corn rent, there was not a receptionist or any equipment that went with it, it was manageable. I successfully made the £500 per month payment.

In business, everyone says you learn by your mistakes. At the start of my business journey, I thought what are the mistakes I need to avoid; being coachable I was willing to hear them, but I was not part of a business group at the conception. My uncle and aunt were uneasy that I was buying a business without a proper lease. I told them it was going to be fine, little did I know.

When the four years started to draw to an end, Martin and I devised an exit strategy of how we would take over the clinic fully and finalise when the old proprietor and associate were going to leave. In the interim, we had all become very pally, dining around each other's houses.

The news of their retirement from the practice did not go down well. I had invested money in the whole practice and clinical space, modernising it and bringing it up to scratch with modern processes and a receptionist. I had taken the stress out of how the clinic used to run. Martin and I had refurbished the old disused kitchen which was falling apart and into another clinical space that was being rented out to an osteopath, acupuncturist, and massage therapist. I was developing a successful multi-disciplinary clinic.

Learning Business, The Hard Way

I went through a phase thinking that you only really learn about business the hard way. You can learn the theory and apply it the best you can, you can engage professionals, but people are unknown entities, and you think you can trust someone and then you find they are pulling a fast one. This happened to me. The proprietor of the Rye clinic and I had a very simple, typed by me, few lined contracts, as I did not pay out for legal advice at the time. The contract stated that I had paid a £5,000 deposit and I would pay £500 per month for four years or I could settle up sooner. When it came, time for us to agree on a date that she was to leave, she said to me that there was nothing in the contract to say she had to leave. I was astounded, to me we had a gentlewoman's agreement that when I had paid for the clinic in full, it was mine. I was due to go on holiday a couple of days later.

I had to quickly get legal advice which at the time was £250 an hour and was estimated at three hours work. I was told on the eve of going on this long-awaited beach holiday that I did own the clinic and that the proprietor, and the associate would have to leave, and six weeks' notice was deemed reasonable. It was such a relief. I could not believe she expected me to buy her clinic that I was not able to work in full-time.

I went on holiday but could hardly relax knowing that on my return, I would have to meet them both and tell them that they had six weeks' notice. It was agreed that the solicitor would send them official letters after I had spoken to them myself. In those meetings, the proprietor changed her mind and said, 'I never said I wasn't going to leave'.

Unbelievable! The stress she had put me under. I then met with the associate who pleaded with me to allow her to carry on for another six months. She refused to understand the complexities of the situation and how I had been legally advised to proceed and that Martin and I wanted to work in and develop our own clinic.

They never spoke to me again. So much for the friendships we had all supposedly built. My ma had thought all along that they had ulterior motives with their friendships. I was hurt by the way it came to an end and I felt outraged for a while, especially when a year later, the proprietor set up business in the same small town. I thought the deed of covenant that stipulated she was not allowed to set up a business in an eight-mile radius would have prevented that happening. I found out after the event that the deed of covenant is valid for only six months, somehow the solicitor omitted to tell me that at the time. You can imagine that came as a shock, but I got over it, to the point that I have parked these memories deep in my mental archives.

I have learnt in business that you 'don't know what you don't know' and that it is amazing how key important pieces of information get constantly omitted when working with professionals. I often joke that one needs to know another professional's business to know the right questions to ask to get the information that you are paying them for.

I have more stories to tell, one about the solicitor who took more than three years to prepare my lease, racking up great expense and causing me anxiety. I took him to the Legal Ombudsman who said I had a case. We settled before the matter was taken any further when the solicitor's partner swiftly completed the lease and agreed to waive all the fees on my insistence of the two different solicitors which would have come to approximately £3K. I also asked for compensation for the stress they had put me through, and he offered me a free will!

I have a new solicitor now, who speaks very fast, and this is not ideal for me either. When we met to renew the lease on the Rye clinic, I wish I had recorded the advice as it was rattled out at machine gun pace using language that went over my head. I did however learn a couple of interesting nuggets about leases which I then had to try and explain to Martin.

In business, it is important to look at new processes that will make a business run more efficiently. Our old accountants are a good example of never reviewing our needs. We had another archaic system in place that was labour intensive and required a lot of micro-managing, resulting in human errors. The information we received on our accounts was historic, usually six months after the year end which did not help us during the financial year.

During the first lockdown of the pandemic, I had the opportunity to look at all the systems of the business and after a very fortuitous conversation with someone who adamantly advised me that it was not the best use of a business owner's time to be dealing with the accounts spreadsheets, I decided to invest in a digital system with a new accountant and let the previous accountants go. After the free 30-minute conversation on 'managing your time better', I literally felt sick that I had been let down for so long by my old accountants. I had always been too busy working in the business that I had not worked on the business and the time out during the lockdown enabled me to rectify this.

Landlords are interesting too. One of my landlords from the beginning wanted us to pay for dilapidation that had occurred in the previous eighteen-year tenancy. I had to really stick my heels in and battle with him. I remember my face was flaming when I walked home after that meeting. This was before I learnt to manage my state! What a cheek!

Later, we found out to our horror that we were responsible for 50% of the building, at the time we understood it to be the area we were renting and not the whole building which meant we were 100% responsible for the whole of the area we occupied. The reception and clinical areas naturally needed redecorating, but the back rooms were a disgrace and apparently, this is considered standard when being leased out. Residential properties need to be of a high standard, but those standards do not apply to commercial properties. Martin and I spent weeks during the first lockdown doing the demolition work of the renovations during the heatwave. The kitchen and toilet had been demoralising but to renovate it was costly, time consuming, dusty and dirty work that could not have happened without shutting down for weeks.

The pandemic made that transformation possible. The new space brings us and the staff such joy now.

Turbines Behind Each Other

Martin and I have had our own roles within the company. I am the strategist and like to see projects through to completion. I got the responsibility of the accounts, finances, invoice payments, staff contracts and maintenance whereas Martin had in my mind the more creative jobs, such as research and development, the website, advertising, display units and networking. Martin has had his wrangles with several website designers over the years and during the pandemic, he was trying to improve the old website.

In the meantime, I had been on a digital marketing mentorship programme and had been picking up useful tips. It was agreed between us that to move forward I would have an active part in the website. A few months later, we excitingly rebranded and relaunched our new more engaging website and have the rebrand throughout the two clinics.

Martin and I are incredibly supportive of each other and that is paramount for any business owner that their partner is right behind them. However, we both have our limitations; I can spend hours on the computer after my day in the clinic working on the next project whereas Martin cannot do that. Martin needs to get a lot more air and be outside than me. He is from Snowdonia after all, whereas I am from southeast London. Whilst I am glued to the computer, Martin will do most of the shopping, cooking, clearing away and looking after the garden.

No Businesswoman Is An Island
The word overwhelm is used a lot. For me it feels like being under pressure. When I have too many things going on, the only way I can feel better about them it is getting on and completing the tasks.

I think there is no point worrying about them, using up precious energy, but to crack on and start getting the tasks done.

If I write a list of the things I need to do, I sometimes end up doing other things that are not on the list, but I will eventually start to do things on the list, and they are more likely to get done than left to memory. Writing new lists in the evening aids better sleep.

Running your own business is a constant revolving carousel of tasks and sometimes I feel I am fighting fire. There are other times when we sit and absorb the good feeling of what we have achieved. It is important to constantly reflect on what you are doing and achieving, how you are learning from it and what you would do differently next time.

One of my sayings is, 'bite size pieces'. Tackling a project and doing small parts of it, helps it become achievable. Also be realistic that everything takes longer than you expect. Some projects do flow and get completed quickly and others do not. That is how it is. Move on to something else if the task is not flowing.

Getting something done is better than nothing.

Also, do not overdo things either. It can be easy to burn your brain cells out and that is not healthy. I confess that I have done that a few times over the last year as I have had an incredible drive to steer 'the oil tanker' our business as I like to call it, in a different direction. Do I put too much effort into things? I am not sure; my ma and Martin keep saying that I must be enjoying what I am doing otherwise I would not be doing it.

During the pandemic, I had time to think about how we could future proof our business and make it work for us better. There was a lot to think about and to strategise and this tied in with me discovering a mindset and motivation coach whose goal is to help small businesses make more money. The pandemic was changing things for him too; he was going online daily with his words of wisdom and after appearing on a TV programme found himself with many more listening ears.

This was a game changer, I had ideas but to hear someone else confirm what I was thinking was all I needed to start thinking much bigger. To get where you want to go, you need a coach and to find your tribe as in like-minded people. Since then, one thing has led to another, and I have been having a massive whirlwind of a year. I am putting as many hours into learning new things as I did for my degree which was a lot.

When I heard Queens In Business was setting up, I had to join. I had met Chloë Bisson virtually on a sales and closing course and knew she was the Queen of Tech. There are five other Queens all with their amazing talents wanting to help female entrepreneurs progress. It is the perfect place to learn and thrive.

Know your value and your values. If there was one thing I knew before I started my business, that would be my value. I would worry about putting the prices up by a pound a year which I did not do in two separate years. I feel I held the business back with this limiting attitude.

Worrying about what people can afford is not my concern. When podiatrists think that people are not going to pay to have their feet done or moan about the price, we feel it devalues what we do and makes us bitter. We have brought this upon ourselves and kept our own profession down. Some people devalue having their feet treated thinking that their feet are not worth it, especially some members of the older generation who are still thinking in 'old money'. The public has no idea how much it costs to run a practice. The clinics are expensive to run, reducing the profit margin and wages. A business must be worth it for all the hard work and responsibility a business owner faces.

To a young person starting out, my advice is to get a credit card and manage your money well and this will ensure a good credit rating. If you are frightened of overspending and mismanaging your finances, you have a lot to learn at a low level. If you cannot manage a credit card, you do not yet have the mindset for your own business. A good credit score will enable you to borrow more money to progress. I built a large proportion of what I have achieved, two clinics and three properties on borrowing money.

One of my shortcomings and I advise against it is: do not be desperate. Whenever I have got desperate, I have not got what I wanted. I have a tendency to rush into some things, but then that is also how I have progressed. I think knowing when to move fast, when something is a no brainer and being discerning to find out more information.

The Phoenix

We are looking for enthusiastic and keen to progress podiatrists to take our places. I want to transition out of the clinical side of the business. I have two things I would like to do, although nothing is ever set in stone with me. I am in the process of learning how to trade stocks and shares and I want to continue my learning and become a successful trader. I fully believe I can do it and I want to share my experiences of how I do it.

Trading is a new exhilarating experience whereby it is me, the computer, and my decisions. It will not involve people directly, but the study of mass human psychology.

The second thing I am planning is to finish setting up my online property business. I want to source deals for investors and help people move on with their lives. At some point, I will increase our existing small property portfolio, but my main aim is to create more wealth. Having been someone who has made enjoying myself a priority, I need money and the freedom to do the things I still want to do with my best buddy Marty.

Vision And Desire

To the next generation of female entrepreneurs, if there is an industry you want to be in, look to find someone who has been successful in that field and find out if they have a coaching programme or find out who coached them. Paying for the advice or being part of a mentorship programme will speed up your success journey. Your success starts with a positive mindset, dispelling limiting beliefs, visualising what it is that you want, so you need to be clear on what that is and with perseverance you will achieve your goals. I wish you all the best on your journey, it will never be dull, and you are welcome to contact me if you have any questions.

About Me

I was born Angela Louise Barraclough in Crayford, Kent, England in 1969, on my sister Julie's eighth birthday. I had adventurous parents that inspired my wanderlust so from eighteen I set off travelling with others at first, then independently and later in groups.

I have traversed the continents from London to Kathmandu, Southeast Asia, Australia, New Zealand, Africa, Europe, and some parts of the USA and South America. I lived in Ulm in Germany for three years teaching English and still visit good friends there today.

Settling in the UK was not easy on my return, but I wanted to be closer to my family. I taught English and practised holistic therapies in Brighton for six years, moved back to Crayford for another two before I made St Leonards-on-sea my permanent hometown. A turning point led me to become a podiatrist and that is when I met my future husband, Martin Parry. Together we have built a successful podiatry business moving people out of their foot pain.

I would like to dedicate my chapter to Marty, together we make the fun happen. No one will ever love me as much as he does, and my drive comes from wanting the best life for us both. A special mention must of course go to my ma, without her support and hard work, I would not be where I am today.

More recently, Jessen James has been a hugely positive influence, Nicholas Lee has helped teach me the important art of 'chunking up' and Emily Wallace my unflappable personal, social media and technical assistant.

I want to inspire people to follow their dreams with perseverance and to enjoy themselves along the way. Anything is possible when you learn how and put your mind to it.

Never Give Up!

Cindy Bansal

MGBL, Founder & Director

Beauty Courses 4 U

"You just never give up. You do a task to the best of your abilities and beyond." --- Debbie Reynolds

Family Life

Growing up in Hyson Green, Nottingham was a great adventure now referred to as 'Nice & Clean'. Terraced houses all lined up like Lego pieces, no keeping up appearances, everyone carefree and happy with a very simplistic lifestyle. I remember you could walk in and out of each other's houses without ever having to ring the doorbell or knock on the door. Just turn the handle and shout that it was you. I have very fond memories of my first house. The families were so close and the atmosphere was electric.

My parents both worked hard to provide for their family at Raleigh Bikes. Most Asian people were given nicknames, my dad's was 'Alan' (from Amarjit) and he was a line manager. My mum, 'Video', short for Vidya, worked on the assembly line fitting bike wheels - very tedious and such a dirty job that she did for so many years.

Mum's second job was at home with the family. All fifteen of us that lived in the terrace house joined in the family activity, pulling the threads on lace sheets to separate them. I remember the same man in a van used to drop off the big black bags and pick them up from our home when done for years. Nottingham was famous for bikes and the lace Industry; I wished it wasn't in my house. Referred to as piecework, volume equals little money, something I vowed I would never do as I got older.

I remember how much my arms were hurting pulling these threads and my grandma saying, "A little more and then more", echoed throughout my life. I was brought up with the mindset that in order to get on in life you had to work hard to earn a good living.

And I also remember the line, "Money doesn't grow on trees!" I wish the concept of working smarter was known back then. Families worked so hard to keep a roof over their heads.

Although it was fun living in a terraced house, three stories and three families, there were a total of fifteen people living there – OUCH! Boy it was noisy, but so much fun.

We all looked forward to Friday night's Chips Night. We'd be all huddled together eating fish, sausage, egg and chips. Families were so close back then. As times gone by, we have become more separated and distanced but not in heart.

Saturdays were cleaning days. By myself, it was impossible and it felt very unfair, so I insisted on equality amongst all and I used to delegate the responsibilities. Even back then, I recognised that I couldn't do everything by myself. Years later, the families became more self-sufficient and went their separate ways.

I went to an all-girl grammar school after completing my 11+. For my parents this was a very proud moment. Community expectations upon working class families were always frowned upon. In everything after that, I always excelled in all that I did to make them proud.

My first emotional brush with what I thought was sure death, leaving secondary school and my best friends, was quickly swooped in by my dad with the following comment, "You're on a constant bus ride; your bus hasn't reached its final destination yet.

You will get on and off, sometimes you may see the same familiar faces, Doll, but you will meet so many new ones, now stop crying."

I remember replying with a frown forehead, "Dad, what are you talking about? I'm not on a bus. I've left my friends. How can I possibly cope with life?" I was crying uncontrollably back then, but now I'm in fits of laughter. I wished my younger self believed him then.

Love Of My Life

My dad passed away in 1988, six months before I got married. This was a very emotional time for the family. Although I tried my hardest to put my wedding off, I went ahead following traditional values in honour of my father.

I met the love of my life, and in June 1988, aged 24, I got married. It was supposed to be a very happy time but there were mixed emotions. There were a lot of changes in such a short space of time and this impacted on my mum's mental health. For her, not only had she lost her life partner, but on top of that was letting her first-born leave the family home to pastures new. Life was never going to be the same again for my family or for me. However, knowing I was with a good man that was going to look after me and does to this day was our shining light.

At the age of 24, I thought I would have my four children by the age of 30, but life had other plans for me. Time was ticking and I was getting worried. After my 30th birthday, my husband and I both decided we would give six months and then pursue another path if needed. Society and cultural expectations were challenging but I had a very understanding mother-in-law that would shut anyone down if they said anything, for that I thank her. The thought of me not having children was a very emotional battle I had with myself. And then six years later in January 1994, after six home tests and a doctor's test, I was expecting my first child at the age of 30, Devan. That feeling of being so overwhelmed will stay with me forever, when they handed me my child.

Now aged 34, I had my second child, my baby boy Nishan, I just remember feeling so emotional. I felt complete and blessed. In our culture having boys was seen as a blessing but for me either way I felt blessed. All I ever wanted was to be a mum, especially with the beautiful relationship I had with my own. That unconditional love was so powerful and nothing came in its way.

In 2014, my whole world came crumbling down. My mum, after eleven years of dialysis, sadly departed. A void that to this day, I find very difficult to fill and I do miss her dearly. Everything I do is in the honour of my parents especially my mum. Just a few months ago I had a tattoo ਵਿਦਿਆ – Vidya, to honour my mum. Her name translated means 'teacher'.

Now in 2021, I live my life with my unit of four in a lovely home, I am very close and cherish the relationship I have with my brothers, sisters, their partners and all the eleven children between us.

However, the saddest part for us as we grow older is that our parents can't see where we are in our lives. We all long to have our parents back and that thought of no parents chokes me up every time. My dad passed away before seeing any of his children get married or his grandchildren but at least my mum had spent quality time with them all and for me that's a blessing.

Adversities And Strengths
My first adversity was back in 1965, in Kenya when I suffered with Chicken Pox. Doctors didn't think I would survive, all wrapped in bandages with the openings for my mouth, eyes, nose and ears.

Given round the clock care, as a mother I can now understand the pain my parents must have gone through.

I am holding on strong after so many adversities in my life, the loss of my father aged 48 and my mum aged 68, only seven years ago has been an incredibly sad time for my family. For me, especially losing my mum, there are times when life feels so empty that I try everything to fill that void and nothing can replace that emptiness.

When I had to think back on all the adversities, a friend pointed out to me "what about all your operations?" I nearly forgot to mention these. As I write about all the operations I have had on my legs alone, I'm shocked because from keyhole surgery, to having my legs realigned the titanium plates removed and my last operation for a left knee replacement in November 2020 during the lockdown going in alone. I have had a total of ten operations on my legs! OMG! It shows how resilient, strong and determined I am to face any challenge that comes my way and it doesn't stop there. I am on the waiting list to have my right knee done as soon as possible.

Along with my health issues, I experienced financial challenges in my businesses. But together my husband and I worked through these. Sometimes when we look back, we cannot believe we managed to get through that journey. We have come out of it stronger than we ever were.

No doubt in life I will face many more challenges but I have built a better dealing mechanism now and know how to ask for help if need be. In the meantime, I have started to climb the ladder and I am so excited about what the future holds for me.

Birth Of The Academy

Having a natural creative flair for makeup, my friends and family would ask me to teach them how to apply makeup. For a short while, I did this for free and then realised enough was enough. I came up with the idea of setting up a beauty academy.

In May 2007, after extensive research, creating my courses and getting them accredited, I launched my training academy; Beauty Courses 4 U was formed. This was a way for me to finally pass on my knowledge, skills and tips. I would now be able to award students with a Nationally Recognised Diploma Certificate to take away and I would be rewarded.

In my business, I am a Makeup, Henna Artist, and Beauty Therapist, Tutor, Assessor and Mentor inspiring women in business with my '7 Step Strategy - Journey to Success Formula'.

In 2009, I opened two salons, one in Leicester and one in Peterborough, with 12 members of staff over two locations. I ran these over nine years until 2018 when I sold them both. How lucky was that before this pandemic!

I provide a personal approach to teaching. The relationship I build with my students is so important to me. Sometimes I teach 1:1 or 1: many. I am very conscious to teach at a pace that they can understand. Sometimes I have to use anecdotal stories to make them understand and I don't move on until they do. I teach to a standard and not a time. Talking to them and not at them is what they value. I do stress to students that money is energy and that money has been exchanged so I want to give that energy back in value.

Having the right connection, interaction and communication helps them to relax. My business would not be able to survive without repeat customers, so when students come back for more courses for me this is a massive bonus and a huge boost that I'm definitely doing the right job and they are enjoying my teaching.

Stresses In Business And In Health

Over the years, I have, like so many of us, experienced emotional stresses. Each of our stresses are personal to us, but on so many levels, there are common threads that we can all relate to.

Back in 2007, I opened a salon in Coventry, my third attempt in a different location. I took on my first paid member of staff. Two months later, I received a letter from the hospital regarding difficulties I had been having a year before with my knees. The letter confirmed my operation to have my legs realigned, not at the same time but a year apart.

Having only opened two months before, I had been feeling apprehensive, anxious, and confused about the salon. Do I stay open or should I cut my losses and close up? But at the same time feeling relieved that finally they could correct the problem from side effects all those years ago in Kenya when I had had chicken pox.

My body back then had a bacterial infection, which affected my bones. The X-rays revealed pressure from my hips was by passing my knees and going straight to my ankles. Over time, I became knocked-kneed, to the point that my feet were at least a foot apart. My weight gain was not helping. I would turn to food for comfort eating. I started my new diet plan to lose a few pounds before the op, and to this date I have managed to lose two and half stone and still continuing to do so, albeit at a snail's pace. And for me this has been a huge win and confidence booster at the same time.

I had been floating through life unaware I even had this condition until I started to have problems in 2006 in the middle of a henna party booking. Out of the blue, I found myself unable to get up off a client's sofa. Oh my goodness! I was so embarrassed but in so much pain I had to ask for help to get up. They helped me to perch myself on a kitchen stool in excruciating pain to finish the bridal henna. I couldn't let them down after all it was their family wedding.

After finishing the booking, I drove home in such agony with tears strolling down my face. When I got home, my husband had to rush me to hospital as the pain was worsening and both extremely worried.

Writing this has reminded me how for years I never used to wear trousers, leggings or even possessed a pair of jeans (something I've always wanted) because of the way I looked in them. To disguise this impairment, I always wore long skirts and dresses to hide the way I looked and give me the confidence to 'fit in'.

Even though the operation had been explained to me, my operation to realign my legs was a big one. The outer knee bones were broken, some bone had been taken from my pelvis (didn't even know I was having this bit done by the way) to insert in the triangle gap they had created when straightening my legs. The rest was injected with synthetic bone to rebuild all held with a bracket to straighten the legs.

Once I was home, I was laid up for six weeks with a leg brace from the top of my thighs to my ankles that had dials on the side of them, so that each day I would increase the movement in my legs. I had to live upstairs in my house whilst in recovery mode.

The journey was very, very difficult and physically draining. I relied on my family and close friends. They were amazing during my recovery time and helped me emotionally. I found this quite difficult especially when I was so used to being independent and strong headed but I took their help.

Added to my physical stress, I was experiencing some financial stress with just one income coming in and a new salon so it was hard. I was in a very vulnerable and low state. Anything and everything were getting to me. But my reading, prayers and meditation helped me during this time.

My mum would ring me up every day, sometimes twice a day just to check in on me, bless her she used to worry about me more than I did for myself. Every day, "How you feeling Dolly?" I'd reply, "I'm fine mum. Just remember there are so many other people worse off than me and they have no one so I'm a very blessed mum please don't worry!"

Six weeks later after my op, I had my first check up and it was all good news on my left leg. A year later, back to my right leg and the same procedure. Six-week check-up came again but this time it was not so good news. Unfortunately, on this occasion two of the screws had come undone so was told I had to have this procedure done again.

What I didn't realise was the effect the anaesthetic was to have on me this time. My overall health and wellbeing took a bashing, my body reacted really badly against the anaesthetic and my body went into a trauma. Completely unaware of what was to come.

I ended up with a condition known as 'Lichen Planus' this is an inflammatory skin condition believed to be an autoimmune disease. I was advised that this type of condition would last for eighteen months in my system. But no, not for me! The doctors when discussing this condition mentioned that I may get one or two of the symptoms. I'm an overachiever so I had to have all the symptoms didn't I. Purple red blotches on the skin, white patches in my mouth and bald patches on my scalp. Eating was so uncomfortable. This condition lasted in my body for over six years.

I was very low in mood and anyone who knows me, knows my hair was my biggest personal asset that I cared so much for; I loved creating drama and an entrance with my hair but now it was no longer thick and was very patchy. I spent so much time covering all the patchy areas up with hair thickeners, powders, root cover sprays, back combing my hair to create a nest of hair to make it look fuller. You name it, I did it, but it wasn't the same.

The visible marks on my legs and lower back could be hidden, so for me that was ok but I do remember a time when my mum saw my back and got really upset, somewhat more than me. Bless her, she was upset her baby's body didn't look the same anymore, but again I used to say, "It's ok mum I'm fine. So many other people are in worse conditions that me. It's not like anyone will see it."

The blotchy marks on my hands and gums were hard to disguise. Hurtful comments such as, "What's happened to you?" didn't help but I managed to get through this horrible phase. It was a very emotional journey but working around these adversities, I got through it. It was sad but I had to close the salon in Coventry and focus on my health.

Now in 2021, I sit here with no visible marks on my hands. My gums so much better. The patchy areas on my scalp have grown back, not fuller, but at least seventy percent better than before. My sheer determination to push myself each day and not give up was how I got through this testing time. I had end goals in mind that I wanted to achieve so I couldn't give up.

However, there have been a lot of emotional stresses, which heavily affected me. Losing my mum was the biggest emotional journey I faced. I remember losing my dad and it was very sad but when I lost my mum, even writing about it now, I feel upset and tearful. It was like losing half of me. And if truth were known I am happy but I don't think I will ever feel complete as a person again. I've tried filling up that void I have with work and food but it still feels empty. And then there, I am back again with weight gain.

Betrayal, Trust And Love

In life, I have faced many problems alone; I'm not in the habit of wanting to burden others with my problems as they have enough of their own. But I will do whatever it takes to make the other person smile. In business I have been betrayed so many times, shockingly with people I thought I could trust. What I find most difficult is when my trust is broken. For me, that is difficult to deal with and I would rather walk away with my head held high than to be lied to.

There was one experience, back end of 2018, when I sold one of my salons. The betrayal and financial loss I incurred was hard to deal with and kept asking myself, "WHY? What had I done wrong? How did I not see it?"

It took me over six months to realise it was not my fault that someone had broken my trust. I was angry with myself for months. Right under my nose, underhanded activities were covertly taking place. I was completely unaware of what was going on. I felt so betrayed and so depressed.

Before selling the two salons, I had businesses with a six-figure turnover. How was it that now in March 2019 was I sitting here with only £5 in my purse? It wasn't even enough money to put diesel in my car.

This feeling of betrayal was having a massive impact on my family and me. I kept snapping at them and I would be moody, irritable and felt so low. Letting go of someone you thought you knew is tough, I know I am tougher for doing so, and I'm also a great believer in "what goes around comes around!" For me, there are three things that you should never break:

1. Promises
2. Trust
3. Your heart

I remember speaking to my cousin's wife Rani. I was telling her my problems back in March 2019, what I didn't realise was how much I had offloaded with her. Before I knew it, they had transferred money into my account the next day. True giving from the heart is an expression of love and this was given in love. I was so emotional. I didn't actually use it. I left it there for a completely dire situation when I needed it, but for now I had been given a safety net.

Struggling financially is never an easy topic to discuss. I couldn't even speak to my own siblings. I didn't want anyone to know I was struggling but most of all I didn't want anyone to know I was failing. Reaching out as a mother to your own kids is even harder. I know they would have given the money to me but it was hard to ask. I know in time my situation would improve. Good things happen to good people, I believe that and I kept manifesting so that it would all get better.

I never imagined my life without any daughters when I got married, I thought I would have at least one daughter, but I find myself blessed with two boys. For that opportunity, I will be eternally grateful. I am so lucky to be surrounded by more and more inspirational women each day, especially my new Queens In Business Club family.

As a headstrong woman, my mindset, strong beliefs and the love of my family with a handful of dear friends are what keep me going. "You are the average of the five people you spend the most time with" - Jim Rohn

Just Keep Moving To Win
At my darkest point I made a few calls that particular day in April 2019, when I only had five pounds in my wallet. I called a few friends to check if they fancied having any beauty treatments, and within a couple of hours I booked in £120 worth of treatments.

That is definitely one of the traits, just sometimes it can be difficult to self-motivate. Receiving my cousins' money was the energy I needed. I'm not prepared to give up. When I'm struggling, I will do whatever it takes to feed the family.

A family win was when I was brave enough to travel out of the country aged thirty-two. For me it felt like the first time, but I must have flown in when I came from Kenya. I don't remember that at all. I was really scared, but I did it!

Setting up my women's group in Coventry was a very emotional win. 'Women2Aspire2' was set up in April 2019 to give women a platform to meet, discuss and network with like-minded women in an environment they felt safe in. Although face-to-face has been difficult, we have managed to stay connected online and looking for the go ahead to meet again.

I am so proud of my achievements with all the digital marketing side of stuff that I have managed to learn this year. I have developed my beautycourse4u YouTube channel, which has been exciting. I have created my first online henna course, which is available for all to download. I have now created a daily motivational Facebook live event to help connect with people.

Lessons

I remember waking up one day after when I was at such a low point in my life. I decided to contact a tarot card reader I knew. Made an appointment to go see her, she put her hands on my shoulder and the first thing she said was, "Your dad is proud of you; keep going, you can do this and don't worry mum is happy!"

Oh my gosh! Tears were gushing down my face. I had not had any connection with my dad for over 30 years and found this quite uplifting and upsetting at the same time. But refreshingly, it put me at ease.

I felt so blessed and determined that this is the day that my life will be changing and only I could make this change.

If my mum hadn't been this strong independent woman, I would not be where I am today. She was one of the first Asian women who learnt to drive in Nottingham, and always pushed us out of our comfort box to be independent strong women.

All pain is an emotional journey, and I don't think it's ever going to stop, as I get older, I am dealing with things in a way that makes me proud of myself.

Getting a mentor was the day my life changed, it was like being at school, but embracing the knowledge and soaking the information I was being fed. The knowledge when so many entrepreneurs come together to share their lives experiences is powerful. My mentors and inspirational speakers have given me the confidence that I am able to tackle anything.

Each day I start with my meditation, do my gratitudes and affirmations. Listening to the right motivational speakers to get me through each day, however, none of these motivations are anything unless I am dedicated to put the time in for them.

My daily manifests to myself are "I've got this! I am enough! I am loved! I am, I am, I am!"

Not all emotional stresses have been bad stresses. There have been some good ones like losing weight, learning to deal with family losses and meeting deadlines such as for this book.

My last lesson learnt in lockdown was how to use my creativity to help with my mental wellbeing. It has given me the opportunity to express my inner thoughts, while helping me to understand and make sense of the emotions I was feeling. It has helped me have better mental health.

Communication during lockdown, and in general for me, has been so important to stay connected. Speaking and staying in contact has helped me with my mindset. Not being able to have human contact was hard as I am such a tactile person. But one of the things that I realised is that each and every one of us is dealing with this pandemic in different ways. Be patient, be understanding and be there. Keep on showing up.

Never Give Up
There's so much that is still possible for everyone. We at least have to have a go. If at the ripe old age of 57 (one of the biggest course

Queens out there) can do it I believe we all can, as long as we dedicate the time.

Motivation is so important but not half as much as dedication. It doesn't matter how many times I fail, for me it's the lessons I have learnt along my journey. The growth I see and my determination to work towards my legacy inspires me to keep going. And you will amaze yourself like I do on what you can do by showing up.

My networking is crucial for growth and connections. I know when I pay for a course that may be thousands of pounds, not only am I paying for that, but I am paying for the knowledge that is brought to the table by so many from all walks of life. That for me is priceless. Like the chapters in this book, each chapter will connect with people in so many different ways. The most important thing is the message reaches you all.

I am blown away when I realise how much is still out there for us to embrace. One clear message that I want to make sure that I get across to my students, my customers, anybody who's actually interested in any of the services that I have: It's not what the academy has to offer, it's what I have to offer. I've had over 35 years of experience as an entrepreneur running various businesses from boutiques, salons and beauty training academies and dealing with people both internally and externally from all walks of life.

That knowledge is priceless when running a business. My message is quite clear. Believe you can do this. Believe that you are enough to be able to do this. There is no age limit if you're passionate about something. Make sure that everything that you do, is creating as much happiness in your life as possible and giving you fulfilment.

"Make what YOU love your HOBBY, make what PEOPLE love your BUSINESS!" - Warren Buffett

Being Heard

The Queens In Business Club has given me an opportunity to share and hear my voice; I am very blessed and grateful for the opportunity to get my message out there.

Remember in everything you do or want to do, simply show up. Showing up gives me, not only accountability, but it shows others that I am willing to learn. I am dedicated to the cause to achieve my goals and leave a legacy that not only I will be proud of but my family, my children and my grandchildren. I want to make sure my motivational and mentoring training will continue forever.

I like to be a team player. Going alone you know you're not going to get anywhere but going together with someone helps me to achieve all this and more.

And so, a wise man once said to me, I have been given a voice to make a difference and it's up to me to share this with the world. NEVER GIVE UP! Life is too short and this is not a trial run to get right next time; it's now or never!

I'm like a jigsaw puzzle - it doesn't matter how many pieces of mine are missing. As long as the piece I'm giving away will make the other person whole and feel good about themselves, that's all that matters to me. Why do I think that? As I hand my pieces of nuggets and knowledge out, it's like being on a conveyor belt. As I pass out on the right, or on the left I'm also given another piece to replace. Perhaps not immediately, but I get it back. Giving hope, belief and time to people is an important trait in my duty to serve.

My advice now to my kids and the next generation is please expand your minds, be creative and ask for help but most of all, NEVER GIVE UP!

I want people to appreciate where they are in their journey, even if it's not where they want to be. It's the opportunity to make a difference to their lives that I want to spread.

My upbringing and culture have taught me to serve others. I've learned to share as well as have compassion. Generosity and hospitality are part of my makeup. I am a natural feeder albeit knowledge or food. I am always willing to look at new ways to evolve even at this age.

My belief is that I have the ability to inspire others to believe in themselves. And the time is always right to do what is right for them.

About Me

I believe that each and every one of us has a gift, a fire that needs to be ignited and a seed that is waiting to flower. Never give up on your dreams, just believe that your time is NOW!

I am an Asian woman of Sikh heritage aged 57, full of confidence, vitality and abundance for life. I am strong, infectious with a cheeky personality that likes to put a smile on your face. I embrace my looks, mind and body. I am very ambitious, dedicated and a highly motivated entrepreneur who is itching to feed.

My name is Chatinder (prefix chat...say no more) my nicknames are Doll-Dolly that is my family name and Cindy is my stage name - ha-ha!

My birthplace is Kenya (Nairobi). We moved to Nottingham, England aged three, having just survived my first health adversity. I have two brothers and two sisters and I am the eldest of eighteen grandchildren in the family, referred to as the 'Don' of the family.

Aged eight, I remembered playing games with my siblings always making sure I was the shopkeeper or teacher and not them. Low and behold I am doing the same two roles now albeit slightly different as a trainer and owning my own business.

Fast forward, I got married at the age of 24, soon to be celebrating 33 years of marital bliss. I feel blessed with my family, I have an amazing husband, friend and soul mate that who puts me first in all that he does. Laughter and communication have been the key to our success.

My time to Empower, Inspire and Motivate as many women as possible to believe they have so GOT THIS is NOW! I believe I am the vehicle that will help to guide them on their Journey to Success!

I dedicate this chapter to My mum,

Since the moment I entered this world, you had cared for me like no other, protected me with unconditional love and made me the Independent woman I am today – all because of you mum.

Girl Boss

Henna Patel

Business Growth Manager

"Just try new things. Don't be afraid." --- Michelle Obama

Where It All Started

'An empowered woman who knows exactly what she wants, has the drive and determination to succeed, take control of her life and achieve her dreams is a formidable force, a girl building her empire.'

That's me, well so I thought...

I grew up in a typical Indian family, lots of aunts, uncles and cousins. I am the eldest of three and all are ambitious. In my generation, there was a lot of expectation - get a good education and marry well! Marriage comes before career; you are brought up knowing that you have to be ready to marry when you leave university.

I guess I would say I am one of the lucky ones. I met my husband in my final year at university and we were engaged as soon as I was home from my final exams. That was 20 years ago and gosh have I changed. My husband has been my rock and always encouraged me to do what I want. So, I pushed myself further.

I wasn't the most academic growing up. I'd rather clean the house and help my mum cook than do my school work. I just didn't find it interesting. I was always the odd one at school, never seemed to fit in. I guess my background was different from my friends so when they were meeting outside of school I didn't. You see 'good'

Indian girls don't do this. I was always one to please and do as I am told. How I got through school, I'm not sure. But I did, I got some GCSEs and went on to do A-levels at my sixth form. It was here I started to find a little of myself, I had some amazing teachers who nurtured me.

Being one to please, I went on to help the college with all sorts of things from being treasurer in the National Union of Students to helping choose a new caterer for the canteen. I was always one that could be relied upon. In some ways I still am. There are parts of you that never leave and stay with you.

I did fairly well in my A-levels and went on to University. This is where life got interesting for me. It was that time of self-discovery. I was far from home. It was a four-hour drive for me to get home so I couldn't go back every weekend. The first term was terrifying. I had never been away from my family and never stayed away with strangers. In the past, if I went anywhere it was with family or to stay with family.

This is what made me. I was able to come out of my shell and discover what I wanted. I was always a determined woman but that isn't what my culture is about. So you learn to suppress it to make sure you are 'right'.

Now I was in an environment that meant I could be anyone I wanted to be. I had an amazing group of friends and they helped me to come out of my comfort zone. What I remember is how competitive I became. The girl that didn't worry about school and wasn't that bothered all of a sudden wanted the first place. I would work so hard on my essays and project, all night studying. I had changed.

The real competitive nature came out of me in my second year at University. I was doing a four-year sandwich degree which involved working in industry in my third year. I had been applying for positions for accountancy jobs - it is after all a very respectable career. I remember going for an interview at a small firm. I got through to the second round and the interviewer said something interesting, "I think this company may be too small for you". I told him that I would love the small nature of it etc, but he was right, it would have been small for me!

Then came the ad, a job within the Securitisation team at a Japanese bank. Wow, banking and me, surely not. I was talking to a few friends about it. We were all excited and the boys were all applying, that is when I perked up and said I'm going to apply for it. They laughed. Yes, laughed. Well I was a bull with a red flag! Hell, I was applying and why shouldn't I!

The first round interviews were held at our university and the interview could not have gone better. There were about 20 people they interviewed and I was one of the three that was selected for a second round at their offices in London. I felt amazing! The only downside was one of my good friends had gotten through and only one of us would get it, but we knew if either of us got it we would be happy for the other one.

I got the call the next day, my application had been successful and I was going to work in London! OMG, this hadn't even been something I had ever dreamed of, not even something I had thought I could ever do. That year of working helped with my confidence, but it was also a fight within myself. I had been brought up to follow a path, a path now I wasn't sure I wanted anymore. My eyes were opened to so much and I didn't think I wanted the marriage thing. Perhaps I wanted the career thing. Luckily, my husband came into my life at the right time and he was exactly who I needed. When you meet someone special, you'll know. Your heart will beat more rapidly and you'll smile for no reason.

A New Chapter

Newly engaged and with a degree, life was wide open for me. With the type of work experience, I had pretty much walked into a job. I didn't have to go through the graduate route. I had a job working within the banking industry. I was flying high and about to get married. Talk about ticking the boxes. I was marrying well and had the career I wanted. Unlike what I was presented with growing up, I didn't have to choose. I could have my cake and eat it too.

I loved working in the city. I moved around a couple of organisations, working 14-hour days. It was fun for me. I think what I loved most was closing deals! A £2 billion deal can do that to a person, spending the whole night negotiating words in a contract; that was my kind of fun. My husband always pushed me and we even had some healthy competition. When one of us earnt well, the other one had to try and beat it.

It's nice to have valid competition; it pushes you to do better.

Shockwaves Close To Home

In July 2005, we were on holiday in Dubai, having a lovely time. We'd spent the day by the pool topping up our tans and keeping cool in the water. We headed back to our room and I jumped straight into the shower. My husband decided to put the TV on. I still remember the shock on his face when he saw the news. There had been a terrorist attack in London, our home town. When we switched on our phones there were so many messages people asking if we were ok. We were fine but the thoughts of those lost stayed with us.

That evening at dinner, we had a long chat about what had happened, how sad it was and how close to home. Even with everything going on in the world you don't expect it to happen around you. I guess you have to have an element of denial to get on with life. We chatted long into the night and came to the same conclusion. This had been a bit of a wakeup call, we wanted to move on to the next chapter, we wanted to start a family.

Coming home from that holiday, I was so excited we were going to have a new part to our lives but six months later and nothing. I had never been a patient person, but there was a part of me that wondered why. I didn't want to wait so I booked a doctor's appointment. I decided it was best to double check but there wouldn't actually be anything wrong.

My doctor was very supportive, she had a chat with me and said it wouldn't do any harm in getting some tests done. In our area the waiting list is long and it would be a good idea to get on it. If anything happened in the meantime, we can cancel. It took about a year, if not more, to get all the tests done. They were unpleasant and invasive, for me anyway. Men get off so easily!

About two years into it all, we were told there was no reason we couldn't get pregnant. In a way not what you want to hear. I mean if there is nothing wrong why hasn't it happened? If we don't know what's wrong, how do we fix it? The only option was to have an Intrauterine Insemination (IUI). The NHS option to this isn't great so the only option was to have privately. Luckily, we both had good jobs so were in a financial position to pay for it. Three IUIs later and still nothing - it was very frustrating and disheartening.

This was the point we were told the next step would be IVF. We were told before embarking on IVF we would have to see a counsellor, to make sure we knew what to expect and not to have a high expectation. That was one of the worst experiences. I walked out so angry. She kept asking how would we feel if this didn't work and we never had a baby. Well that wasn't an option - we were going to have a baby! It was going to happen one way or another and no one was going to tell us otherwise. As you can imagine, we never went back for any more sessions.

This sparked something in us. We were in our late twenties and still had plenty of time - what was the rush? We spoke to our GP and agreed we would put a hold on IVF and booked an amazing holiday. We wanted to have a bit of fun and forget about our dream for a little bit of time. We took time out and had loads of fun. Then we felt ready to start the process again, were put on the list and had to wait.

I had moved jobs and decided I didn't want to climb the career ladder. I wanted to focus on having children and was happy staying where I was. The drive and ambition I had was now going to be used to become a mum. In 2008 the credit crunch hit, it affected my field enormously, but I didn't think it would affect me. That is the day my life came crashing down. It was the day before my first appointment, and I had been told I was being made redundant, everyone at my level had to go.

Sometimes bad things happening in our lives put us on the path to the best things that will ever happen to us.

Where To Go Now
My husband came to the rescue again. Phoning him to tell him I had been made redundant wasn't great. He came to meet me for lunch and said, "Well now you can focus on having a baby." My first instinct was to call everyone I knew and start looking for a new job, but he helped me to see that was not what I wanted. It was going to be tough, a salary down and the start of a new lot of

fertility treatment. But he was right. We had wanted it for so long, so we focused on that.

The journey of IVF can be a tricky one, numerous appointments, lots of holistic appointments, people telling you to relax when that is almost impossible. But like anything that I do in my life, it was all consuming, I lived and breathed IVF. I ate all the things I was told to and drank lots of water, did some gentle exercise and got a little bored.

This is when I started my cake business. While I'd been working in banking, I had been learning how to decorate birthday cakes, wedding cakes, any type of novelty cakes. Why? One of the companies I worked for encouraged us to take up a hobby that had nothing to do with work because when you're working such long hours, it's always a good idea to have something else to do. I was somewhat good at cake decorating and thought whilst I'm at home I may as well do some cake decorating.

A good friend of mine was looking at doing the same thing. She was coming to the end of her maternity leave and looking to do something that didn't mean leaving her children for long in childcare. So we started this cake business together and it was good fun. We actually got some orders, set up our websites and worked as individuals because we didn't know where we were going. At the same time, I collaborated on a lot of cakes, and made some beautiful ones. It was a lovely little business from home. A lot of our orders came from Facebook and word of mouth. This was more of a fun business for me, using the profits to pay for my new equipment.

Alongside running the business, I spent most of the year going to hospital appointments. Having one of these visits resulted in requiring minor day surgery. Unfortunately, the hospital lost my notes resulting in me not having the operation until October. I'd been home since February, it was now October, and I still hadn't started my fertility treatment. When I finally got this operation, I was able to go straight to the top of the list. I'd already been waiting for a long time, and I started my treatment in November 2008.

IVF is tough. Your body goes through quite a lot during this process. It's draining and stressful. I was glad to have my cake business to focus because it kept my mind occupied.

In December 2008, I got the news. I was pregnant!

It was one of the happiest days of my life and I remember it vividly. I had a conversation with my husband the night before, I told him it hadn't worked. My body felt odd, so I knew I wasn't going to get the result I wanted. When you have IVF, you are told to take a pregnancy test on a certain day. I didn't actually bother getting up early on that day to take the pregnancy test. I took the test not expecting anything of it. When I got those lines to tell me, I didn't know what to do with myself. My husband had already left for work, and I remember the doorbell going thinking, who the heck was ringing my doorbell at that time of morning? It was actually my husband who'd forgotten his keys! It was lovely to be able to give him the news face to face.

I didn't have the easiest of pregnancies. I had gestational diabetes, chronic anaemia and pretty much spent nine months in and out of hospital. But I was in such a good place because it didn't matter – I was going to get what I had wanted. In the meantime, I was still carrying on with my cake business until I was about seven months pregnant, and couldn't actually roll icing anymore. It kept me busy and gave me something to focus on.

I wasn't working with my friend anymore because she wanted to grow the business, which was completely understandable. I wanted to focus on having a baby. Our business visions weren't aligned anymore. She has been working in cakes now for over 11 years and is doing brilliantly!

In August 2009, we were blessed with the birth of our beautiful son, and he is everything we could have ever dreamed for. I then spent the next six months enjoying motherhood bliss, doing every activity under the sun and I guess I kind of took motherhood like I did my corporate world. Everything was organised and structured, and I enjoyed it.

Where To Go Next

When my son was about nine months old, I looked at going back to work. But the thought of going back to what I used to do didn't fill me with joy. The job market wasn't great. Having spent two years out of the industry I was in didn't look great on my CV. The kind of positions I was being put forward for were not things I wanted to do. That's when my husband and I sat down, had a serious conversation about what we were going to do. I remember talking to a friend of mine who had recently bought a franchise. Her daughter was six months older than my son. She encouraged me to look at a business. She sent me a long email with lots of information and I remember clicking through it half-heartedly.

I came across the tutoring business; it was something I knew about. I had nothing to lose investigating it further. It took me about two weeks to fill in the application form, and then low and behold, a few weeks later I got a letter saying that the centre near my house was actually up for sale.

I took the opportunity and called the business owner. We got on well and agreed a price, I then went through the interview process.

In September 2010, my application was approved! I could buy the business. I took over in January 2011, I was a fully-fledged business owner. It was a lot of hard work. I had a one-year-old at home, and now I also had a team of 15 people and a thriving business.

I guess this is where the reality of being an entrepreneur kicked in. As a new business owner, you are responsible for everything. I was HR, accountant, trainer, support staff, and maintenance - the lot. I knew it would give me flexibility but I guess I didn't think about all the work that would be involved with being a business owner. Having a very young baby at home made it challenging. The day I took over my business, I had a team of 15 people to manage. Buying an established business meant I was thrown in at the deep end.

Why Do It All Yourself?
Owning a franchise, I had some support, but at the same time also rules and deadlines from the team at head office. There are strict procedures to follow. Working with children you also have safeguarding and first aid in place.

I ran my business from home and hired a church hall to run my classes. In addition, I was customer service, sales, and marketing which had never been my strong point. It's not something I ever understood, I didn't know how to market. Luckily the business I'd taken over from was fantastic, and had been run well by the previous owner. She had an excellent record, so a lot of my new customers came via word of mouth, and I was able to capitalise on it.

There was a lot to learn and I was enjoying the challenge. There were a lot of late nights. I only had two days of childcare plus the few hours I was at the centre. So, it meant a lot of working in the evenings when my little boy was asleep because I was trying to do it all. I was trying to be a mum and I was trying to be a business owner.

My business is also quite a cyclical business so it follows the school year. Some parts of the year are far busier than others times of the year. This is something I had to learn very fast within my first year. The business was very successful. I had a good income right from day one. I ran a big campaign nine months into the business, growing my business by about a third, which was huge.

The part of the business I didn't enjoy the most was the customer service. People project their own ideas on to you and more times than not want to tell you how it should be done. I started to lose track of what was happening. I began letting these comments get into my head. It's not what you want to take on board. There were days I wanted to throw in the towel. I knew how hard I had worked for the children and knew I only had their best interests at heart. Working with children is an absolute pleasure. I love helping children develop, helping them progress. It was an amazing part of what I do.

But juggling it all is tough. I remember in the eighth month of business my little boy got chickenpox. And all of a sudden, I'm there thinking, I can't put him down. If you have children you will understand. When they are sick, they want to be glued to you and I've got to get to class. Luckily, I had trained my staff well and they were able to take over from me for class. I had to drop everything off and they were able to carry on. I always made a point of making sure that my business would run if I was sick. It was important that if I couldn't be there for the day it wouldn't affect my business. I was able to move the business forward in that way.

The parts of the job I enjoyed was the sales, taking on new students, talking to families, knowing I could help them and not only the children in some cases it was the parents as well. Having the pleasure of talking to so many different people, it was humbling seeing how much people put their faith in you. When you see their children developing and they can see their children developing, it was great to know that I was helping people.

That's what my business is about, helping. Sometimes it can be stressful when parents have had some feedback from school and the kids haven't taken the feedback well or the parents don't know how to support their children. I've always made sure I took the time to talk to them to help them with how they can also support their children at home. I'm no expert, but I am able to read people and see how they see and understand how different people react to different things.

There were also tough parts of the business. Things like my accounts bored me; doing bank reconciliations was the worst. There was a lot of admin to do and it wasn't the most exciting. For the first good few years of my business life, I was doing all of it and that point is when I stopped enjoying it. How can you enjoy something that you don't like doing? It got to the point where almost 70% were things I didn't want to be doing. That is when I started to learn to delegate. That's when things got very interesting because a part of business is doing what you enjoy.

You are the business owner; you don't have to do all of it. I learned to delegate a lot of the admin tasks. I had someone come to my house to help me. It allowed me to focus on the bits that I enjoyed which are the parts of my business I could actually add more value to. We all only have 24 hours in the day. And what do we want to spend them doing - boring admin that we could delegate? Even if you have the time to be able to do it, do you want to spend it during that time? Do you want to be working all those hours?

Whilst I was undertaking the bulk of the work, I started to feel burnt out. I remember that feeling well. I learnt to take time out. You need to be rested and recuperated for the business. I think there was a lot of time, especially at the beginning, where I never saw the value in that. It was all about work. In my head I always thought you have to work hard. We're brought up to believe that we have to work hard all the time.

Something I've learned along my business journey is you don't have to work hard; you have to work smart. When you work smart you have more energy. Your business is going to thrive because you've got that more to give to your customers because that's ultimately what my business is. Without the customers, there is no business. By delegating, it helped me to take a little bit more time back. In reality, it took me about five years into my business to actually realise this.

I thought as a new business owner, you had to do it all. I almost stopped enjoying it but it was serving a purpose so I carried on. My business allowed me to be around for my son, do all the activities and things that I wanted to do at the school, cook him dinner, and be there for him. But I kind of stopped enjoying what I wanted to do, moved on to almost going through the motions. And when you start going through the motions, your business does start to struggle a little and it's not ideal.

At that point, I should have taken a little step back and looked at what I wanted to be doing but I was very much stuck in a rut and thought this is what I've got to carry on doing. Then I decided that growing the business or taking the business in a different direction would be a good idea so started to look at going commercial. I was still working out of the church hall and home; I was lugging boxes backwards and forwards from home. I had taken over my house with all the boxes or the products that the business needed. I needed to change something and looked at what else I could do.

I took the leap and started looking for a property. As with buying a house, looking for a commercial property for business can often be the same. We had a couple that fell through. We had to get planning permission so that was another spanner in the works that a lot of landlords didn't want to go down that route. The best things came to those who waited and found the best location was right next door to the church that I was in and negotiated a fairly good rent.

In September 2017, I got the keys to the property. It needed a little bit of work done to it and that took a couple of months to do. In November 2017, we moved across into our new premises. This did give me a new lease on life.

Everything was out of my house. I was able to differentiate between home and work, which had become difficult. It gave me that little bit of time back so when I was at home, I was at home and when I was at work, I was at work. When you run a business from home, it is very difficult to switch off. I remember hearing the business phone line ringing at night and I'd be thinking I should answer.

I settled into my new premises and things were going well. I have a great team around me. I actually managed to reduce the team down. I needed to streamline and have everybody working more productively. I actually went down to a team of five which happened quite naturally because I used to hire a lot of 16 to 19 year olds so a lot of them were going off to university in September. I didn't replace them and I was able to reduce the team very efficiently.

Things were ticking along nicely but in about 2019, I started to feel tired. We had a lot going on, my son had had his 11 Plus exams, it was go-go-go, at home and at work. I took a holiday to India in February 2020. It was what I needed. I came back, rested and recuperated and thought I need to give my business everything I can and start to drive it forward.

Two weeks after coming home, the reality of COVID-19 hit home and how serious it was. In the UK on 26th March 2020, we went into lockdown. I had to stop running face to face classes and I had to work out how to get work out to the students. Luckily, I have great team members and one of them helped me organise the work and the delivery addresses. Between the two of us, we went out and delivered all the children's work. From that point for the next four months, the children all had their work packs hand delivered to them. They weren't in school. I wanted to make sure that I supported them in the best way I could. Instead of face to face classes, I moved all classes to Zoom.

Through the process, I started posting a lot more on my social media. I tried to give parents tips on things they could be doing. I did a huge download of lots of other resources that are available, and put it in one place so parents could access it. I did 'read along'. We even got some local authors to come in and read to the children, which is fabulous.

I did book reviews and the children absolutely loved it. I was running lots of competitions and sending loads of positive messages every month, so every month they would get something fun in their work pack to keep them going.

In August 2020, we were allowed to open again. It was lovely being able to welcome children back into my classroom. It all looked very different and had to be very COVID secure but a lot of parents loved the way we worked online and actually chose to stay that way.

I'd gone from this business which was a purely face to face with no reliance on technology to one which was a hybrid, half online half face to face. It worked well so I had to learn fast. I had never used Zoom before and now my business is surviving because of Zoom.

I did loads of marketing, using social media and offline over the summer. There was an incredible amount of interest to join my centre. September and October are incredibly busy months and my business actually grew by 30%. The value I'd been adding was more than most others. I cared about the children and I wanted them to do well. It wasn't about me growing or the business growing. It was more for them and that showed.

Always Another Level

All the work I had been doing made me realise I had to self-develop. This is when I came across Jessen James. I had watched him on TV and there was something about him. I followed him on social media and ended up listening to a webinar. He was running a course. I thought it was the perfect time to take the leap and do something. I enrolled myself and it was life changing for me. What Jessen taught me was about mindset and a lot of what I'd been teaching to the children for the last 10 years. But you often can't be your own teacher. If we all often took our own advice, we would do better than we often do.

I loved the course and worked hard. I am one of these people that if I do anything, I do it properly and throw myself right into it. I passed with flying colours and I ended up with a CPD qualification. I went on to further myself and work with Jessen.

What the future holds for me, I have no idea. I know that investing in myself and investing in my education is what changed. Often, we are told that education ends when we leave school, and if we go on to any other further education it's usually to do with professional qualifications or something that has an element of our work.

I wasn't thinking big, thinking how else can I run my business or what else can I do to make my business more efficient. By training and taking the time out to learn different elements of the business and actually learning which parts I should be delegating, I grew organically. Although I was delegating, I wasn't delegating enough or the right parts. I have learned to delegate the right parts. I'm working far less than I ever have been and am so much more efficient.

When I'm at work, I'm so much more present because I am the face of my business and that's what I want to be. I want to be the one who's there for the children. I don't want to be doing all the admin or chasing payments. I've now delegated that out which means I can focus on the parts that I enjoy.

This also gives me time for my own self development. What the future holds, who knows? Am I going to be in this business forever? No idea, but what I do know is that I now have the tools to allow me to go on to do so many more things. I know that I love working in sales and talking to people. I know that could be a great option for me in the future. My little boy is not so little anymore and is now at secondary school which gives me so much more time to be able to do other things such as develop myself further.

I'm a driven woman. That's what I want to show the younger generation - you can be anyone you want to be. I am a mother, wife and successful business owner. I love being all those things! I'm also an individual with my own personal goals and ambitions. I am blessed to have a family that completely supports me, and my husband has always pushed me to follow my goals.

The most important part of having a business is to have a good network. After all, you are the average of the five people you spend most of your time with. Be around people that celebrate you, push you, pick you up when you are down. Being a business owner can be lonely at times and it is important to have that close network.

My life has taken a lot of ups and downs, twists and turns but that is the key. It is never too late to start a new chapter. There is nothing wrong with restarts. There is nothing wrong with trying new things.

My sister blessed me with a beautiful niece, my little girl Sienna. She doesn't know it, but she drives me every day. I want her to grow up doing whatever she wants, no bounds and no restrictions. If I can be ready to change things at my age, the world is hers for the taking!

You're the author of your own life story. You can start a new chapter any time you choose.

About Me

I am a mum, wife and business owner with over six years within the banking industry. After the arrival of my son in 2009, I took the decision to leave my career and start something new that would give me a balance between career ambitions and being there for my son.

Through sheer dedication and commitment, I juggled a successful business with motherhood, ensuring I was there for the concerts, sports fixtures and after-school activities, all while growing my business to support thousands of families in my local community.

The world is full of amazing women and to be in a book with some of them is an honour and privilege. Often in business it is about competition, but supporting women help other women is something close to my heart. I understand the personal and societal pressures that often come with being a woman in business. They juggle various roles and can feel like we have to be perfect in every one of them.

Through this chapter, I hope to have shown you that you can start at any time and inspire other women to take the next step in their journey.

Legacy To Empower And Enlighten

Jackie Latty

Director

4me2Thrive Ltd

"Never doubt who you are." --- Stephanie Lahart

Selfish Or Selfless

As a child, having to take on the duty as the eldest girl in the family was a tough role. Looking after my terminally ill mum was emotional and testing. Always in a situation of having to choose within constraints was a task in itself. It was either too selfish or selfless. Do I go out to play or stay in to be the carer? Either way, it left me questioning my own judgment. I had no words to articulate it; maybe that's why I write!

My experience as a carer in the 70s has left me with the ability to recall very clinical smells and visual images that will remain with me forever. I remember taking our mum out of her bed, bathing her, and giving her breakfast with a cup.

My brother and me would place her in an armchair and leave her in front of the open coal fire that we had to light at such young ages. We had no knowledge of health and safety, praying and hoping for the best. All day swaddled in a blanket; front door unlocked waiting for the district nurses. Connection with the help was very difficult due to the number of helpers coming in and out of our place we called "home".

Where my friend's houses had furniture, we had a hospital bed, hoist, disposable bedding, bedpans, and special equipment. It was a very emotional experience to live through. I vowed never to be a nurse. To watch mum's tears roll down her face day upon day left me feeling numb and nervous. I used to read Bible stories to her and plait her hair, creaming her very dry body. Our ultimate concern was making sure she was comfortable as possible.

My brother had a paper round, and I would leave at the crack of dawn to help him deliver newspapers. It was scary down the country lanes on the homemade broken bike. We shared it between both of us with me as the pillion passenger. No helmet or safety gear, occasional grazed knees, bruises and tears. Never being as fortunate as other children in our street, we didn't get to access toys and playtime like them. We made homemade toys out of boxes, cans and strings. I know that's where my creativity comes from. I am so grateful to so many charities that gave people like us in need gifts so we all had something because they opened their hands in benevolence to us. Even of the jigsaws we got had pieces missing; we were just happy to get a gift.

I remember many times, dad would go to work as a shot blaster at Wickman's, early in the mornings to earn his pay, leaving his precious family to fend for themselves. The next part of the routine was imperative that we ensured our dignity as a household in crisis remained intact.

I love music even to this day. I remember how much we danced to the sound of reggae music from dad's sound system and Top of the Pops on Thursdays. Every week, we would go to the launderette and had a bag of chips as a treat. We had soup on Saturdays and rice, peas and chicken on Sundays. Being Caribbean, we loved sharing our food. Many times, we would sell our food to the neighbours to make a profit.

My dad would be pulling his hair out because at times he would be looking for the shopping, but we had used it to cook the food to sell. At times, we went hungry. We hadn't realised that one packet of biscuits was to last a week, but we as kids got so excited and ate them on that one night. The boundaries were stretched beyond the parameters. My dad would be fuming and threatened to beat us – but they were words. It was Jamaica in the house and England outside - what a great experience!

Discovering Ourselves And Our Legacy In Life's Troubles

In 1975, mum sadly passed away at a tender age of thirty-one. I was eleven. It was a very depressing time for us all. I remember becoming insular, watching the clouds pass by for hours. My life was still and grey, yet it was a turning of the tide and new beginnings for us.

Dad eventually found happiness, a new love of his life. We were all happy. Due to the merging of two families, my stepmother and her three daughters joined us in becoming a blended family. I finally realised the importance of having a mother figure to talk to and to nurture me. I can't say that it was easy. At times, it was hard to accept another woman telling me what to do and taking charge of me. I guess that the impact of losing mum was deeper than I ever thought possible. But the Creator knew my needs and answered my cries for help.

Love conquers all. I am proud of making it this far with so much love and gratitude for my family. This love extended to foster children over the years. I heard that it was thirty-eight in total that my dad and my stepmum cared for, and that's amazing. My dad had a big heart and he shared it with the masses. He left a beautiful legacy before his passing four years ago. We practice what we see and learn when we are young. Through these lessons, when we are older, we know how to make our way.

With too many living in the family home, I was led to leave home in my early twenties. I had knowledge of the world, but I recognised that it is not easy to live alone. I soon determined in my mind that I needed to make it, and I needed to do it regardless. Working harder and smarter, I secured a mortgage. I've had many more challenges and I now know that troubles won't last forever!

When you are a carer, nothing can prepare you for empty hands, and nothing prepares you for the time that appears in your life when you ask yourself, "What's next?"

Good news is that I made I through that dark time. My ability to serve dates back to my childhood. I have had to fight for my right to be, to do, to go, to have. I'm still here, pushing for the rights of the less fortunate of us. I believe that I have already become a gifted and talented individual. I have used my experiences in life to beat the negative things I have endured along the way.

I enjoyed my school days with my friends who we called 'The Possie'. There are too many to name, and I will always remember them and those who have now passed on. It was a laugh every single day. We shared a lot of love and compassion between us. I couldn't wait to leave school because it all felt new and exciting. Little did I realise that school life had formed a big part of me, and I missed everyone so much once we had departed. I am still in touch with most of them and that means a lot to me.

I eventually settled down to college and life working in a nursery began. It was tough working with babies from six weeks old to the age of eight and their families. I have always had an extra connection with the challenging ones who others found hard to understand. I would always go the extra mile for the children. We would laugh whilst sitting at the dinner table and I would make jokes about the scoffing noises and relate them to animals' sounds. I would whisper and ask, "Children, do you think we have a little piggy at the table today because I can hear a scoffing noise?"

The young one that was scoffing would stop immediately and we would all fall about laughing. I know that this was not the best way to behave but I loved to hear them laugh uncontrollably.

We would then go to the bathroom and give the boys side partings or middle partings that we called 'Cecil's'. I don't know why we called them Cecil's, but it sounded so comical all those years ago. My dad had a good friend called Cecil and the name was universal in those times. Of course, we asked their permission, but it was so funny to see them all scrubbed up, waiting for their parents to collect them.

It is so important to me that children feel free to express their feelings. Whether good or bad, there is always a message that they are trying to convey. It's up to us to ensure that their voices are heard and correctly interpreted.

As the years rolled on, I moved over to adult services and was successful in securing a job as the Project Manager at The Black Mental Health service in Coventry. This catered for people in the local community who were facing mental health issues. The role of the organisation was to support minority ethnic people to navigate through the NHS systems. They were able to access community support and to have a place where they felt safe to speak about their concerns and poor experiences. This was a massive task that I held for over nine years. At times, I experienced some challenges that had me near breaking point.

Discrimination featured heavily from external and internal factors. I worked with the team and found allies within local services, in whom I could trust to offload and for them to share their issues. I saw many skilled workers come and go. From there I supported the team to turn what was called a failing organisation around, moved location, re-named it. I am proud to say that it is still in existence and named the Tamarind Centre. I believe in creating legacy. Making something that lasts beyond yourself is something to boast about.

I used my knowledge working for the city of Coventry with the local city leaders, helping to set the standards and a pace for women and children as part of the community care plan volunteering. There were varied community panels, Joint Health Committees and chairing panels where I was recognised. Learning that my voice made a difference was powerful. As a young person myself I had felt lost in hardly ever been heard.

Now I encompass my skills, knowledge and expertise in the work that I do. I drew upon my life experiences to build my character from the pain, hurt, disappointments, lack of playtime and nurturing of a mother at a young age. Out of this, I began creating my lifestyle. I had no idea at that time that this was what would form my interests. I understand the sheer agony of loneliness, relentless crying, anxiety and emotional distress - but it also made me strong. My belief is that what we learn when we are young, can be used for the good or the bad when we get older. Often, times like this determines the style of our character. It builds our tenacity and gives us the impetus to use our skills and knowledge in our adult hood.

Another Level Of Service

I secured a role as Deputy Pastoral Manager at an Independent school; many had been left feeling hurt from broken families. My job was a testament to my ability, and I was regularly called upon. The students began letting me in to help them heal, to gain back courage and confidence. This was how it all came to light. It confirmed to me that all voices count. I wanted to spearhead something new and accessible for the seldom heard.

Chasing missing children, working with children from care homes, children with autism and so much more became a work in progress. Making new relationships with police, social workers and, multi-disciplinary teams and early helping for families became second to none. Unfortunately, I moved on from the position that I enjoyed due to many reasons beyond my control.

My new roles then became varied, rich in more experiences in mainstream schools. I developed my repertoire even further. Every school I attended for my agency was a winner and I secured medium to long-term work, sometimes invigilating for school exams. I created a platform to ensure access to services and appropriate information. The wins have been challenges in securing employment at a diverse range of settings in pupil referral units.

As a volunteer Prison chaplain, I joined the team after a visit to Coventry Chamber of Commerce. I pitched my business idea and history was in the making. I met with a brilliant advisor named Helen and informed her that I wrote poetry. She listened to two of my pieces and asked me if I had ever thought of joining prison ministry. Little did I know that she had a husband who was a prison officer. Helen passed my name to the Chaplain and I soon joined the West Midlands Team at a Young Offenders Institute. I have been attending there for around seven years with phenomenal results. It is an institute for young men aged eighteen to twenty-five, and my role is to bring inspiration through reciting my poems. Inspiration works.

Sometimes our congregation consists of double figures that attend from their cells voluntarily and bring their friends. To see the faces and the countenances change, smiles emerging and spirits lifting makes it all worth it. How do I create my poems? Imagine you talk to me and together we create a poem, an inspirational piece from the topic that's affected your life, whether negatively or positively. I support you to authentically find yourself and to have something tangible that you will be proud of to help you to move forward.

I've since learned to understand that right can sometimes feel wrong and wrong sometimes can feel right. It doesn't always pay to listen to the masses. I guess that we each must learn to listen to our inner selves, our hearts and minds. My perspective being, that no one ever walks in your shoes and will never realise what it feels like from within the inner place of another person.

Business Idea

My business idea came to light after two redundancies, one resignation and a range of experiences in my other jobs. I was supported in naming it lovingly, with the help and support from some of the special young people that I have the pleasure of working with. They helped me create the logo and choose the colours. They are my champions for helping me with this side of the business. We collectively came up with the name '4me2Thrive Ltd' for people with challenging behaviours and traumas. I realised that I always had something that was unique about me, and this was my time to get my message across all sectors.

My audiences are professionals, police and those within the educational establishments. The coaching and mentoring programme helps to nurture others in a different kind of way that will allow them to identify the gaps within their services. Coming together in a platform that offers a listening ear and creative outlet to share in a safe environment is something tangible that is changing lives.

Using sounds, words, music, educating and feeding minds in a bespoke programme for your unique qualities and requirements is a huge part of supporting young people with challenging behaviours to attain positive results and adults in gaining back their self-esteem. Seeing them learn to smile makes it all worth it.

How about if your life became a song and dance, a walk in the park or even a sketch? Fancy that! My coaching program consists of my life experience, my abilities, gifts and talents, including educational packages and problem-solving toolkits. Unique opportunities to help you to turn up, show up, to be present and to be honest with yourself. Come as you are, and we work together. We offer coaching support and mentoring to people who are in need, helping the broken and in need, moving forward from personal issues and life's negative circumstances.

I share, I listen, I hear, I pray, I support, I love, I offer hope by using experiences and knowledge to navigate the systems. It's an outlet to have better, to be better, to do better.

This can be for art, music, dance, painting, sketching where you talk, and we create. We gain new life, release and new meaning. Purpose comes to you, through you and in you.

My winning formula out of the challenges was built on determination and courage to bounce back. Having honest conversations with myself, hiding out but always showing up. I learned to look in the mirror to accept and love myself as much as I loved others.

What I did not realise, is that I did not have a plan, not even a written one. I learned the art of paying my bills and noticing the lack of money in my account at the end of each month. My dream at that time was to become a midwife but unfortunately, that did not come to pass. I studied, but I did not go to university (that was a conscious decision). I did not like sitting exams and stayed away from any type of pressure. I was not strong in that sense at the time, and I was aware of how far to push myself.

I must admit that I also had a negative mental picture about the system; about racism and about how little I felt embraced within the culture that I lived in. In the seventies there was a lot going on politically within the climate and the community. Young black people were finding their feet and coming up against discrimination and oppression. Bands were emerging, singing about unemployment. I related to the realities and pressures of life they faced.

I heard of people going to prison or being sectioned in mental health hospitals. Jobs were hard to come by and poverty was rearing its ugly head. Realising the need to walk with wisdom, knowing myself was my key to getting through. Throughout my childhood, I have had to fight for my right to be, to do, to go, to have. I'm still here pushing for my rights and for those of the less fortunate of us.

I have already become a gifted and talented individual because I have used my experience in life, to beat the negative things I have endured along the way. I now understand that I had entrepreneurial skills from a young age but I was without the knowledge to apply it to gain a much higher quality of life. We all need cheerleaders, and I see that joining QIB is a sure response and option to develop a new perspective that will help me to achieve by following their great advice, experience and support.

Finding Myself

Over the years of being made redundant and it was called a 'pity party' at the age of fifty. I sat in my bedroom thinking how did I get here? I felt stuck, lack of energy and like stagnant water eventually that starts to smell. That was a wake-up call to get moving and get back into work.

Joining an agency was one of the best moves I had ever made. I soon was earning at a slightly higher rate and in the top five employees with a brilliant track record across a range of schools including a Pupil Referral Unit (PRU). My unique self-development happened over time and look at me now. "Pow!"

So, for my disappointments and rejection, I realised that going from different workspaces, meeting new people brought something different and unique to the table. It was all my quirkiness and the gift of building great relations with troubled young people that helped me to stand out.

From breakdowns to breakthroughs, the comments from people who tried time and time again to get through to a young person without being successful were a testament to my ability to ensure positive change. In a very short space of time, when that young person was afforded space, they were able to understand what was happening for them. By my showing up, being authentic while capturing their feelings changed everything. I offered respect where respect was due and I commanded respect in return. It was an agreement with sensitivity, warmth and care with safe boundaries.

My journey in all the paths that I cross, the people that I meet and the lessons and teachings I leave behind are to create my legacy to empower and enlighten not only the professional but the next generation.

My desire is to be the light in the darkness, to bring words and actions to show the way that one can go. Come along with me and on a journey we will ride together.

I arrived here out of sheer determination and willpower from tears pain, disappointment and heartache, mental challenges, toil, sickness and now in health. Surfing the net for jobs and going back to basics in my earning capability, pushing and being pushed and pulling myself along. Sometimes not even knowing how I was going to get from one day to the next but knowing that I would arrive by having grit and determination to make it.

Unstoppable in All That I Do

Not being able to say goodbye to my mum was one of the toughest lessons of my life. My mother going so suddenly was a very difficult process to deal with, the pain has never been forgotten. It was hard to overcome and that will live with me forever. Nothing can prepare you for death of a loved one. Even if you've been given a timescale, it still smacks you in the face or in the guts. Yet I've learned that you can recover and you can use your experiences for the better.

I believe that all things are possible so I needed to make sure that I was unstoppable. Even during the storm, remember there's always going to be a calm after all the problems and situations that we go through.

Every day is a lesson if you can learn to embrace these trying times. You will overcome. One ought to develop being a better person, stronger, and more reliable. We can become someone who loves themselves, putting away the self-loathing. We can wake up each morning ready for a new day with new opportunities.

Embracing people and controlling my internal dialogue in my head was the biggest hurdle to becoming unstoppable. It wasn't always a positive dialogue. I grappled with it and was determined to win. I believe that a positive mindset makes all the difference; it is okay to have negative thoughts, just don't wear them as a badge of honour.

My feelings help me to embrace myself for who I am, to look at my strengths and opportunities and weaknesses and my threats. Asking myself questions like,

"Is it really real?"

"Am I making it up?"

"How much will this prevent me or accelerate me?"

Having passion enthused with desire to make it, I've had to become courageous and savvy in learning. My internal barriers such as negative self-talk and all other undesired emotions must be shifted in our bodies and minds. I took the time to mentally break them down because many of them seemed to belong to me, but they were mostly built on false evidence appearing real.

You've got to learn to believe in yourself, especially in moments of adversity. Sometimes it's a choice not to speak out, and it's a choice you must make. No matter how painful it is, no matter how unsolicited the words are that are thrown at you, as women, we need to know who we are. The asset we are adds value; we all have a purpose.

One thing I wish I knew before I started my business is the need to have a written clear and concise business plan with dates, forecasts and budgets. Failing to plan is planning to fail. It is imperative to have support from crucial peers. You must be courageous and believe in your dream. Most importantly, ask for help.

To my younger self I would love to have said, "Never be concerned if others don't get it. Keep on moving forward and be tenacious. Expect everything good and be prepared for negativity. Tough times will come but you will get through them."

My advice to women: do not tolerate great suffering and pain. We have the art of finding what we believe in as valid reasons to make our lives worth living, even when exhausted. We have the ability to show up and be present. It is okay to say it's not okay with you. When you need to rest take some time out, but with caution. I would add that you should not take too much time out because it's harder to get back up again.

Embrace and believe in yourself. Invest in yourself. Celebrate your success. Take a few calculated risks with your opportunities. Look after yourself. Forgive yourself and go, go, go!

About Me

I am Jacqueline, affectionately known as Jack-Jack by my nieces and nephews, Jackie at work and play, Reverend Jackie in the church and 'G' to some special friends who have never met each other. G is particularly special to me because it was my dad's middle name.

My parents arrived from sunny Jamaica to settle in a new life in the UK. I am a Coventry gal from a large, blended family, married with two beautiful daughters. My eldest Cara is 33 and my youngest

Naomi is 21. I have a wonderful son-in-law and a very smart grandson who already talks about becoming a famous rockstar. My family constantly makes me proud and my love for them is unconditional. I am the second eldest of my brothers and sisters, with an abundance of foster siblings. It has been a privilege with lots of lessons learned along the way.

I am a woman who is always availing myself to serve others in an altruistic manner. Studying as a nursery nurse, I guess that my nurturing side got the best of me, mainly caring for children aged 0-18 and adults including those facing mental health challenges. My career has given rise to me managing services and to voluntary sector roles.

I am a good listener, encourager and all-round inspirational person. My creativity allows me to write poetry and songs along with expressing myself through my visual art. I am very popular and deeply admired, believing this is a trait from my upbringing. I love to inspire others with a desire to help people release their inner potential, overcome their fears, negativity whilst realizing their place in the world. My vision has been to become a household name for all the right reasons bringing HOPE!

Acknowledgements
To my creator for my LIFE!

To my parents, and my stepmother who supported me in good and bad times.

To my family, friends and young people whom I have met along the way, who trusted me, inspired me to enable us all to become better and wiser.

To the Queens In Business Club who have embraced me and helped me to move closer to my goals.

Remember to finish the race you do not have to WIN IT!

I thank God for all He has done in my life.

Laugh At Sh*t!

Sandra Ammerlaan

Founder

Laughatshit.com

"Life always waits for some crisis to occur before revealing itself at its most brilliant." --- Paulo Coelho

Once Upon A Sh*tty Time....

I never thought it would happen to me, that I would get in a relationship with a narcissist and suffer mental abuse. You hear these stories from other people, and think how do they end up in those situations?

Well it starts small and goes really slow. So slow that I had no clue; I grew into it, and it became normal.

After a year, I moved from my parents into a house with him. Working in his family's business, which was like a ship with two captains who didn't agree on anything, and someone had to pay the price. Unfortunately, that was me. Daily blaming me for things I had nothing to do with, if I was lucky only once a day. But that was on a very lucky day, all in front of co-workers, his family and customers who were looking on at me. Walking on eggshells constantly trying to keep quiet. Maybe if I would listen, be better, do better and act better then maybe, just maybe I would live one day in peace.

When my childhood friends from England came over, I could only spend one day with them. He already ruined the day before I left, by yelling and screaming that I was going out and having fun. I can write a whole book on examples like that.

One time when he was sick, he blamed me while it was his dad doing something and said he wanted to shoot himself. While I had to go back to their shop, I was sick all afternoon and so scared to go home later not sure what and how to find him. For no reason, he would literally punish me by turning his back on me, and sleeping on the other end of the bed for nights.

Being the manager of his band, I got them gigs due to my connections but he suddenly wanted me to quit. I was not good enough. Whilst I called the other members with an excuse why I couldn't do it anymore, they almost begged me to keep doing it.

His daughter from a former relationship got back in contact, she was lovely. A young teenager who was so vulnerable and missing love, care and attention so much that she got involved with a lover boy. By yelling at her and screaming, she was drawn into the arms of this bad guy. He and his friends attacked my partner's shop, where my partner got beaten up.

She was missing for a few weeks. As I called the emergency number while we were attacked, this was a huge mistake. For years, I heard I should have fought instead and his mum said "Don't you ever think that you will ever be a part of this family, because you won't".

God, I have never been so lonely, never felt so ashamed and scared. After being kicked out of my own home three times, I decided I could not live there anymore, I was too far from my own family who had no clue what was going on. I was too ashamed and scared to look them in the eyes and tell them. He said he would come to move in with me in time, but never did. It was already hard to even come over once a week. The weekends I would go to him, to the house that used to be my home, although it never felt home ever again.

I got a great chance to go to a beading show in Toronto, Canada. I even asked if it was okay with him. He would drop me off at the airport and at the same time pick up my parents as they came back from Toronto. Two days before, he started yelling and swearing at me for going and having fun. I didn't deserve it, but he said I was selfish, and not loveable, and a whore for going on a trip on my own. (I always paid everything myself, he did not provide me anything!)

Right after he hung up on me, my dad called from Canada asking how things were and if I was ready to go. I couldn't tell my dad what happened. I don't know how I managed to pretend nothing was wrong, but I did.

During the trip, he did not respond to any of my messages. Even though I tried to remind myself I am here now, and he should not take away the joy of this. I was so scared to come back and have weeks full of shouting, swearing and whatever sh*t he would put on me.

Saved By A Miracle In Painful Disguise

Even while I was so unhappy, I was getting to the age of 34, if I ever wanted to have children, then now would be the time. Otherwise it would be too late. I mistakenly believed that this was the best life had to offer me, so I had to settle with this. I did not think I deserved any better.

15th March 2010. I know it has happened, I can feel it, something changed, and this will change my whole life. While my partner was late as usual, I took the test already. Wait for it... Wait for it... How long do a few minutes take?! OMG.... oh yes, it's real I was pregnant! I am crying... I am going to be a mum; I have a baby growing inside me. My partner said don't be happy, go see a doctor to make sure first. He, as usual, was not supportive to say the least.

I couldn't wait to tell my parents, my dad wanted to be a grandfather for so long. I can already see them go on the lawn mower together, or my mum playing hide and seek with him. I know it is a boy, I couldn't explain how I knew but mums just know things, right?

31st March 2010. Middle of the night, I was in bed, something didn't feel right. I lost some blood a few days before. As I got out of bed and had got to the bathroom, I saw that I was losing blood again, but a lot this time. This was not good. I got back to bed, I closed my eyes, it looked like I was dreaming even though I was awake. I saw my baby, as if it was sleeping in my arms, satisfied, and I heard the message, "Sorry mum I can't stay with you, this was all we had, we have to let go now, I love you…"

In the morning, I went to the obstetrician, who checked and confirmed that I have lost the baby. As I got into my car, I felt paralysed. How will I tell my parents? I saw the disappointment in my daddy's eyes, even though he didn't say it. I saw he's sad too. I felt as if I disappointed him.

My partner took the whole effort to come. The first thing he said was "Oh this was nothing, we can try again, this is definitely going to be a problem that you will moan about for months, right?" As I heard him say it, I thought, What the heck?! I am never talking to you about this again! Then he said "You know this is your fault that you had the miscarriage." I knew why he said that, since he was the one who initiated sex days before I lost blood the first time, I was now to blame for that too. I believed it and felt horrible about it. Never ever was anyone to know this, I might have killed my own baby?!

For two days, my partner didn't even bother to give me a call. I am upset as my whole body is upside down, and gave him a call crying, and said, "Don't you wonder how I am doing?" As usual he started yelling and swearing at me, he told me that I am a selfish, useless b*tch. I should be supporting him and not thinking about myself. It was my fault that I had lost the baby. I shouldn't act so pathetic, what the hell was I thinking?!

I was literally looking at my phone thinking, what?! From all the times I heard this, this is the first time I realised that it should be the other way around. That was the one time that he should be there for me. He hung up the phone angry. It took me hours to get him back on the phone. The only reason I had for that is that I didn't want to go to the Easter brunch with my family alone, I didn't want them to know.

He showed up in time to go to the family. Since I was in pain, I wanted to get back home. We drove up to my house, he kept the engine of the car running. "Aren't you coming in?" He said, "No, the cat still needs to eat... " THE CAT NEEDS TO EAT?! Before I had the key in the lock of the door, he was at the end of the street.

This is the moment... I finally realised.

Am I out of my bloody mind?! I have been taking this bullsh*t for 10 years now, ENOUGH IS ENOUGH!

I can't keep living like this, it will cost me my life, it almost had already did several times.

It was real torture. Every Saturday night after dinner, he would start playing his guitar, over and over "Tears in heaven" from "Eric Clapton". Looking back, I wonder how I ever got through that, at some points I wanted to grab that guitar and hit him on the head with it, it hurt so bad. I kept my word, as I never spoke about the whole pregnancy again. And as far as the let's try again, hell no, there is no way that you will put me through that again.

It took me another six months to get the courage, before it came to an end. Ten and a half years, almost a third of my life so far. I was so used to the abuse, feeling inferior, being belittled, yelled, sweared at and getting the blame for everything. Praying for one day in peace without being punished, it finally was silent.

Starting To Live Again
All the things I lost along the way, my dignity, my confidence, my self-esteem, the laughter and cheery vivid young woman and a lot of money. But most of all my identity. It took time to recover, to feel free, do whatever I wanted with whoever I wanted whenever I want. Wow this was great! I could do anything I want!

I went to the biggest consumer beading show in the world. As a jewellery designer, I even made it into even teaching a class! What a great experience! I remember standing in front of the hotel thinking "I need to take this experience in with every sense I have". I will always remember the sound, the smell, the temperature, and most of all this great feeling of joy, being grateful and happy.

I loved my job, but my parents owned a party centre and when the manager was laid off for stealing, my dad offered me the job. At the time, it seemed like the right thing. I was on the roll, very talkative, good at bringing people in, and I loved arranging and organising events for people. I always went the extra mile.

On the side, I was still running my jewellery studio. I served in different volunteering activities and committees, joined a political party, and contributed to the community.

At some point, I had to quit my first job I kept on the side. I needed to put everything into managing the whole business. We had a small team, and then our chef found out he had cancer. We were close and in only a few weeks he passed. Not only did it take a toll emotionally, as he was the colleague anyone would wish for, but also all of his work. Suddenly I had to do all the catering too, I was even in the kitchen at night.

It was a difficult time to get the business running successfully, and the stress was taking its toll. I went to see the GP several times with different complaints that were stress related. Only he was not hearing me and most of the time he said to swallow it. So I assumed it was me, I worked even harder, I didn't want to disappoint my parents, and I did not want to fail.

There was someone hired to support the team and do the catering. That was a relief… For a few days… He took over things, no team working, he knew everything better.

I was so overworked, I literally had all my days off from more than a year left, I was so tired, I could not defend myself anymore. At some point he had a whole buffet ready two hours before the guests were supposed to eat, what a mess!

At the end of the month, we had a meeting to decide whether he should stay or not. He got to talk, and he burnt me down to the ground. I was not doing my work properly, even though the proof that I was doing a great job there. According to him I was the worst person ever. Wow I got the blame again, what is this? Going back down memory lane?

I sat there as if I wasn't even there. Since we all got a chance to talk but I was so hurt and tired of the whole BS. I didn't care anymore and thought what the hell am I even here for? My colleague saw it all happening, as we were on the same page, he made it clear that he was not willing to work with him. My parents had to let him go. This was not what I had hoped for. I hoped we would make a great team and do it all together, making people happy, it should not be about power.

Back to reality, let's keep the spirit up and keep working. I had trouble sleeping, and noticed I forgot some things and was not able to manage my time as well as before. And of course, when I noticed I beat myself up over it.

It was a Monday, I was alone at work, great! I could finish a lot without being disturbed. I got a phone call. The person on the other side was not in a good mood and demanding. I listened, but couldn't reply, as if my voice got lost. I hung up the phone as fast as I can. I stood up from my desk, and then boom! It all turned dark....

Next thing I knew was that I was sitting on the floor.... What just happened? Dazed, I looked around me and felt this pain in my chest. Huh? Sweat dropped on my forehead as if I got a fever, all of the sudden. I felt dizzy too. Suddenly this thought about a famous Dutch man my age who was on the news had a heart attack a few days before flashes by.

OMG! This is serious, I had a similar thing. No, that couldn't be, I was young, I was active, I was strong, that wouldn't happen to me, right? I crawled over the floor to reach the end of the desk and pulled myself back up and got back in my chair. Okay breath, just breath... Thank God I am alone, then no one needs to know about this, and it will all go away.

A few days later, the pain was still there, and I was worried. I thought to cover it up, but it was not good. Reluctantly, I called the

GP again. As I walked in, he sat behind his desk, stared at his computer and typed. While I was telling him what happened, I noticed he was not even listening. I took the test on the sum, and stopped talking in the middle of the sentence so he would have to ask.

Instead of asking anything and having not heard the story he said "Oh this is nothing, you are making things up, you have been hyperventilating." HYPERVENTILATING?! WTF?! Since he had a close connection to my dad and knows heart problems run in the family are you freaking kidding me?! He sent me out, just like that as if I don't know my own body, as if I was bullsh*tting him.

As I stood outside, I gasped for air. He was my GP; I should be able to trust him. What the hell do I have to do to get some help? I was drowning, I needed help! It was suggested that I go on a holiday. As it was not a busy time, I could take a week off. I decided to go to Egypt. Really on my own as a blonde woman? Hey I don't care, I wanted to live my life, and who cares where I'll end up. I booked guided tours and sightseeing. As long as I was gone and didn't have to think about anything.

I was scared, I didn't speak the language. If that guy I booked with would not be there to pick me up, I would be screwed and not know how to get to a hotel or whatever. Well at least I was not home. Of course, he was there. I spent two days in Cairo, with two guides, both speaking Dutch, it was very impressive. The third day, I flew to Hurghada and the first guide said "my brother will take care of you, I already called him".

At the arrival, I picked up my bag as the door opened and, in the distance, I saw someone in a green blouse. At the same time, I heard a voice saying "Here comes your life lesson". There's no one there, where did that just come from? How true that was. He

264

changed my life forever, only I didn't know at the time. The next few days were as if I was on a different planet. An unexplainable connection from the moment he shook my hand and we looked in each other's eyes. As if we were electrified. The way he talked to me, the way he took care of me, the way he looked at me.

Though I am not stupid! I mean, besides my so far experience, fairy tales do not exist. I was warned I was blonde, coming from a wealthy country, had my ducks in a row, of course they try to…

He did everything to make me understand, and to understand me. This wall around me was not breaking down, no way Jose! It's complicated enough already.

It was the last day, I did not want to go home, how weird for someone that gets homesick. I realised it was real, and it was too late. Going gift shopping, he went along and bargained about the price and even got the shop owner mad. I didn't take a goddess statue as it was too expensive, but it still got wrapped. I said "But I am not buying that?" He said "No I am, as I want you to remember this forever."

While he looked at me, I saw and felt the truth. He had to work at least two days paying for that, and wasn't even sure if he would have enough money to pay his bills for the next few weeks.

Unfortunately, there was no time left, we only had a half hour before I was leaving. This was probably the most heart-breaking goodbye ever. Waiting for the taxi to pick me up he said he couldn't see me leaving, and wouldn't come along to say goodbye at the airport. As I stood there feeling so stupid, wondering what happened, I heard the same voice again saying, say what you want now, you will never meet him again.

I could not talk, I stared at him while he was saying things no one ever said to me, while we both tried not to cry. There was the taxi, he formally shook my hand and closed the door. I looked at him as we drove off. What kind of movie was I in? At the airport, I got teary and couldn't stop. Oh crap, I have to be a big girl now, come on, this is too stupid! But I couldn't stop crying the whole flight until I landed in Amsterdam.

I felt broken, I couldn't function properly and I couldn't stop crying. My colleague who was close to me understood and carefully said maybe you are overworked and should see the doctor? Well look where that got me so far? He will send me straight home pretending I am being pathetic. I even said I wanted to leave everything and everyone behind and go back to Egypt! While I said it, I knew that was not the solution.

Finally, I went back to my GP, only this time I took control over the conversation and said to him "If you don't recommend me to a specialist and help me now, I will help myself and believe me that will be permanent". I only realised then that I told him that I was about to see if I could commit suicide. This is bad, this is really bad. How did it get this far?

When You Think You Are Being Buried, You Are Actually Being Planted

The psychologist set the diagnosis, a severe depression with burnout. I believe, "I am f*cked up. Totally f*cked up". I accepted that even Duracell batteries run empty, so I had to recharge first before I can do anything again.

The next few months were like hell. Each day was a struggle, to get up in the morning and get out of bed. It took me a half hour to even get a glass of water from the kitchen. I was waiting for the minutes, the hours to pass. When I got to bed, I prayed to the universe to come and get me, this life is too hard for me. I didn't want this life, give it to someone else that deserves it more. I didn't have the balls to take my own life, but I had been through every option possible.

So far, my life has been all about doing what other people expect me to. Trying to be perfect, the perfect woman, the perfect employer, the perfect entrepreneur, the perfect daughter, the perfect sister, the perfect aunt, the perfect partner, the perfect friend. Trying to be perfect sucks!

Things had to change! The only way out is in. What could I do to become better?

I made a big decision and investment. What I now say if you want any advice from me, here it is "The best investment you can ever make is the investment in yourself."

I started a year-long program that made me see things in a different way, make me go outside my comfort zone. With like-minded people things were easier. A New Year's dive in the North Sea? It was January and freezing! But I did it. I noticed how fast the change in me happened, more confidence, and things started to make more sense.

I took the advanced program the year after. If I can come this far in a year, what would happen in 3, 5 or 10 years?

This year they had a "Nature Quest". We stayed in a 2.5m circle for 4 nights and 3 days. We're not supposed to see each other and had no tent and food. I am not a happy camper and I am afraid of all kinds of insects and bugs. It was meant to give you clarity by sitting and being on your own.

Doing nothing is hard, you never know when you are done.

Of course, all the sh*t came up first. After two days crying, sitting there counting bugs, having a wild horse in my circle, I woke up with a snail against my nose! It looked like the air had cleared. As I had been sitting on a bunch of nettles, I moved to a bench with a view on a small lake.

As I was sitting in the sun I thought, "What if everything is possible? What would I do?" I started to fantasise… What if I could make some kind of performance about all the sh*t I went through? To inspire people and make them laugh? What if my sh*t could be my motive? What if it could help other people? Whilst I was fantasising and visualising it grew bigger. What if I could do it in New York too? What if I could make a difference in other people's lives?

At the end of 2017, I fell back into depression. My new GP made me come to check in every now and then. When it got worse, she immediately recommended me for support. Only at least three months waiting list?!

In the meantime, I went to a seminar. This young man came on stage and said the magical words "Listen as if you hear everything for the first time today. Your mind is like a parachute. It only works when it's open, it's like a buffet, just take what you like". At the end of the day I signed up for a Neuro-Linguistic Programming (NLP), starting within a month. No clue where it would take me, but this was the best investment in myself ever!

As we started, I was a grey mouse, very quiet in the back of the room. The first day they asked about our dreams and goals and my arm just went up whilst my best friend and I were both in shock, I stood up and said, "I want to do my own cabaret performance". Everyone in the room was cheering and uplifting and I was processing what I said.

Finally, the new psychologist had time. In two sessions she figured out that she was not able to help me. I was almost the one to help her with all the coaching skills I had learnt by that time.

My GP was still worried and thought it could be dangerous and wanted to put me on anti-depressants and with hesitation I agreed to try it. Very quickly, I had all the side effects and felt even worse. One night I was hallucinating pretending to be an angel in bed, now that was dangerous! I stopped taking them right away.

With NLP, it all went so fast, I was coachable, eager to learn and willing to grow, to become a better version of me. So many things made sense, why didn't I learn this 20 years earlier? On the 7th October I graduated as an NLP Master Practitioner.

I also took the plunge and jumped. On the 13th October 2018, I went on stage, with my own cabaret performance. It surpassed every expectation I had, and it sold out with 300 people in the room!

What a reward it was…. I will never forget the enthusiastic audience, the standing ovations, the reactions afterwards and how long people kept saying that I not only made them laugh but also gave them new ways to look at things. I even inspired someone to pack her bags and move to Spain for months!

That's not all. Nine months after that, I went to New York and did several open mics, just as I imagined in the forest. I performed only two blocks from Times Square! I even got to work with one of the best-known comedy coaches of the US. This whole trip was one of the best experiences in my life so far.

I did crazy stuff even while I felt scared! I broke a wooden board with bare hands, walked over coals, I went rappelling from a 108m high tower while being afraid of heights, I even bent steel and broke a wooden arrow with my throat!

I found that being scared was a sign of trying something new, most things we are afraid of are not even real and will never happen. And sometimes we are not afraid to fail, but to succeed. Now that's weird!

Being scared is just an emotion, it can either paralyse or move you. But whatever you do always brings results. So, what result do you want?

What if we can change and make our limited beliefs and negative patterns into fuel to get us fired up? If we change our self-talk, we will change our own lives. We have so much more control over our lives than we think.

I worked on a new performance, with a premiere on the 20th March 2020. What a great date until COVID threw a spanner in the works. Just a week before I had to cancel.

Four weeks later, at 7:30am my phone rang. It was my dad, seriously that early?! I pick up and said, "Yes dad?" "No, it's your mum." "Huh? why are you using daddy's phone?" "Because he's dead next to me in bed" WTF?! Six minutes later I ran up their stairs where he was laying in bed, nothing I could do. I couldn't believe it, my dad, my rock in the surf, the man in my life was gone.

Just when I thought things were getting on track, sh*t happens again?!

It was a hard pill to swallow. With all the things I'd learned in the past years I managed to keep standing, and found that it was possible to laugh at the same time as feeling grief or sadness.

Due to COVID, all contacts became digital. By joining a Facebook group called "Billions Lives Changed" I got into contact with more like-minded people. I took a sales course, and surrounded myself with more people that believed in me, my dreams and goals, the people that uplifted me, inspired me, make me grow, pushed me forward, and were honest with me.

Nowadays if I don't speak English at least 30 minutes a day something is wrong. I even talk to myself in English! This is what I was born to do. I inspire, guide and help show you how to grab your sh*t, own it and turn it around so you can laugh at it, accept it, and let go of the control it had over you. This will help you to become who you really want to be.

I always use my 3 core values:

- Humour: I help you laugh at your own sh*t first so that you can own it, accept it, and then let go of the control it had over you
- Connection: I help you reconnect with your inner hero, your true self again.
- Love: Once you reconnect with your true self you will feel more self-love, pride, joy and confidence.

In every situation you'll find yourself in, no matter how bad it looks, there are 3 things:

1. Something to learn
2. Something to be grateful for
3. Something to laugh about

There is no failure, there is only feedback. Don't ever give up on that dream, desire or goal. Wish it, believe it and act on it. If one way doesn't work try a new one until you get there, it's our mindset that we can achieve anything once we believe.

It's never the prettiest or smartest people that succeed in life, it is always the bravest ones.

We all have our own story, we all get our share of sh*t. I am not special, my story is not that special, there are more people in the world with similar experiences. But we are all unique and we all deal with our sh*t in our own unique way.

Does this mean that I now never go through sh*t? Hell no!

I believe that depression can become chronical. A week ago, I realised this is what happens with me. Every now and then, I get a trigger by something happening, that could be an old pain, a fear, or shame. Most of the time it has nothing to do with the current situation or person, but goes to a deeper level. Our brains are wired to come up with a past emotion we felt and try to protect us, so when something looks similar they will bring that straight up again.

We all have feelings and thoughts, but we are not them so we should not identify ourselves with them. I found that a tricky thing to do. When this comes up, I throw myself a pity-party. I even visualise balloons for me, when it gets dark and it's completely dark, and I know I just have to sit in the dark and let it all out. Hand myself some tissues, and know that I survived worse things, so I will survive this too.

Feelings want to be felt, not only the good ones. By allowing myself to feel whatever it is, I can find out why I feel it, where it comes from and how I can change it into what I want to feel.

There is no one else other than you responsible for feeling whatever it is you feel, no one else can do it for you. So, no judgement, no blame, just feel. I found by doing this, answers will come and like my dad always said, "It can never be this dark or it will be light again". We always tend to hide the bad stuff not only from other people but worse from ourselves. But without the feelings we don't want, how can we even know what we do want? I found that taking that time which I never did before always makes me a better version of me.

It took me so many years to learn to laugh at my sh*t, and this is the first time I am sharing my story without sugar-coating anything, I am not Willy Wonka. THIS IS ME! The process of putting all the words down made me realise "I love my sh*t and I probably wouldn't want to miss anything, it brought me exactly here to who I am today. And for the first time I can say out loud "I am so proud of myself".

"Life Is About Kicking Ass, Not Kissing It!"
We are all superheroes. We need to be brave enough to put on our cape so that we can be courageous, and live the life we want. To make our dreams come true, to be confident enough to believe that we can create and live our best life ever.

If there is one message I would give to my younger self or anyone else, it would be "Treat yourself as how you would treat your best friend. Don't be so hard on yourself, you are doing the best you can with whatever you have".

Trust the process, nothing happens by coincidence. We are always on time in our lives; you are never late or missing out on anything. Everything will come to you at the right time for the right reason.

Laughter is the best therapy, and love is the best medicine. If it doesn't work? Increase the dosage.

About Me

I am Sandra, Award winning entrepreneur, International speaker, NLP Master Practitioner, author, comedian and the happiness trainer.

I was born in Maarssen a village in the middle of Holland, in an entrepreneurial family, where I was taught no one ever dies from working hard, so I did. I was mostly living life doing whatever was expected of me on all levels, it was never about me or what made me really happy.

To find my inner happiness I took a journey with a lot of self-development and education, that made me find my real purpose in life. I don't want to live forever, but I want to create something that will.

I am the founder of www.laughatshit.com.

"Make your sh*t from the past the fertilizer of your future".

I inspire, guide and help you with how to grab your "Sh*t", own it and turn it around, so you can laugh at it, accept it, and let go of the control it had over you. As a result, you can become who you really want to be, the best version of you.

This chapter is for all the people who cross my path, that contributed in whatever way to my life, and the people that will.

For the people that made things hard, I know you had good intentions. You gave me the chance to grow.

For the people that believe in me, uplift, inspire, challenge and motivate me, that kick my butt and love me just as I am. The people that I can laugh at sh*t with. There are no words that can express how much you mean to me.

For my dad, who always challenged me to try new things. Even though you didn't understand my journey and also wanted to keep me safe. I love and miss you, it's time for me to stand up now…

Redefine YOU To
Connect, Lead, Inspire

Dr. Jo Keith

Transformational Coach and Mentor

Connect.Lead.Inspire

"Stay true to yourself. An original is worth more than a copy."
--- Suzy Kassem

Discovery

Who are we – do we ever truly know? I would have never thought I would be one of these people who wake up one day in a state of utter confusion and feeling deep unexplainable sense of loss they could not shake off. N.E.V.E.R. Of course not. Why would I?

For I am a strong, confident, empowered, determined, unapologetically ambitious, intelligent, and passionate woman.

All my life, my strong sense of achievement helped me plan and get what I (thought) I desired. I have been highly driven by my passions, fuelled by my achievements. This is how I have always seen myself thrive, by setting high standards and expectations from myself and others, smashing it every time.

Then there was my focus – always razor-sharp to keep unshakeable confidence to inspire people around me as a leader, partner and friend, especially as they were losing faith and positivity. I have seen myself as someone who has always recognised unique authenticity in people, encouraging them to 'walk the walk' bravely through the world, with unstoppable courage to show others their light even if they could not see it themselves.

This is who I was, I thought, and it has helped me achieve everything I have had and reach the place I thought I wanted to be at.

Most of my professional career, I felt respected and recognised for my achievements. I had a strong track record for whatever I involved myself in; I was ruthlessly diligent, conscientious, dedicated and delivered excellent results to support the businesses. I spent nearly 15 years transforming strategic risk management practices across complex banking environments. None of this was easy, and that is why I thought it brought me the sense of fulfilment I was searching for.

I worked for an organisation that supported my ambition and passion to transform (yes, I was always passionate about anything and everything transformational). Its vision aligned with mine - people are at the core of any organisational culture and must be the focus of any leadership which is to be fit for the future. With that in mind, conscious and compassionate leadership was what I integrated into my leadership approach as a coach and mentor. I remember every person I worked with - their struggles, beliefs and hopes and how it felt to help them untangle their spider-web-like challenges to create their own strategies for what they defined as a success. And as that version of me I really believed it was bringing me joy.

I was a top performer and the firm has consistently invested in my fast-tracked development. I wanted to become an empowered senior female leader that the banking industry needs so desperately, and I had management endorsement. I was part of leadership training and had C-suite exposure to help me get there, and I loved it! Everything was on the right track.

When I decided I wanted to continue my academic career, the firm supported my decision to start the Doctorate programme granting full sponsorship. It was unheard of but they fully believed that my work dedicated to researching risk management practices across financial organisations would add a lot of value to development of risk frameworks in the industry. It all sounded like an incredible dream coming through, so why wasn't I feeling like it? I really could not answer that.

The next three years were challenging even for someone like me who needs diverse intellectual stimulation. I was working a full-time job and enrolled in a full time PhD programme. It meant a complete immersion into both banking and the world of research to allow me to bring together the best of two worlds – the wealth of academic knowledge and depth of industry practices to create a more strategic and commercially driven risk approach for the banking industry.

On top all of that, I just had a baby and was in an emotional state I cannot even begin to describe. At 30, I did not feel prepared for motherhood. In my mind, you can never be fully ready until you are a mother. I was overwhelmed with fears and anxieties that I will fail to be an exceptional mother and it was pulling me further away from myself than I realised at the time.

By 2018, I had over a decade long successful career in banking. That year had been full of ups and downs, challenging yet exciting, filled with anticipation for what I was convinced I wanted. The Holy Grail of directorship was just around the corner for me. Finally... what I have worked so hard for over the years was becoming a reality and I could picture it all in my mind. I was thrilled for what was coming - I could just feel that everything would change for me with reaching this huge career milestone.

I believed that all of those sacrifices I made over the years, all the times I put myself last (as who has time for self anyway!), moments I missed with my children, my family, all those lost relationships, it would be all worth it.

If I was to be truly honest with myself, I would have to admit that my light was losing its glow over time. But I was too busy achieving to notice what was going on inside. Yes, I was exhausted with all those conflicting responsibilities and long hours in the office. I was feeling overwhelmed with the stress, perpetually tired because of increasingly erratic sleep, and defeated by health issues that I consistently ignored. I kept telling myself, "Who has time for all those distractions?! They will sort themselves out with time."

I was so focused on supporting everyone else, I did not allow much time for me - to breathe, to think and to check with myself, where I was and how I was feeling. I took myself for granted. Every time I felt something that did not feel quite right, I directed my strength and determination and ruthlessly pushed it all the way down so I did not feel 'the uncomfortable' anymore. And I had become a master of suppressing what I later realised were my emotional needs slowly building a foundation of deep unfulfillment.

The darkness was slowly creeping in but I was quite comfortable ignoring all the signs.

As you are reading this, ask yourself:
Do you truly know who you are and what you want?
What really matters to you and why?
How often do you check in with yourself whether you are still living the life you want?

Ego Death

The day I was waiting for with anticipation was finally here. My boss called and I could feel it before he said the words – I was promoted to a Director. It finally happened. Except, instead of feeling an overwhelming pride, joy and excitement, I felt emptiness. I felt numbness I could not understand. Why was I feeling or rather not feeling what I was expecting? What was I actually expecting? I wanted this so much, didn't I? I could not find a logical explanation to what was wrong, but this certainly did not feel good.

Everyone in the office and close to me extended the words of recognition, and genuine happiness for they knew what a challenge it was to get there. So, I kept a smile on, I received it all with gratitude, but inside I felt such an overwhelming disappointment crushing me. I wanted to cry, not the tears of joy but despair.

This was an unfamiliar territory and with that moment my unshakable confidence in myself and what I truly desire started to show some visible cracks. My immediate thoughts were – 'it is my job, I need to quit as it is clearly not 'right for me', otherwise I would not feel this deflated surely'.

I could not shake off this feeling of loss and with each passing day it got worse, and I knew I had to do something.

And then a shiny new object syndrome kicked in when I got a call from a different bank offering me a role that sounded as if it was created for me. I took it as a sign I was looking for and I resigned. It came as a shock when I told my boss, my team and my family. No one could fully understand the logic I followed – I just achieved something unbelievable, was rewarded for it financially and yet I decided to leave. I can still remember all of those conversations over coffee with my colleagues and their bewildered expression when I shared the news.

My confusion started to be dangerously contagious and so I was thankful to start a 3-month gardening leave with hope that I can just be and finally spend time with just me. Be more present for my family, friends and finally travel. Suddenly from having no time at all, I had no work commitments and all the time in the world.

But as time passed, nothing changed for me. The voice inside of my head got louder, and the niggling feeling was not going away. If anything, it was getting more agitated and more impatient. And then a few days later, on one sunny April day, I woke up and it hit me. It was me! The way I was feeling had little to do with my job, career, promotion, money or any of it. It was definitely me, the one and only element in this equation that is constant as I removed all the others – me. No number of external achievements that may be perceived by the rest of my world as extraordinary was going to fix this for me, if I felt as if I was living someone else's life - unfulfilled, disconnected and full of emptiness I was unable to grasp.

And so, I knew deep inside this is where I have to start and it was time to start digging for some answers. And fast.

Now over to you, ask yourself:

- What does your relationship with yourself look like right now?
- How often do you challenge yourself?
- Do you know what your values are?
- Do you have the courage to be vulnerable with you and choose to change what does not feel right?

It Gets Darker Before…

Every day brought on more anxiety, and I felt as if I was on an emotional rollercoaster. I could not sleep; I stopped eating and went into a self-punisher mode to 'motivate' myself to get to the answers faster. I had no patience. I wanted results yesterday.

I remember a conversation with one of my best friends who really understands me, sometimes better than I do myself. He said, "Jo, you have woken up from a dream. It is now time to get real. Go back to basics. Forget what you know today and start digging deeper than you have ever had before." I was terrified as I was trying to get my head around what this meant. He was right. This was not going to be a quick and easy fix. I will have to be patient and I did not like the sound of it.

The logical side of me was rebelling and could not accept what was happening. I did everything right. I was smart, confident in who I was and here I was in a state of fear, mental confusion and paralysis. My mind went automatically into the 'overanalyse-overthink-bypass all emotions-mode'. It felt like I was in the vicious 'washing machine' cycle, seeing myself whirring around, feeling like I am losing control of myself, sinking deeper and deeper into the darkness with each day.

Next came self-criticism, self-doubt and so much disappointment in myself as I failed and let myself down. Thoughts about my work and career forward started to creep in.

How can I possibly lead others if I cannot even lead in my own life? I could not get this question out of my mind. I could not see any reasonable way to move on from this, and it felt devastating.

I did not want to be around anyone as I was not able to articulate anything cohesively. I was scared as it felt as if all I have known and created until then was an illusion.

I decided to take a few days and went to one of my favourite places, Paris. As I was re-discovering all those forgotten parts of the city, I was re-arranging the lost, scattered puzzle pieces inside of me. I remember spending a couple of days in the Louvre, one of my places in Paris. As I was looking at the art I loved, inspiring me to understand other people's expression of the world, I could feel a glimpse of hope that there is another way, and I can find it.

I continued to take the city in, making the most of my time there. My daily runs along Seine helped me along to process thoughts and emotions in my own space and time. I was slowly allowing new awareness in and I felt more certain that things were not lost, as they may seem; they are just hidden from me right now and so I needed to find them. Curiosity was sparked by this new realisation and each passing day I was re-discovering a part of me that I missed and forgotten about. I was learning so much about myself.

Those close to me understood I was on a self-discovery journey. Others, who could not understand my desire to travel on my own when I could just relax at home and be with my family, just judged. But none of that mattered to me. I was focused on what needed to change for me.

I needed a good plan. Just as I did for my career, now it was time to do it for me.

Physical health became my priority. I made some healthy changes in my diet, and it felt great. I became conscious of what I ate and eliminated some foods that did not agree with me altogether.

Vegetables, fruit, super-seeds and healthy protein became the core of my new diet. I reduced coffee intake in favour of water and herbal teas. I started a new exercise regime; running on the countryside trails became my daily routine.

Over time, I could see the changes in my body. I was getting my strength back. I slept better and felt this newly borne responsibility for my physical health supported by new levels of energy flowing through my body. I could hardly even recognise myself when I looked in the mirror. I was transforming into a new person, and the physicality was only the first step.

As I started to get used to my new image and learnt how to answer all the questions everyone was asking "everything was ok with me?", "have I fallen ill?", "did I need help?", "is it cancer?", "is it pregnancy?" and many more. I just smiled.

I felt it was time to go deeper into the other, less 'visible' areas of what really mattered. This meant getting honest with myself, being even more vulnerable, and listen to my intuition's whispers – it was time to re-define my needs, goals, priorities and really understand what was holding me back to redefine my 'why'.

I was ready.

...You See The Rainbow

Every day, week, month brought new emotions, thoughts, and experiences strengthening my realisation that as I was reconnecting with me and redefining all that my old version of me understood. I had to do that before I could fully be there for anyone else. I had to redefine what leadership meant to me first to become a leader I always wish I had. I had to redefine what I want in my life only then to have a bigger impact on other's. I understood then and there that by being the best version of myself, I can drive real change in other's life and my own.

I started to be naturally drawn to and re-connected to aspects spirituality I have always been intrigued about and so I allowed it back in my life. The more I opened my mind and my heart to this new reality, seen through my awakened self, the more connected I felt to myself, more intuitive and in flow.

I connected with spiritual leaders, learning their insights and approaches to spirituality. I became in tune with my own energy, as awaken empaths often do, feeling so much more than ever before. I allowed myself to continue my long-forgotten journey with tarot and it became one of my strategic tools I still use for myself and others to provide guidance when they need it.

I knew I found the key to the door that held the answers.

I started the journey of re-defining me on all levels - emotional, mental, physical, spiritual, and intellectual, and it felt just right to walk through it with trust and courage.

Ask yourself:
- When was the last time you honestly asked yourself: 'if my life ends tomorrow, have I lived it to the fullest being the best version of myself?'
- Do you know what your emotional, mental, physical, spiritual and intellectual needs, goals and values are?

Choice Is Freedom
Fast forward to last year and many, many lightbulbs moment later. I find myself reflect on the last few years – the choices I made, who I was back then and who I am today.

As I stepped onto the 40th floor to start my new job, June sun shining on my face, I could feel all the anticipation and curiosity built up over the last several weeks. But I knew whatever was going to happen, it was going to be a lesson I chose to learn. I was going to stay authentic to who I really was and trust my intuition this time.

I was stronger, more determined than before. And if there was only one lesson to learn from all of this for me, it was this – Choice is Freedom. No matter what you decide in any given moment, it is the best you can do, with what you know. So, keep it simple, know what you want, why you want it and just do it. If the outcome is not what you imagined or expected, try a different approach, adjust, be flexible. Try again. Stay connected to your vision and goals as you make those changes and do not lose sight of why you are doing it to begin with.

I remember one September day, I sat down in my favourite garden spot, wrapped up in a blanket, sipping my favourite Pukka Peppermint tea. And suddenly I felt this creative flow rushing through me and I realised I had to share all I have learnt to support others on their journey. I recognised the value I could create for others if I dared to share my knowledge, if I dared to connect my strategic mind, with my intuitive empath's heart and wisdom.

As I created time and space for me for the first time in forever, it allowed me to understand that we all need balance in life – balance of what we understand, how we see the world, how we choose to articulate our thoughts, process our feelings and emotions, and reflect it in our decisions, behaviours and actions we take.

To help you visualise, here is my picture defining what being in this balance and flow meant to me:

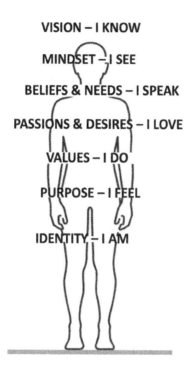

VISION – I KNOW

MINDSET – I SEE

BELIEFS & NEEDS – I SPEAK

PASSIONS & DESIRES – I LOVE

VALUES – I DO

PURPOSE – I FEEL

IDENTITY – I AM

This is how my new life philosophy came out of my head onto a piece of paper.

Three simple words.

Connect. Lead. Inspire.

Connect with yourself first before you can fully connect with others. Define what that connection means to you and how it feels.

Self-lead with authenticity and courage before others choose to follow. To do that, you must become aware of all your inner voices and what they have to say to you. They will make you angry, scared, frustrated and doubtful as you make unprecedented choices leading to unknown outcomes. But they are there for a reason, protecting you, so continue to get to know them better, befriend them, and let yourself have vulnerable heart-to-heart conversations with them, in your head. Connect with them.

Lastly, find ways to inspire you first before becoming truly inspirational to others. Yes, it is that simple, you start with you every time.

And you do not stop there, you continue to challenge yourself relentlessly and with compassion.

With that new truth, confidence, and clarity, I committed more of my time and energy to coaching and mentoring people, with a goal to guide them through their transformation as they redefine how they want to live, lead, and inspire, when faced with challenges.

And every day I check with myself if this still feels right. When it does, and is aligned with my authenticity, I know I want to dedicate more of me to it as it will continue to lead me towards my true fulfilment.

Making It Happen. Making It Stick.
If there is one thing I want you to remember after reading this chapter, it is this - there is no magic pill to changing your life.

There are strategies and tools you can learn and use to create your unique recipe to stay in your magic when life gets tough.

And if there is a guarantee in life, it is this - there will be challenges, and it will get tough. The more risk we decide to take, the more we grow, the scarier our fears become. Our fears and insecurities will fuel our self-doubts; they will try to 'warn us' to slow down by helping us to self-sabotage to protect us from any potential failures.

It is not the question of trying to avoid it, it is the matter of staying aware, prepared, and being strong to manage them as they come up.

And if right now, you are at a point of feeling a bit overwhelmed, wondering where to start first and not knowing what you do next, I will give you a little inspiration and share my own practical examples to Connect.Lead.Inspire philosophy I created based on 5 Ps:

Person – Priorities – Performance – Power – Plan

Breaking it down into 5 key areas of life is how I have defined each into what I felt right for myself.

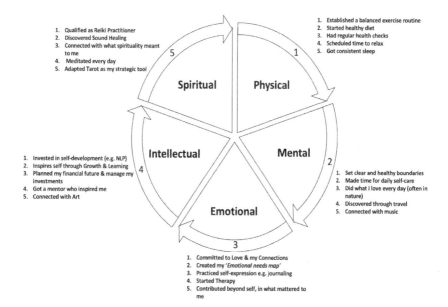

And if you are looking at this wondering … 'ok looks great, but so what? What really happens when I do this?' And most importantly, 'how do I make it stick and create sustainability?'

I will let you in on a little secret that may be hard to hear. The truth is, it does not all happen all at once - it is a process that takes time, patience, consistent effort, and determination followed by trust in yourself, your abilities and relentless discipline to keep going.

The first step is to become aware that where you are is not where you want to be; who you are is not who you want to be. You start with you, the 'Person', your beliefs (empowering and disempowering), values that will influence your state of mind, behaviours, and ultimately sense of your identity and what you see as your purpose.

The clarity about you as a person will naturally take you to the next step – setting 'Priorities' for you. Questions that may come up here for you:

a.   What do I really want to focus on? What matters to me and why?
Action - Must prioritise and understand my 'why's.

b.   How do I know and assess what is important and how important is it to me?
Action – With guidance, must design and adapt the right tools to assess importance.

c.   What do I do next? Where do I start?
Action – Must decide on practical actions, right for me.

d.   And what if things out of my control come up?

Action – Must understand and adapt tools to self-regulate emotions to manage out-of-control changes that allow to stay calm, agile and flexible.

e.   How do I have the strength to keep going?

Action – Must make time, space, be accountable (to me and / or buddy) to create consistent, simple, sustainable approach that works for me

Once key priorities are clear, you shift your focus and go into the third step 'Performance'. You set tangible and measurable goals to allow you achieve what you want. You measure and track your progress. And you are specific what results you want and what impact (changes) you want to see and implement. Connecting priorities with the performance plan drives your strategy that will take you there.

As you are going through the process, you will have no shortage of challenges to deal with. Some of it may be you and your limiting beliefs:

'I do not have time'

'And what if it works?'

'What if it doesn't work and I wasted all this time I don't have?'

'Do I really need this change? Maybe it will all go back to normal on its own'

'Can I really sustain this?'

… others will fall into your environment, connections (or there lack of).

Therefore, the next, forth, step 'Power' becomes even more important to stick to your values, be authentic and have courage to keep moving forward. In the 'Power' stage you focus on (re)defining what being in your power actually means to you. This means understanding your strengths, triggers (what can challenge you to procrastinate), doubts (good old imposter syndrome), fears and limiting beliefs.

Any, some, all of them can become your 'show stoppers'. Awareness of what they are and how you best manage them is really important to move forward to create the ultimate plan for your new way of being and living translated into connecting, leading and inspiring you (and others) into your new life.

So, what is the last step 'Plan' then? Simply put, it is the decision you take from here on to create your own daily (realistic, balanced, sustainable) habits and routines. As you do, you also reinforce your boundaries to align your physical, spiritual, emotional, mental and intellectual health.

Imagine, how would this feel for you? Waking up each day feeling this incredible sense of peace, fulfilment, and joy? Feeling like each day you are one step closer to mastering new skills to navigate through whatever challenges life throws at you with confidence and peace, as now you know you better, and you know how to get back to you, when you drift away.

You know your inner lighthouse will always have the light on, to guide you back to your true self. And that, that feeling fills you with so much empowerment and humility – as you realise you did this, you made it happen, and now you are ready to create and show others the way.

If you find yourself now wondering if all this relentless work is worth it, the answer is short and simple – unquestionably yes!

New Me, New Perspective, New Life

Nobody is perfect. And life is not about being perfect. Perfectionism is an illusion; it only exists in our heads. Life is about continuously redefining yourself as you grow and transform as a person. And when we do, you will still experience failures, and they will become your best teacher. Even the strongest of us will stumble and fall. But each time you will rise stronger than before, and you will use that strength to be a better version of you.

As you followed my story on these pages, you have learnt that as a strong, determined, and confident woman, I found myself in, what I would define as the depth of the worst darkness I have ever known. I underestimated the importance of redefining me and what happens if you choose to ignore or avoid this inner voice telling you to stay connected to you.

It led me down the path of confusion, paralysis with fear of losing control and judgement, drown me in anxiety, self-doubt, shame, guilt, overwhelm, emotionally deprived of my needs, and extremely uncomfortable in expressing my insecurities and vulnerabilities, to myself let alone to others. I allowed my ego to silence my intuition consistently. I disconnected from myself, and whether it was a result of self-neglect or an intention, the impact was still the same – indecision, constant overthinking, mental paralysis what to do next and avoidance to make changes I so desperately needed.

With time, effort and dedication, as I followed my own 5P's approach to Connect.Lead.Inspire, I accepted that I reached a new level of awareness and there was no going back. I brought back balance by integrating physical, mental, emotional, spiritual, intellectual aspects of my life and designed a strategy to guide me back to me, and to move forward with authenticity and courage.

I was now fully committed to continue to challenge myself on this journey and have the courage to overcome whatever comes up, whilst make necessary changes supporting my continuous and sustainable growth.

I became more empowered in my decisions in all aspects of life. I've become a conscious and much more emotionally intelligent leader, leading with humility, kindness and compassion for myself, my family, loved ones, friends, and at work, for my teams. I gained confidence in how much more impactful I can be when I show up as the best version of me.

I decided to invest in what was best for me to grow, rather than making self-sacrificing choices others wish to make for me. I strengthened my boundaries, being clear to myself about my non-negotiables, about what serves me and can best support my capability to serve others.

When I got COVID last year, it was all one big test of integrity to myself. It brought about a lot of emotional, mental, and physical trauma, along with disappointment, anger, rage and so many more feelings. Each time I felt those negative emotions resurface, I found myself intentionally bring me back to balance, leveraging everything I have learnt. I kept reminding myself to feel compassion for my body and mind as there was an internal battle going on, and it was not an easy one. Here I was, vulnerably humble again, learning every day that the illusion of control we may think we have over our life is best to be let go off sooner rather than later. For our own sanity and peace of mind.

As soon as I recovered, I realised it was time for another change in my life. I learnt through my COVID experiences that you never truly know how many more days to live you have left, and so it is irresponsible to waste it away if we know in our hearts that it no longer feels right.

And so I decided to change jobs in the middle of the pandemic. If I were to be more impactful, I had to move on. Once again, I took the lead in my own life.

I remember one conversation, when I said to someone, I was changing jobs. I spoke with utmost confidence, describing what it is I would be doing and the impact I was going to have. I could visualise it all - in my mind it was real as if it had already happened. When asked where I was going, I said calmly 'I do not have the job yet, but this is what is happening'. The reaction I got was an expression of shock and bewilderment, as if I was insane followed by "Good luck, I guess". We were in the middle of pandemic, no one was hiring and my next job was an ambitious one.

As I was in the process of redefining my new life, I had no doubt in my mind that it was going to happen before the end of 2020.

And just like that, one day, it happened. I took a senior position, in a bigger team, having a broader mandate and impact, in a culture and environment I knew would allow me to thrive, build winning teams who feel inspired and drive incredible results. Just as I visualised it would, as we create what we think and want.

All my experience of the last few years certainly changed the trajectory of my current life. I do not regret any of my decisions, no matter how hard they appeared to have been in the moment. They led me to a place I am at right now, and it is a good one.

None of it would be the same without my connections, the people I love and choose to share my life with. They have helped me appreciate the world through many different lenses and led me to become the person I am today. I have always believed each person we connect with is unique in how they see and feel life experiences. And life is about sharing those moments with people important to us, and that's how meaningful connections are created when we show up consistently, being truly present and with undeniable, unshakeable, and unconditional reciprocity. And this is how we drive real change in the world.

I have met some incredible people over the years. We have learnt from each other, grown together, cried through some of the toughest challenges. We celebrated our wins. We stayed connected. And I am incredibly humbled and thankful for it all.

My intention for you when I share my experiences and lessons, I learnt is this - in any given moment of your life, always be honest with yourself. That is a non-negotiable for us all.

Do not be afraid to ask yourself difficult questions, challenge relentlessly but with compassion, even if the answers you get are not what you expect. Be patient as change happens with time.

Live and lead authentically and with courage, allow yourself to grow. Keep the consistent alignment of your mind, words, emotions with your behaviours and the way you act in the world.

Be proud. Be present for you. Stop, appreciate, and celebrate as you grow and achieve each new level of you.

And keep redefining you as you Connect. Lead. Inspire!

About Me

My soul journey into this world began in 1982 on a cold November evening in Poland. My parents were young, excitable and always ready for a new adventure. For as long as I can remember, despite living in the restrictive Cold War regime, they did what they could to live life fully, always protecting our family from the toxicity of that environment.

Travels have always been part of my life. From an early age, it hugely influenced my natural curiosity of all things different from what I knew - my love for adventures, an insatiable passion for learning and discovering through constant movement and traveling. My decision to study abroad followed by a choice of career in the US and the UK was an easy one. It allowed me to create incredible memories of moments I would have otherwise never experienced.

As a transformational coach and mentor, I help those highly driven to Connect.Lead.Inspire with authenticity and courage to grow. I have always believed that we can only inspire others to be, think, connect and act in our true power by first being the best version of ourselves.

Both of my parents have been an important influence on becoming me. My mum, a driven and determined woman, always encouraged me to 'show the real me to the world', leading with wisdom and knowledge. My dad, the most patient and composed person I have ever known, always challenged me to bring joy, playfulness and movement through sports in my daily life, and has taught me so much about spirituality.

My life has been a series of unforgettable moments that made me who I am, and I am so thankful.

I dedicate this chapter to all of the people in my life who I love - for making me a better person, and choosing to share part of you and your life with me, as we learn and experience it all together. Thank you for seeing who I truly am and loving me unconditionally; for inspiring me and bringing fun, laughter and play to my life.

And most importantly, thank you for challenging me and giving me the strength to persevere when things are hard and having the patience to help me stay in my magic when life has other plans. I dedicate this chapter to you for being you. I love you.

I also dedicate this chapter to all of you:

- who are strong, driven and passionate, aspire to become the best version of yourself and are not afraid to admit you too got lost and disconnected as you have walked through life;
- who lead with unshakeable authenticity and courage in face of life's adversities, choosing to challenge yourself with kindness as you step towards the fears of the unknown;
- who understand the power of connecting with yourself first before leading and inspiring others;
- who dare to live and lead with compassion and open heart to grow and inspire others to grow.

Conclusion

Queens, we hope that you found inspirations in our stories to reign in your own Queendom. There are commonalities throughout these stories that happened all over the world:

- Stepping out of the undesired situation of painful undervaluation
- Moving through the doubts, fears and ridicules
- Trusting our own inner voice and intuition
- Shifting identity to become something new
- Finding a way to serve others with what we know
- Mastering our craft
- Creating a supportive environment of people
- Learning to properly value ourselves
- Honouring our mental, emotional and physical strength
- Creating businesses where we reign, in love and authority

We hope you see that you are not alone in how you are feeling. The things we imagine separate us are actually the humanity that binds us. When we allow ourselves to be authentic, honest and real, a new identity emerges. We are able to create, build and reign like never before.

Wouldn't now be a great time to use the lessons you just read to begin your own business, or level-up in the business you have? Do you have strong communities around you to help you in your business and in life like the outstanding Queens In Business Club? The right people cheering you on every day is so important to success.

No Queen ever needs to be alone or lonely. We share our knowledge, hopes and challenges. We get to brag openly about our successes, receiving full celebration with our fellow queens. In our community, we are able to be authentically us, without fear or shame. We are accepted for all of who we are, and cheered on as we become who we can be.

If you would like this in your life, please connect with us. We believe that you have something special inside of you to offer the world. We see you. We hear you. We understand.

About Queens In Business

Our Why

Today women are making waves in the world of entrepreneurship. There have never been more women rising up, standing up for what they believe in and building their own vehicle for freedom.

It's our belief that each and every woman has what it takes to be successful. Everyone has a gift inside of them, a skill or knowledge that could help someone who is struggling right now.

Women have the ability to contribute to the world and deserve the opportunity to be successful, feel fulfilled and have the freedom to start or scale their own business.

As women, we have always been nurturers and problem solvers – it's in our biology and many of us spend our lives thinking of others and putting others first. But who is looking after us?

The journey of entrepreneurship can be challenging at times and with just a fraction of women taking the leap to start their own businesses it can be a lonely ride.

That's why we created the Queens In Business Club.

The Queens In Business Club is more than just a community. It's a movement created to recognise the achievements of women, to support and guide female entrepreneurs and give them the tools to build and grow their own successful businesses.

Co-founded by six of us, it's the first of its kind, created by female entrepreneurs for female entrepreneurs:

Chloë Bisson – The Automation Queen
Carrie Griffiths – The Speaking Queen
Marjah Simon-Meinefeld – The Wealth Queen
Shim Ravalia – The Health Queen
Sunna Coleman – The Writing Queen
Tanya Grant – The Branding Queen

Before starting the QIB Club, we'd all built our own successful businesses, spent huge amounts of money on training and mentorship and invested years in growing our businesses.

We learned and mastered specific strategies and methods to get our businesses where they are today and we are now sharing those learnings and experiences with the members of the QIB Club.

Whether it is having a successful business or becoming financially independent, we aim to provide female entrepreneurs with the tools they need and a community to support them along the way.

Our Methodology
We believe that in business the ability to achieve success comes down to three core pillars:
- Education
- Empowerment
- Execution

Education for us means having the right skills, knowledge and strategies to achieve your goals and if you don't have them right now, having access to learn from experts that do.

Empowerment is about surrounding yourself with the right people to support you and cheer for you on the journey. It is about creating an empowering environment that nourishes you to be the best that you can be.

Execution means having the motivation, determination and drive to do what it takes to get to your end goal. Where we may struggle to find the motivation within ourselves, it's about having mentors to encourage you and giving you a kick up the bum when you need it.

At Queens In Business, we've created a powerful methodology that combines all three of the core pillars.

We provide the hands-on business education from world class experts with the push you need to execute your strategies whilst surrounding you with supportive members to empower you overcome any roadblocks that come up on the way.

Our Mission

We're on a mission to change the world of entrepreneurship.

We want to create a movement that empowers women and encourages their drive for success, not belittles it or judges them for putting their career first.

We want to eliminate the fear of judgement and the fear of failure. We want to create a world where it's ok to ask for help, it's ok to express your challenges and it's ok to make mistakes.

We want to support women in becoming powerful role models for their children, paving the path of the future generations of women who will believe in their abilities and believe they can achieve what they want.

It's our mission to provide support to Queens all over the world regardless of their age, background, or their position in their business. Whether they want to take their business to the next level or just get started, there is always a place for them in our community.

It's time now for women to rise up and be leaders, fight for what they want for themselves and for others.

It's Time to Reign.

To find out more about the Queens In Business Club, go to:
www.queensinbusinessclub.com

Contact us on:
team@queensinbusinessclub.com

Printed in Great Britain
by Amazon

69521296R00180